Department of Education and Science and the Welsh Office

South East Essex College
of Arts and Technology, Southend

Discipline in Schools

*Report of the Committee of Enquiry
chaired by Lord Elton*

30130504087684

02/05

371.5
DIS
STL

©Crown copyright 1989. Published with the
permission of the D*f*EE on behalf of the
Controller of Her Majesty's Stationery Office.

Applications for reproductions Should be made
in writing to The Copyright Unit, Her Majesty's
Stationery Office, St. Clements House, 2-16
Colegate, Norwich NR3 1BQ.

ISBN 0 11 270665 7
Second impression 1997

Enquiry into Discipline in Schools

Elizabeth House   York Road   London SE1 7PH

Direct Line   01-934 0507
Switchboard 01-934 9000
GTN Number 2914

Telex 23171

The Rt Hon Kenneth Baker MP
Secretary of State
Department of Education and Science
Elizabeth House
York Road
LONDON
SE1 7PH

31 January 1989

Dear Kenneth

In March you asked me to lead an enquiry into discipline in schools in England and Wales and to make recommendations. I have had the good fortune to be supported in this task by an energetic committee, experienced assessors and a small but exceptionally able and hard working secretariat. I am grateful to them all. Their names, our terms of reference and methods of work are given in our report which I enclose with this letter.

A copy of this letter goes to Peter Walker.

Yours ever

Rodney

THE LORD ELTON

Table of Contents

000 777 498 9 00 10

NOTES

1   Abbreviations most commonly used in the text.

Secretaries of State: The Secretary of State for Education
                         and Science and the Secretary
                         of State for Wales

DES   :   Department of Education and Science

LEAs   :   Local education authorities

2   Other abbreviations are explained when they first appear in
a chapter.

Foreword

1   This report contains recommendations which apply to many people who are not professional teachers or educational administrators and we hope it will be read by them. We have therefore avoided using the technical language of education whenever we have felt that this might conceal our meaning from the general public. Some of our comments may seem to specialist readers to be statements of the obvious. We have included them in order to present a picture that is complete for those unfamiliar with our subject. This is important as we believe that some of them may have prejudices firmly based on incomplete knowledge.

2   Many specialists will also find some of our recommendations to be proposals of the obvious. These are included for a different reason. We were surprised to find that some schools are not following what seemed to us to be obvious good practice in simple matters. Our report would be incomplete if it did not deal with these lapses.

3   We were particularly concerned by reports that physical attacks by pupils on members of staff were commonplace and the cause of widespread anxiety among teachers. Although our evidence indicates that there are few such attacks and that teachers do not perceive them as a principal disciplinary issue, we still regard this as a very serious matter indeed.

4   As with other matters that have attracted widespread concern, such as vandalism, we have made some proposals dealing specifically with the individual problem. But these are not the most important of our proposals for the prevention of these very serious lapses in discipline. It is not enough to avert a lapse when it is imminent, or to rely on putting things right afterwards. The aim must be to create a school community in which pupils do not begin to consider behaving in such a way.

5   The behaviour of pupils in a school is influenced by almost every aspect of the way in which it is run and how it relates to the community it serves. It is the combination of all these factors which give a school its character and indentity. Together, they can produce an orderly and successful school in a difficult catchment area; equally, they can produce an unsuccessful school in what should be much easier circumstances. Our recommendations relating specifically to serious incidents of indiscipline will not, therefore, stand on their own. They are part of a range of proposals which, if taken together, can have a profoundly beneficial effect on conditions in our most difficult schools.

Foreword

6   Our recommendations also relate to the great majority of schools that
    are generally well ordered but in which significant improvements could
    still be made. Our broad objective was to make recommendations that
    would help all those who are responsible for schools and their pupils to
    create the orderly conditions in which pupils can learn.

7   We believe that, if the full range of our proposals is adopted, it will
    produce a general improvement in the behaviour of pupils, and that this
    will improve both the quality of their education and the job satisfaction
    of those who teach them.

8   Our recommendations are addressed to the whole range of people
    involved with primary and secondary schools – from parents to pupils,
    and from Government to caretakers. If our report does nothing else it
    should demonstrate that our schools do not operate in isolation. They
    are an integral and immensely important part of society for which we all
    have a responsibility at some time in our lives. We hope that its
    publication will lead to a practical recognition of this; to a shared and
    general sense of commitment to our childrens' education; and to a
    realisation of the great potential latent in our schools.

Membership of the Committee

Chairman

Lord Elton

Vice-Chairman

Dr R Bennett — Emeritus Reader in Educational Studies, Derbyshire College of Higher Education

Members

Mr R Atkinson — County Education Officer, Northamptonshire Education Authority

Mr J Phillips, OBE — Headteacher, Graveney School, Wandsworth

Mr L Spencer — Chief Executive, Project Fullemploy Ltd, London

Mrs G Thomas — Headteacher, Blaencaerau Junior School, Bridgend, Mid-Glamorgan

Mrs C Thomson — Teacher, Alderbrook School, Solihull, West Midlands

Assessors

Mrs J Reisz — Department of Education and Science

Mr D Soulsby — Her Majesty's Inspectorate of Schools

Secretariat

Mr A Sevier — Secretary to the Committee

Mr R Mace — Assistant Secretary to the Committee

Mr R Rampling — (from June 1988)

Miss J Offen

Mr J Bryce — (to June 1988)

Summary

THE ENQUIRY

1 The Committee of Enquiry into Discipline in Schools was established by the Secretary of State for Education and Science in March 1988 in response to concern about the problems facing the teaching profession. Our task was to recommend action to the Government, local authorities, voluntary bodies, governors, headteachers, teachers and parents aimed at securing the orderly atmosphere necessary in schools for effective teaching and learning to take place. We decided that the focus of our enquiry should be on maintained primary and secondary schools (other than special schools), which the overwhelming majority of pupils in England and Wales attend.

2 Our report is based on a large volume of evidence gathered from a wide range of sources. We visited institutions here and abroad, had discussions with expert witnesses, received written submissions from numerous organisations and individuals, and commissioned the largest structured survey concentrating on teachers' perceptions of the problem ever carried out in Britain.

3 Press comments have tended to concentrate on attacks by pupils on teachers. Our evidence indicates that attacks are rare in schools in England and Wales. We also find that teachers do not see attacks as their major problem. Few teachers in our survey reported physical aggression towards themselves. Most of these did not rate it as the most difficult behaviour with which they had to deal. Teachers in our survey were most concerned about the cumulative effects of disruption to their lessons caused by relatively trivial but persistent misbehaviour.

4 We regard any incidents of physical aggression in school, however infrequent, as a very serious matter. Some of our recommendations deal specifically with such serious incidents. It is also important to find ways of creating an atmosphere in school in which pupils do not even think of being aggressive towards teachers. We regard our recommendations on changes in school atmosphere as being as important in tackling aggression in schools as our specific recommendations on serious incidents.

5 Our recommendations relate to a wide range of discipline problems, particularly persistent disruption. We find that most schools are on the whole well ordered. But even in well run schools minor disruption appears to be a problem. The relatively trivial incidents which most concern teachers make it harder for teachers to teach and pupils to learn. Our recommendations would secure a real improvement in all schools.

6   A wide range of causes of, and cures for, bad behaviour has been suggested to us. We conclude that any quest for simple or complete remedies would be futile. Our report highlights the complex nature of the problem and the variety of measures required to deal with it. It contains many detailed recommendations for action at classroom, school, community and national levels by all interested parties to promote good behaviour and tackle bad behaviour. It recognises the importance of clearly stated boundaries of acceptable behaviour, and of teachers responding promptly and firmly to pupils who test those boundaries.

TEACHERS

7   We conclude that the central problem of disruption could be significantly reduced by helping teachers to become more effective classroom managers. We see the roles of initial and in-service training as crucial to this process. This leads us to make two key recommendations. The first is that all initial teacher training courses should include specific practical training in ways of motivating and managing groups of pupils, and of dealing with those who challenge authority. The second is that similar in-service training should be provided through school-based groups. These groups should aim not only to refine classroom management skills, but also to develop patterns of mutual support among colleagues.

8   Our evidence suggests that the status of teachers has declined in recent years, that this decline was accelerated by their recent protracted industrial action, and that it may have reduced their authority in the eyes of pupils and parents. We recommend that all interested parties should give urgent consideration to establishing a framework of relationships between teachers and their employers which will minimise the risk of future industrial action. We also ask the Secretaries of State to clarify the legal basis of teachers' authority.

9   We emphasise the serious implications that any teacher shortages would have for standards of behaviour in schools, and the need for their pay and conditions of service to be such as to ensure the recruitment, retention and motivation of sufficient teachers of the required quality.

SCHOOLS

10   We draw attention to the growing body of evidence indicating that, while other factors such as pupils' home backgrounds affect their behaviour, school based influences are also very important. The most

effective schools seem to be those that have created a positive atmosphere based on a sense of community and shared values.

11   We recommend that headteachers and their senior management teams should take the lead in developing school plans for promoting good behaviour. Such plans should ensure that the school's code of conduct and the values represented in its formal and informal curricula reinforce one another; promote the highest possible degree of consensus about standards of behaviour among staff, pupils and parents; provide clear guidance to all three groups about these standards and their practical application; and encourage staff to recognise and praise good behaviour as well as dealing with bad behaviour. Punishments should make the distinction between minor and more serious misbehaviour clear to pupils, and should be fairly and consistently applied.

12   We see the headteacher's management style as a crucial factor in encouraging a sense of collective responsibility among staff, and a sense of commitment to the school among pupils and their parents. We recommend that management training for headteachers should pay particular attention to team building and the development of a whole school approach to promoting good behaviour.

13   We point out the links between the content and methods of delivery of the school curriculum and the motivation and behaviour of pupils, particularly those who are not successful academically. We emphasise the importance of the Secretaries of State ensuring that the National Curriculum offers stimulating and suitably differentiated programmes of study for the full ability range, and that the national assessment system is supportive and not threatening. We urge schools to achieve the best possible match between the needs and interests of individual pupils and the curriculum which they are required to follow.

14   We stress the importance of personal and social education as a means of promoting the values of mutual respect, self-discipline and social responsibility which underlie good behaviour, and we recommend that personal and social education should be strengthened both inside and outside the National Curriculum.

15   We emphasise the importance of the pastoral role of class teachers and form tutors, and the need for schools to maintain regular contact with the education welfare service and other support agencies rather than calling them in as a last resort.

16   We draw attention to evidence indicating links between the appearance of school premises and the behaviour of pupils. We stress the need for

appropriate building design. We recommend that the Government should give positive encouragement to local education authorities LEAs and governing bodies to ensure that adequate funds are made available for building maintenance. We urge all schools to develop policies to deal with litter, graffiti and other damage, and to follow the good example set by the best primary schools in displaying pupils' work.

17 We highlight the problems that many schools are experiencing during the lunch break. We recommend that the Government should encourage LEAs to ensure that adequate funds are available for lunchtime supervision, that LEAs should devolve these funds to schools so that the best match between local needs and supervision arrangements can be achieved, and that training in the management of pupils should be given to midday supervisors.

18 We draw attention to evidence indicating that the most effective schools tend to be those with the best relationships with parents. We urge heads and teachers to ensure that they keep parents well informed, that their schools provide a welcoming atmosphere which encourages parents to become involved, and that parents are not only told when their children are in trouble but when they have behaved particularly well.

19 We recommend that schools' policies on discipline should be communicated fully and clearly to parents. If children are excluded from school for an indefinite period, the school should re-admit them only after an agreement setting out the conditions under which they will be allowed to return has been signed by their parents.

PARENTS

20 We highlight the crucial role parents play in shaping the attitudes which produce good behaviour in school. Parents need to provide their children with firm guidance and positive models through their own behaviour. Not all parents appreciate the degree of commitment and consistency required to provide such guidance. We think schools have an important part to play in preparing pupils for the responsibilities of parenthood. We therefore recommend that education for parenthood should be fully covered in school personal and social education programmes, and that the Government should develop a post-school education strategy aimed at promoting socially responsible parenthood.

21 We recommend that parents should take full advantage of all formal and informal channels of communication made available by schools, and

that parent-teacher associations should ensure that their activities are accessible and rewarding to as many parents as possible.

22 We conclude that there is a need to increase parental accountability for their children's behaviour. We ask the Government to explore the possibilities for imposing civil liability on parents for damage or injury done by their children in school.

PUPILS

23 We draw attention to evidence indicating that pupils tend to behave more responsibly if they are given responsibilities. We recommend that schools should create opportunities for pupils of all ages to take on appropriate responsibilities, and that they should recognise pupils' non-academic achievements. We welcome the Government's support for the development of records of achievement, work experience and compacts with employers as means of promoting a sense of responsibility among pupils.

24 We stress the need for the rapid assessment of the special educational needs of pupils with emotional and behavioural difficulties by all LEAs. We recommend that LEAs should employ enough educational psychologists to enable this process to be completed in less than six months. We urge schools and LEAs to ensure that failure to identify and meet the learning needs of some pupils is not a cause of their bad behaviour.

25 Our evidence indicates that, while all LEAs make alternative provision for the most difficult pupils, its pattern tends to be a more or less improvised response to needs and difficulties. We recommend that all LEAs should review their alternative provision and, in determining its future pattern, should aim to provide adequate, appropriate and cost-effective support services for schools and individual pupils. We suggest that the most effective provision is likely to be based on support teams of specialist teachers working in mainstream schools with access to places in on-site units and, in exceptional cases, off-site units. We ask the Secretaries of State to make Education Support Grant funding available to encourage innovative projects for meeting the needs of the most difficult pupils and their schools.

26 We highlight the strong concerns expressed to us about the effect that violent television programmes may be having on childrens' attitudes and behaviour. We emphasise the need for careful regulation and monitoring of this aspect of broadcast, cable or video material, and the

responsibility of parents for restricting their children's access to anti-social images. We recommend that broadcasters should take full account of their educational responsibilities for all television programmes, and that teachers and parents should make positive use of popular programmes as an educational resource.

ATTENDANCE

27 Our evidence indicates that, while overall attendance rates seem to have remained relatively stable for many years, there are significant differences in the rates for individual schools which cannot always be explained by differences in their catchment areas. We encourage heads and teachers to take action to minimise unauthorised absence and internal truancy. We urge governors to monitor patterns of attendance in their schools. We recommend that LEAs should carry out regular attendance surveys and employ enough education welfare officers to ensure that cases of unjustified absence are properly followed up. We suggest that joint LEA – police 'truancy sweeps' should be considered as a means of improving attendance, and that the Government should consider increasing the penalty for the illegal employment of school age children.

POLICE

28 We encourage headteachers to develop clear understandings with local police forces about how intruders in their schools should be dealt with. We emphasise the value of school – police liaison projects and, in particular, the contribution that the police can make to education for responsible citizenship.

GOVERNORS

29 We identify two major areas in which governors can help to promote good behaviour in schools. One is the positive contribution that they can make to developing and monitoring their school's policy on discipline. The other is through the decisive part that they play in the appointment of staff, especially the headteacher. We emphasise the importance of governors looking for the personal qualities required for managing a school or a classroom effectively, and for working as part of a team.

LOCAL EDUCATION AUTHORITIES

30   We urge LEAs to develop their management information systems so that they can target their consultancy and support services on schools in difficulty. We stress the need for them to provide more effective consultancy services, particularly in the areas of school management and institutional change, and to ensure that the guidance and support systems which they provide for schools are coherent and properly co-ordinated.

31   We draw attention to the behaviour problems which are sometimes associated with the use of supply teachers, and suggest a variety of steps which could be taken to minimise their use. These include exploring the possibility of moving more in-service training out of teaching time. We ask schools to adopt codes of good practice for the use of supply teachers.

32   We conclude that attacks on teachers are relatively rare, and that our recommendations on better training and whole school approaches to behaviour should help to reduce the number of violent incidents involving school staff. We recommend that all LEAs should monitor such incidents systematically, and that a national serious incidents reporting system should be established. We urge the employers of school staff to offer comprehensive support to the victims of violence, and the police and Crown Prosecution Service to prosecute attackers.

GOVERNMENT

33   We point out that most teachers see smaller classes as an important contribution towards reducing the problem of classroom disruption but that it is difficult to identify relationships between class size and pupils' behaviour. We recommend that the Secretaries of State should commission research to investigate these relationships.

34   We highlight concerns about the power of LEAs under the Education (No. 2) Act 1986 to order the reinstatement of excluded pupils to most schools against the wishes of their heads and governing bodies. But we conclude that it is too early to say that this part of the Act, which came into force very recently, is not working. We recommend that the Secretaries of State should monitor its operation for five years and consider any necessary changes in the light of the information gathered during that period, and that a special reporting procedure should be established for cases in which pupils have been reinstated by the LEA against the wishes of the governing body or by the governing body against the wishes of the head.

Summary

35 Implementation of our recommendations would require a re-ordering of priorities and additional expenditure by some LEAs. We ask the Government to encourage adequate expenditure by LEAs and governing bodies with relevant responsibilities on building maintenance and lunchtime supervision arrangements in schools. In relation to the support services provided by LEAs for schools and pupils in difficulty, we note the marked differences in local levels of provision and recommend that all LEAs should ensure that they provide services which are adequate in terms of our report. At national level we draw attention to the part played by pay and conditions of service in securing the necessary supply and quality of teachers, and the need to investigate the relationships between school staffing levels and pupils' behaviour. We ask the Secretaries of State to make classroom management a national in-service training priority and to make an Education Support Grant available to fund work with the most difficult pupils.

Recommendations

These are listed in the order in which they appear in the full text of our report and should be read in conjunction with it.

3 TEACHERS

R1 Teachers and their trainers should recognise and apply the principles of good classroom management.

R2 Initial teacher training establishments should give full weight to the personal qualities required for effective classroom management, particularly the potential ability to relate well to children, when selecting applicants.

R3.1 Initial teacher training establishments should encourage students to undertake a period of pupillage, or other work with children, before starting their courses.

R3.2 Schools should offer opportunities for intending teachers to undertake such pupillage.

R4 The Secretaries of State should, when reviewing the criteria for the approval of initial teacher training courses, incorporate the following requirements:

R4.1 all courses should contain compulsory and clearly identifiable elements dealing in specific and practical terms with group management skills;

R4.2 these elements should aim to enhance students' skills in relating to pupils by increasing their understanding of group behaviour and the techniques available to manage it;

R4.3 they should involve practical learning methods, and the skills which effective group management is based on should be an explicit part both of college work and school experience;

R4.4 teaching practice should be systematically used to consolidate these skills;

R4.5 the development of the ability to relate well to pupils should be a key consideration in assessing a student's overall competence to teach.

R5 When reviewing the criteria for the approval of initial teacher training courses, the Secretaries of State should specify a minimum requirement for regular classroom teaching experience for staff providing training in teaching skills equivalent to one term in every five years.

PUPILS	TEACHERS	HEAD TEACHERS	OTHER SCHOOL STAFF	GOVERNORS	PARENTS	LEAs	TEACHER TRAINERS	CURRICULUM COUNCILS	GOVERNMENT	OTHERS	REFERENCE IN TEXT
	T						TT				3.28
							TT				3.32
							TT				3.34
		HT									3.34
							TT		GT		3.37
							TT		GT		3.37
							TT		GT		3.37
							TT		GT		3.37
							TT		GT		3.37
							TT		GT		3.40

Recommendations

R6   Initial teacher training establishments should introduce students to the concept of peer support and its uses.

R7   LEAs should ensure that their induction programmes for new teachers take full account of the need to provide on-and off-the-job training in classroom and group management skills.

R8   If the proposals in the consultative document on Qualified Teacher Status are implemented:

R8.1   governing bodies should take full account of the personal qualities of candidates when appointing or recommending the appointment of licensed teachers;

R8.2   induction programmes for such teachers should be strongly reinforced with tailored in-service training, particularly in the area of classroom management.

R9   The management of pupil behaviour should become a national priority for funding under the Local Education Authority Training Grants Scheme from 1990/91 until at least 1994/95.

R10   Urgent consideration should be given, by all the interested parties, to establishing a framework of relationships between teachers and their employers which will reduce the risk of future industrial action to a minimum.

R11   The Secretaries of State should consider introducing legislation to clarify the legal basis of teachers' authority.

R12   The Secretaries of State and LEAs should give due weight to the serious implications of any actual or predicted teacher shortages (whether specialist, regional or general) when considering future pay levels and conditions of service for the profession.

R13   The Secretaries of State, LEAs, governors and headteachers should encourage the recruitment of teachers from minority ethnic backgrounds.

PUPILS	TEACHERS	HEAD TEACHERS	OTHER SCHOOL STAFF	GOVERNORS	PARENTS	LEAs	TEACHER TRAINERS	CURRICULUM COUNCILS	GOVERNMENT	OTHERS	REFERENCE IN TEXT
							TT				3.43
						L					3.46
				GS							3.48
						L					3.48
						L			GT		3.50
						L			GT	Professional Associations	3.66
									GT		3.74
						L			GT		3.86
		HT		GS		L			GT		3.87

Recommendations

4 SCHOOLS

R14 The School Management Task Force should ensure that management training programmes for headteachers and other senior staff give specific emphasis to personnel management in its broadest sense and to the management of institutional change.

R15 Headteachers should review and, wherever necessary, improve channels of communication within the school and between the school and parents, governors, the community and outside agencies.

R16 Headteachers should use all the means available to them to build up a sense of community in their schools and to encourage staff, governors, parents and pupils to play an active part in that community.

R17 Headteachers should:

R17.1 take the lead in defining the aims of the school in relation to standards of behaviour;

R17.2 create the conditions for establishing the widest possible measure of agreement on these standards and how they will be achieved;

R17.3 ensure that these standards are consistently applied throughout the school.

R18 Headteachers should ensure, by consistent policy-making and encouragement, that all teachers accept responsibility for maintaining good behaviour throughout the school and that they model the types of behaviour encouraged by school policy.

R19 Headteachers should promote the development of both management support and peer support within the staff team, and the professional development of its members.

R20 In making all major management decisions, headteachers should consider their likely effects upon the commitment and morale of teachers and pupils.

R21 Headteachers and teachers should, in consultation with governors, develop whole school behaviour policies which are clearly understood by pupils, parents and other school staff.

R22 Schools should ensure that their rules are derived from the principles underlying their behaviour policies and are consistent with them.

PUPILS	TEACHERS	HEAD TEACHERS	OTHER SCHOOL STAFF	GOVERNORS	PARENTS	LEAs	TEACHER TRAINERS	CURRICULUM COUNCILS	GOVERNMENT	OTHERS	REFERENCE IN TEXT
						L				School Management Task Force	4.21
		HT									4.25
		HT									4.28
		HT									4.32
		HT									4.32
		HT									4.32
		HT									4.34
		HT									4.36
		HT									4.37
	T	HT		GS							4.51
	T	HT		GS							4.55

Recommendations

R23	Schools should strike a healthy balance between rewards and punishments. Both should be clearly specified.
R24	Pupils should learn from experience to expect fair and consistently applied punishments for bad behaviour which make the distinction between serious and minor offences apparent.
R25	Headteachers and teachers should ensure that rules are applied consistently by all members of staff, but that there is flexibility in the use of punishments to take account of individual circumstances.
R26	Headteachers and teachers should avoid the punishment of whole groups.
R27	Headteachers and teachers should avoid punishments which humiliate pupils.
R28	Headteachers and staff should:
R28.1	be alert to signs of bullying and racial harassment;
R28.2	deal firmly with all such behaviour;
R28.3	take action based on clear rules which are backed by appropriate sanctions and systems to protect and support victims.
R29	Pupils should tell staff about serious cases of bullying and racial harassment of which they are aware.
R30	All parties involved in the planning, delivery and evaluation of the curriculum should recognise that the quality of its content and the teaching and learning methods through which it is delivered are important influences on pupils' behaviour.
R31	The Secretaries of State should ensure that the National Curriculum offers stimulating programmes of study suitable for the full ability range.
R32	Schools should not use rigid streaming arrangements to group their pupils by ability. They should take full account of the implications for pupil behaviour when reviewing their arrangements for grouping pupils.
R33	Schools should:
R33.1	distribute their teaching and other resources equitably across the ability range;

PUPILS	TEACHERS	HEAD TEACHERS	OTHER SCHOOL STAFF	GOVERNORS	PARENTS	LEAs	TEACHER TRAINERS	CURRICULUM COUNCILS	GOVERNMENT	OTHERS	REFERENCE IN TEXT
	T	HT		GS							4.56
	T	HT									4.57
	T	HT									4.58
	T	HT									4.59
	T	HT									4.60
	T	HT	S								4.66
	T	HT	S								4.66
	T	HT	S								4.66
PP											4.67
	T	HT		GS		L		CC	GT	School Examinations and Assessment Council	4.71
								CC	GT		4.77
	T	HT									4.84
	T	HT									4.85

Recommendations

R33.2 provide a range of rewards accessible to pupils of all abilities.

R34 Schools should make full use of off-site learning as a means of motivating their pupils.

R35 The Secretaries of State should ensure that multi-cultural awareness and equal opportunities become identifiable cross-curricular themes and are used to promote the attitudes on which respectful and tolerant behaviour are based.

R36.1 The Secretaries of State should ensure that personal and social education is effectively covered as a cross-curricular theme within the National Curriculum.

R36.2 Schools should also provide personal and social education programmes outside the National Curriculum.

R37 Secondary headteachers and teachers should base pastoral systems on the strengths of the traditional integrated academic, welfare and disciplinary role of the teacher.

R38 Secondary headteachers and teachers should identify clear aims for the use of tutorial time. These aims should include reinforcing the school's behaviour policy.

R39 Headteachers and teachers should:

R39.1 recognise the importance of ascertaining pupils' views;

R39.2 organise systems for doing so and for taking the information gathered into account in the management of the school.

R40 Headteachers should ensure that there is regular and effective communication between their staff and support services, and that these services are given early warning of developing problems.

R41 Headteachers and teachers should ensure that pastoral care in schools is characterised by a healthy balance between challenge and support for pupils.

R42 Initial teacher training establishments should introduce all their students to basic counselling skills and their value.

R43 LEAs should provide in-service training in basic counselling skills for senior pastoral staff at least.

PUPILS	TEACHERS	HEAD TEACHERS	OTHER SCHOOL STAFF	GOVERNORS	PARENTS	LEAs	TEACHER TRAINERS	CURRICULUM COUNCILS	GOVERNMENT	OTHERS	REFERENCE IN TEXT
					L						
	T	HT									4.85
	T	HT									4.87
								CC	GT		4.93
								CC	GT		4.97
	T	HT		GS							4.97
	T	HT									4.103
	T	HT									4.105
	T	HT									4.106
PP	T	HT									4.106
	T	HT				L					4.108
	T	HT									4.110
							TT				4.111
					L						4.111

Recommendations

R44 Headteachers and staff should adopt comprehensive policies for the care of premises, with responsibilities allocated to specific people, including pupils.

R45 LEAs and governing bodies which employ school staff should include the repair of minor damage and the removal of graffiti in the duties of caretaking staff where such arrangements do not already exist and can be negotiated.

R46 Headteachers and teachers should recognise the importance of displaying pupils' work in creating an attractive environment, increasing pupils' self-esteem and fostering a sense of ownership of the premises.

R47 The Secretaries of State, LEAs and governing bodies with responsibility for buildings should ensure that school buildings are designed with durability (consistent with attractiveness), ease of maintenance, avoidance of circulation bottlenecks and good sightlines for the supervision of pupils in mind.

R48 LEAs and governing bodies with responsibility for buildings should ensure that large scale maintenance and other building work are carried out only with due notice after consulting the headteacher and, whenever possible, in the school holidays.

R49 The Government, in its expenditure plans, should give explicit encouragement to LEAs and governing bodies with responsibility for buildings to ensure that adequate funds are made available for the maintenance of school premises.

R50 LEAs and governing bodies with responsibility for buildings should help schools to create a better environment for both staff and pupils by providing soft floor coverings and other noise reducing features wherever possible.

R51 Headteachers and their senior management teams should recognise the importance of efficient and sensitive timetabling as a management tool which can be used to reduce problems of circulation, supervision and classroom management. The annual timetabling cycle should involve thorough consultation with staff.

R52.1 Senior staff should be visible and strategically placed during mass circulation periods between lessons.

PUPILS	TEACHERS	HEAD TEACHERS	OTHER SCHOOL STAFF	GOVERNORS	PARENTS	LEAs	TEACHER TRAINERS	CURRICULUM COUNCILS	GOVERNMENT	OTHERS	REFERENCE IN TEXT
PP	T	HT	S								4.117
			S	GS		L					4.117
	T	HT									4.117
				GS		L			GT		4.121
				GS		L					4.123
				GS		L			GT		4.124
				GS		L					4.125
	T	HT									4.130
	T	HT									4.133

Recommendations

R52.2	Headteachers and teachers when moving about the school should be aware of and take responsibility for pupils' behaviour.
R53	Headteachers should ensure that pupils have access to school buildings outside lesson times.
R54	LEAs and governing bodies which employ school staff should ensure that midday supervisors are given adequate training in the management of pupils' behaviour.
R55	The Government, in its expenditure plans, should give explicit encouragement to LEAs to ensure that adequate funds are made available for lunchtime supervision.
R56.1	LEAs should devolve the funding of lunchtime supervision to schools.
R56.2	Headteachers should use these funds to devise schemes which meet the needs of their schools and encourage participation by teachers.
R57	Headteachers and teachers should ensure that parents receive positive and constructive comments on their children's work and behaviour as a matter of course.
R58	When disciplinary problems arise, headteachers and teachers should involve parents at an early stage rather than as a last resort.
R59	Teachers should recognise that pupils' behaviour at home may differ markedly from their behaviour at school. They should take this into account when discussing pupils with their parents.
R60.1	Headteachers and teachers should develop an active partnership with parents as an aid to promoting good behaviour.
R60.2	They should ensure that their schools provide a welcoming environment for parents.
R60.3	Particularly in primary schools, they should encourage parental involvement in the classroom and in home learning schemes.
R61	Headteachers and teachers should develop policies to secure easy access to them by parents and good communications between them and parents which go beyond the provision of formal parents' evenings.

PUPILS	TEACHERS	HEAD TEACHERS	OTHER SCHOOL STAFF	GOVERNORS	PARENTS	LEAs	TEACHER TRAINERS	CURRICULUM COUNCILS	GOVERNMENT	OTHERS	REFERENCE IN TEXT
	T	HT									4.133
		HT									4.134
			S	GS		L					4.137
						L			GT		4.139
						L					4.140
	T	HT									4.140
	T	HT									4.144
	T	HT		PT							4.145
	T	HT									4.146
	T	HT		PT							4.152
	T	HT									4.152
	T	HT		PT							4.152
	T	HT									4.153

R62	Schools should ensure that:
R62.1	written communications to parents are in a language easily understood by them;
R62.2	where significant numbers of parents use first languages other than English, communications are in these languages as well as in English.
R63	Headteachers should ensure that their schools have effective induction arrangements for parents of new pupils.
R64	Headteachers should ensure that their schools' behaviour policies are communicated fully and clearly to parents, who should be reminded of them regularly and informed of any major changes to them throughout their child's school career.
R65	Headteachers should use re-entry agreements, specifying the conditions under which an excluded pupil can be re-admitted to school, as a means of ending indefinite exclusions.
R66	In appropriate cases, LEAs and headteachers should make time available for home visits by teachers, who should consult with the education welfare service and other agencies where necessary.
R67	LEAs, headteachers and governing bodies should give serious consideration to providing community access to school facilities, where it does not already exist, as a means of fostering good relations with parents and the wider community.

5 PARENTS

R68	The Government, LEAs, governors and headteachers should consider means of impressing on parents that the ways in which they bring up their children are likely to have a significant influence on their behaviour in school. Parents should recognise the need to:
R68.1	provide firm but affectionate guidance in the home, which is most likely to produce the attitudes on which good behaviour in school can be based;
R68.2	ensure that they set a good and consistent example to their children by their own behaviour;

PUPILS	TEACHERS	HEAD TEACHERS	OTHER SCHOOL STAFF	GOVERNORS	PARENTS	LEAs	TEACHER TRAINERS	CURRICULUM COUNCILS	GOVERNMENT	OTHERS	REFERENCE IN TEXT
	T	HT									4.154
	T	HT				L					4.154
		HT									4.155
		HT									4.155
PP		HT			PT						4.160
	T	HT				L					4.161
		HT		GS		L					4.164
		HT		GS		L			GT		5.15
					PT						5.15
					PT						5.15

Recommendations

R68.3	avoid permissive or harshly punitive responses to aggressive behaviour, particularly by boys, which can encourage attitudes which are incompatible with schooling.
R69.1	The Secretaries of State should ensure that education for parenthood is fully covered as a cross-curricular theme in the National Curriculum.
R69.2	Governors and headteachers should ensure that education for parenthood is fully covered in school personal and social education programmes.
R70	The Government should develop a post-school education strategy aimed at promoting socially responsible parenthood.
R71	Parents should take full advantage of all channels of communication made available by schools and develop good working relationships with teachers in order to help their children to become constructive members of the school community.
R72	Parent–teacher associations should ensure that their activities are accessible and rewarding to as many parents as possible.
R73	Parents should make every effort to attend parents' evenings and annual parents' meetings.
R74	The Government should explore the possibilities for imposing on parents civil liability for their children's acts in school.

6 PUPILS

R75	Headteachers and teachers should give pupils every opportunity to take responsibilities and to make a full contribution to improving behaviour in schools.
R76	Headteachers and teachers should encourage the active participation of pupils in shaping and reviewing the school's behaviour policy in order to foster a sense of collective commitment to it.
R77	The Secretaries of State, LEAs and schools should ensure that records of achievement give due weight to a wide range of achievements and personal qualities.

PUPILS	TEACHERS	HEAD TEACHERS	OTHER SCHOOL STAFF	GOVERNORS	PARENTS	LEAs	TEACHER TRAINERS	CURRICULUM COUNCILS	GOVERNMENT	OTHERS	REFERENCE IN TEXT
					PT						5.15
								CC	GT		5.17
		HT		GS							5.17
									GT		5.18
	T	HT			PT						5.21
	T	HT			PT						5.24
					PT						5.27
									GT		5.34
PP	T	HT									6.8
PP	T	HT									6.9
	T	HT				L			GT		6.14

Recommendations

R78 Employers should give balanced consideration to the full range of a young person's achievements when appointing school leavers.

R79 Schools, LEAs and employers should increase their co-operation in developing means of increasing pupils' motivation, such as compacts.

R80 Pupil records should cover their pastoral as well as their learning needs. They should be in a format which could be adopted by schools and LEAs throughout England and Wales.

R81 All local authorities should ensure that adequate provision for pre-school education for severely disadvantaged children is available in their areas.

R82 The Government should evaluate preventive schemes aimed at primary age children with a view to encouraging the development of such schemes if they are found to be effective.

R83 All LEAs and schools should ensure that the special educational needs of pupils with emotional and behavioural difficulties are assessed and met.

R84 LEAs should set and maintain an establishment of educational psychologists adequate to achieve the target of six months for the processing of statements of special educational needs specified in the draft circulars recently issued by the DES, the Department of Health and the Welsh Office to replace DES Circular 1/83 and Welsh Office Circular 5/83.

R85 LEAs and schools should ensure that the learning needs of pupils involved in disruptive behaviour who may not be suffering from emotional and behavioural difficulties are properly identified as part of any plan for remedial action.

R86 All LEAs should review the alternative provision that they make for the most difficult pupils. In determining future patterns of provision they should take full account of:

R86.1 the need to provide adequate, appropriate and cost-effective support for schools and individual pupils;

R86.2 the importance of keeping pupils in and, if they are removed, returning them to mainstream schools wherever possible;

PUPILS	TEACHERS	HEAD TEACHERS	OTHER SCHOOL STAFF	GOVERNORS	PARENTS	LEAs	TEACHER TRAINERS	CURRICULUM COUNCILS	GOVERNMENT	OTHERS	REFERENCE IN TEXT
										Employers	6.14
	T	HT				L				Employers	6.16
	T	HT				L			GT		6.20
						L				Local Authorities	6.22
									GT		6.25
	T	HT				L					6.36
						L					6.37
	T	HT				L					6.38
						L					6.53
						L					6.53
						L					6.53

Recommendations

R86.3 the balance between the inherent disadvantages of off-site units and the need to maintain a minimum number of off-site places;

R86.4 the benefits that can accrue from the work of support teams in mainstream schools with access to on-site units;

R86.5 the need to ensure that support teams are adequately resourced to carry out their work effectively.

R87 The Secretaries of State should establish an Education Support Grant to encourage innovative projects aimed at providing comprehensive yet flexible support for the most difficult pupils and their schools. All LEAs should be eligible to bid for this grant for three years.

R88 On- and off-site units should take full account of the recommendations in this report wherever they are appropriate.

R89 Teachers should take account of the gender differences involved in pupils' behaviour, for example by not reinforcing attention-seeking and aggressive behaviour.

R90 Headteachers and staff should work to create a school climate which values all cultures, in particular those represented in it, through its academic and affective curricula.

R91 Teachers should recognise the potential for injustice and the practical dangers of stereotyping certain kinds of pupils as troublemakers.

R92 Teachers should guard against misinterpreting non-verbal signals and speech patterns of pupils from different cultural backgrounds.

R93 Teachers should avoid modelling any kind of insulting or discriminating behaviour.

R94 LEAs and governing bodies which employ school staff should regard the racial harassment of pupils or colleagues by teachers or other staff as a disciplinary offence.

R95 Broadcasters should take full account of their educational responsibilities for the content of all television programmes, including those broadcast after 9.00 pm. The Broadcasting Standards Council should encourage them to do so.

PUPILS	TEACHERS	HEAD TEACHERS	OTHER SCHOOL STAFF	GOVERNORS	PARENTS	LEAs	TEACHER TRAINERS	CURRICULUM COUNCILS	GOVERNMENT	OTHERS	REFERENCE IN TEXT
						L					6.53
						L					6.53
						L					6.53
						L			GT		6.56
	T	HT									6.57
	T	HT									6.62
	T	HT	S								6.63
	T	HT									6.64
	T	HT									6.65
	T	HT									6.66
				GS		L					6.67
										Broadcasters BSC	6.74

R96 Teachers and parents should make active use of television as an educational resource, reinforcing the positive messages presented by programmes and encouraging children to become more discriminating and critical viewers.

R97 Parents should monitor and, where necessary, restrict their children's access to network, cable, satellite or video material transmitting violent or other anti-social messages.

R98 The Government should continue to monitor research findings on links between children's diets and behaviour and should take appropriate action if any causal connections are identified.

7 ATTENDANCE

R99 Headteachers and teachers should make full use of education welfare officers to maximise attendance.

R100 Senior school staff should carry out frequent random attendance checks on individual lessons.

R101 Governors should obtain regular reports on attendance, including internal truancy, with a view to encouraging and supporting action by the school.

R102 All LEAs should regularly gather data on attendance at their schools and should use this information to plan the deployment of their resources in the most effective ways to improve attendance.

R103 Those designing school-based computerised information systems should take account of the possibilities of including programmes for monitoring attendance in them.

R104 All LEAs should maintain adequate numbers of education welfare officers to ensure that cases of unjustified absence can be followed up systematically and promptly.

PUPILS	TEACHERS	HEAD TEACHERS	OTHER SCHOOL STAFF	GOVERNORS	PARENTS	LEAs	TEACHER TRAINERS	CURRICULUM COUNCILS	GOVERNMENT	OTHERS	REFERENCE IN TEXT
	T				PT						6.76
					PT						6.77
									GT		6.83
	T	HT				L					7.10
	T	HT									7.11
		HT		GS							7.12
						L					7.13
	T	HT				L					7.14
						L					7.16

Recommendations

R105 LEAs and chief officers of police should jointly consider the use of 'truancy sweeps' as a means of maximising school attendance and reducing juvenile crime in local circumstances.

R106 The Government should review the penalties for the illegal employment of school age children with a view to substantially increasing penalties for employers, especially those who make use of illegal child labour during school hours.

8   POLICE

R107 All LEAs and schools should recognise the practical and educational value of good relations with the police and promote the development of school–police liaison projects.

9   GOVERNORS

R108 When governors choose to draw up a written statement of general principles for a school's behaviour policy, they should take account of the principles of good practice identified in this report as well as the professional advice of the headteacher and the chief education officer.

R109 Governors should obtain regular reports on the standards of behaviour in their schools from headteachers.

R110 Governors' annual reports should contain a section on the standards of behaviour in and attendance at the school.

R111 In selecting applicants for interview and appointing headteachers, or recommending them for appointment, governors should take care to select only those candidates who have the leadership and management qualities necessary for establishing whole school behaviour policies on the lines set out in this report.

R112 In selecting applicants for interview and appointing other teaching staff, or recommending them for appointment, governors should take care to select candidates temperamentally suited to staff team work and mutual support and able to form relationships with pupils based on mutual respect.

R113 In making or recommending appointments, governors should give full weight to the professional advice offered by chief education officers and headteachers.

PUPILS	TEACHERS	HEAD TEACHERS	OTHER SCHOOL STAFF	GOVERNORS	PARENTS	LEAs	TEACHER TRAINERS	CURRICULUM COUNCILS	GOVERNMENT	OTHERS	REFERENCE IN TEXT
						L				Police	7.17
									GT		7.18
	T	HT				L				Police	8.9
		HT		GS		L					9.7
		HT		GS							9.8
				GS							9.9
				GS							9.17
				GS							9.18
		HT		GS		L					9.19

R114 LEAs and governing bodies which employ contractors should make adherence to the relevant parts of the school's behaviour policy a condition for the letting or renewing of contracts.

R115.1 Governors and LEAs should recognise that teachers who are unable, with the training and support recommended in this report, to control their classes in a school should cease to be employed in that school.

R115.2 In such cases, as in all personnel matters, governors should follow professional advice on good employment practice.

R116 LEAs should ensure that governors' training includes their role in forming school behaviour policies and in the appointment and dismissal of staff.

R117 Governors should take full advantage of the training opportunities which are becoming available to them.

10 LOCAL EDUCATION AUTHORITIES

R118 All LEAs should provide effective management consultancy services for headteachers.

R119 LEAs should develop information systems covering pupils' behaviour in their schools which will enable them to make timely and effective use of their consultancy and support services.

R120 If an LEA is convinced that a breakdown of discipline has occurred or is likely to occur in a school, it should not hesitate to use its powers of intervention under section 28 of the Education (No. 2) Act 1986.

R121.1 LEAs should develop effective strategies for supporting the behaviour policies of their schools based on clear aims and procedures and backed up by the necessary communication systems and resources.

R121.2 They should regularly evaluate these strategies in relation to their aims and the perceptions of schools, parents and pupils of the quality of service being provided.

R122 LEAs should ensure that schools and education welfare officers establish regular pastoral contacts and early warning systems to identify pupils 'at risk' at the earliest possible stage, so that preventive action can be taken.

PUPILS	TEACHERS	HEAD TEACHERS	OTHER SCHOOL STAFF	GOVERNORS	PARENTS	LEAs	TEACHER TRAINERS	CURRICULUM COUNCILS	GOVERNMENT	OTHERS	REFERENCE IN TEXT
				GS		L					9.20
				GS		L					9.22
				GS							9.22
						L					9.23
				GS							9.23
						L					10.6
						L					10.11
						L					10.13
						L					10.15
PP	T	HT			PT	L					10.15
	T	HT				L					10.16

Recommendations

R123 LEAs should, wherever possible, ensure continuity of family and school contacts by using education welfare officers to service clusters of secondary and related primary schools.

R124 LEAs should encourage closer working relationships between schools and educational psychologists to develop consultancy services providing advice on the management of behaviour in groups and in the school as a whole.

R125 Local authorities should promote better co-ordination between the various local agencies dealing with pupils with behaviour or attendance problems and their families.

R126 LEAs should encourage schools and youth services to explore the possibilities for developing closer links within particular catchment areas and, where appropriate, for basing youth workers in schools.

R127 LEAs should make the improvement of the motivation and self esteem of lower achieving pupils one of the objectives of their careers services.

R128.1 LEAs and schools should select supply teachers with as much care as full-time staff.

R128.2 LEAs should provide them within in-service training in classroom management.

R129 In order to increase the amount of in-service training undertaken out of school hours, the Secretaries of State should consider the extent to which it would be possible to finance such training from savings achieved by a consequential reduction in the use of supply teachers to replace full-time teachers absent on in-service training courses.

R130 LEAs should make it their normal practice to attach individual supply teachers to specific schools or groups of schools.

R131 Headteachers and teachers should ensure that schools provide a welcoming and supportive environment for supply teachers and adopt a code of practice for the use of supply teachers based on the model provided in this report.

R132.1 An LEA/DES/Welsh Office working group should be set up as soon as possible to develop serious incidents reporting systems with the aim of having a pilot system in place by September 1989.

PUPILS	TEACHERS	HEAD TEACHERS	OTHER SCHOOL STAFF	GOVERNORS	PARENTS	LEAs	TEACHER TRAINERS	CURRICULUM COUNCILS	GOVERNMENT	OTHERS	REFERENCE IN TEXT
						L					10.17
	T	HT				L					10.18
						L				Local Authorities	10.19
	T	HT				L					10.21
						L					10.22
		HT				L					10.25
						L					10.25
									GT		10.29
						L					10.31
	T	HT									10.33
						L			GT		10.39

Recommendations

R132.2 As soon as possible thereafter, all LEAs should establish serious incidents reporting systems and should monitor and act upon the information that these systems provide.

R133 LEAs and governing bodies which employ school staff should establish clear procedures for dealing with attacks on staff by pupils, members of pupils' families or intruders.

R134.1 In considering whether to refer cases of physical attack on school staff to the Crown Prosecution Service, chief officers of police should take into account the effects of their decisions on staff morale as an aspect of public interest.

R134.2 The Crown Prosecution Service should also take staff morale into account as an aspect of public interest when deciding whether to prosecute such cases.

R135 LEAs and governing bodies which employ school staff should, either through insurance cover or ex-gratia payments, ensure that adequate compensation is available to school staff for non-accidental injury, or for damage to their motor vehicles or other belongings which they bring into school but cannot be expected to supervise properly while they are working.

11   THE GOVERNMENT

R136 The Secretaries of State should commission research to investigate the relationships between school staffing levels, class size and pupils' behaviour.

R137.1 The DES and Welsh Office should systematically monitor for five years the operation of the procedures for the exclusion of pupils from schools established by the Education (No. 2) Act 1986.

R137.2 At the end of this period the Secretaries of State should decide, in the light of all the evidence then available, what amendments, if any, should be made to these provisions. They should act sooner if the accumulating evidence warrants it.

PUPILS	TEACHERS	HEAD TEACHERS	OTHER SCHOOL STAFF	GOVERNORS	PARENTS	LEAs	TEACHER TRAINERS	CURRICULUM COUNCILS	GOVERNMENT	OTHERS	REFERENCE IN TEXT
						L			GT		10.39
				GS		L					10.42
										Police	10.45
										CPS	10.45
				GS		L					10.46
									GT		11.18
									GT		11.29
									GT		11.29

Recommendations

R138.1   The appropriate Secretary of State should require any LEA which directs the reinstatement of a permanently excluded pupil to a school against the wishes of the headteacher and governing body to supply him with a written report of the circumstances contributing to this decision within 14 days.

R138.2   The headteacher should be asked to supply his own account to him within the same period.

R138.3   Similar procedures should apply in cases where the governing body directs the reinstatement of a permanently excluded pupil against the wishes of the headteacher.

PUPILS	TEACHERS	HEAD TEACHERS	OTHER SCHOOL STAFF	GOVERNORS	PARENTS	LEAs	TEACHER TRAINERS	CURRICULUM COUNCILS	GOVERNMENT	OTHERS	REFERENCE IN TEXT
						L			GT		11.30
		HT							GT		11.30
		HT		GS		L			GT		11.30

1 The Enquiry

1   In November 1987 the Professional Association of Teachers (PAT) wrote to the Prime Minister suggesting that a committee of enquiry should be set up to look at discipline in schools. The PAT drew attention to the results of a survey that it had carried out with the help of the Daily Express newspaper. The survey found that the great majority of those members who replied believed that indiscipline was on the increase, and about one in three reported that they had been attacked by a pupil at some time in their careers. Other press reports of violent incidents in schools helped to increase public concern about pupils' behaviour.

2   The establishment of the **Enquiry into Discipline in Schools** was announced by the Secretary of State for Education and Science in March 1988. The Secretary of State's announcement pointed out that education can take place only if there is good order in schools. It emphasised concerns about the behaviour of some pupils in some schools, and the need for society as a whole to support teachers in pushing for acceptable standards of behaviour.

3   Our enquiry, which covers schools in England and Wales, was given the following terms of reference:

    'In view of public concern about violence and indiscipline in schools and the problems faced by the teaching profession today, to consider what action can be taken by central government, local authorities, voluntary bodies owning schools, governing bodies of schools, headteachers, teachers and parents to secure the orderly atmosphere necessary in schools for effective teaching and learning to take place.'

4   Over 90% of pupils in England and Wales attend ordinary maintained primary and secondary schools. We decided that the focus of our enquiry should be on these schools. We agreed that, although some of our recommendations might be relevant to special schools and units, we would not make specific recommendations about their internal organisation. It was clear, however, that the ways in which special schools and units are used to support ordinary schools and their pupils were directly relevant to our terms of reference.

5   We also agreed not to assume from the outset of our enquiry that discipline problems were increasing or that schools were facing a major crisis with which they could not cope. The concerns expressed in press reports and the PAT survey were real and strong, but we knew that we would need to consider the widest possible range of evidence before we could come to any balanced conclusions on the matter.

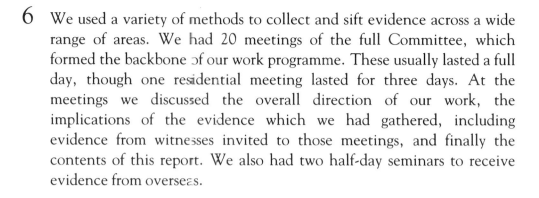

6   We used a variety of methods to collect and sift evidence across a wide range of areas. We had 20 meetings of the full Committee, which formed the backbone of our work programme. These usually lasted a full day, though one residential meeting lasted for three days. At the meetings we discussed the overall direction of our work, the implications of the evidence which we had gathered, including evidence from witnesses invited to those meetings, and finally the contents of this report. We also had two half-day seminars to receive evidence from overseas.

7   We started by identifying four key questions. These formed the basis of all our enquiries. They featured in an advertisement published in May in the educational supplements of national newspapers inviting written contributions to the Enquiry. The questions were about:

7.1   definitions of good behaviour and discipline (and their opposites) in the school context;

7.2   the extent of any discipline problems in schools;

7.3   the principal causes of these problems; and

7.4   action which could be taken by relevant organisations and individuals to promote good behaviour in schools.

8   We sent a more detailed list of questions to all LEAs and all institutions providing teacher training in England and Wales. 68 LEAs and 59 teacher training institutions replied – a response rate in both cases of over 60%. Many other national organisations also supplied written evidence, either in response to our advertisement or to a specific invitation. In all, we received a total of 476 submissions from these other organisations and individuals, including many serving teachers. This makes a total of just over 600 written submissions. Details are given in Appendix A. We are most grateful to all those who contributed in this way.

9   We also invited a number of witnesses to our meetings. They included representatives of the seven major teacher unions in England and Wales, other national organisations and expert witnesses on various topics. Our discussions with them helped us to explore some of the more difficult issues raised in the written evidence. We were also able to learn at first-hand from their experiences. Once again, we are most grateful for all their help. Their names are listed in Appendix B.

10   Visits were an important part of our work programme. We were anxious to see for ourselves schools and other institutions in different regional and social settings. In particular, we hoped to draw lessons from any

good practice we observed. We also wanted to talk to serving teachers, pupils and others at the 'chalk-face' about the issues at the heart of our enquiry. We therefore set up a varied programme of visits, particularly to schools in the kind of inner city areas where difficulties might be expected. Small groups of us visited a total of 25 schools, teacher training institutions and special units throughout England and Wales. Details are given in Appendix C. We should like to record our thanks for the co-operation, courtesy and frankness with which all of these institutions received our visits and enquiries.

11   Other useful evidence was gathered from abroad. Concern about discipline in schools is not unique to this country. We quickly recognised that there might be lessons for us in the experiences and the practices in education systems overseas. We divided into small groups for our three overseas visits to the Netherlands, Norway and the USA. In each of these countries, we were able to meet with senior educationalists and to visit schools. We also held two special seminars with expert witnesses from Japan and Australia. Details are included in Appendix B.

12   We also commissioned the largest structured survey concentrating on teachers' perceptions of the problem ever carried out in Britain. This is described in chapter two.

13   We were given a challenging timetable for our task. Our report, which covers a wide range of complex issues, was completed in just over 10 months.

1 Every organisation depends on people behaving in certain ways to achieve its purposes. Companies cannot achieve good results without co-operative effort. Neither can schools. A school's central purpose is that children should learn. Good behaviour makes effective teaching and learning possible. Bad behaviour disrupts these processes.

2 The two questions most frequently asked about bad behaviour in schools are how much of it is there, and is there more now than in the past? We quickly discovered that these questions could not be answered directly. No relevant national statistics exist. We recommend a way of filling this information gap in chapter 10.

3 We looked for other kinds of information which might indicate the size of the problem and recent trends. Two seemed directly relevant. One was the records kept by LEAs of pupils excluded from their schools. The other was the results of postal surveys carried out by heads' and teachers' professional associations which asked their members how they saw the problem.

4 Pupils are excluded (suspended or expelled) from school for misbehaviour which headteachers consider serious enough to warrant such punishment. In theory, the number of exclusions could be used as a crude indicator of how much serious misbehaviour had occurred in a year and whether it was becoming more of less frequent. The evidence we received on exclusions is too fragmentary to be used in this way. Some LEAs provided us with figures showing the number of pupils excluded from their schools over the last few years. Others told us that they do not keep such records. Some of those that do had started recording exclusions too recently to give any meaningful indication of trends. Records are also kept in different ways which makes it very difficult to compare and combine figures from different LEAs. We looked at the total number of exclusions in the small number of LEAs which had provided figures going back several years. We could see no clear overall trend, but the data are too patchy for us to be certain that none exists. In chapter 10 we suggest that exclusion figures should be collected more systematically.

5 We received written and oral evidence from the seven major professional associations representing heads and teachers in England and Wales. With different degrees of emphasis they told us that their members saw disruptive behaviour and violence to staff as serious problems, and that many believed that they were now more common in schools than they had been five or 10 years ago.

6   The National Association of Headteachers (NAHT), the National Union of Teachers (NUT) and the Professional Association of Teachers (PAT) included the results of surveys in their submissions to us. The National Association of Schoolmasters/Union of Women Teachers (NAS/UWT) referred us to survey results previously sent to the Department of Education and Science (DES). Strong concerns were expressed in these surveys about indiscipline and violence to teachers. Some of these figures did indeed seem worrying. About 80% of the teachers who responded to the 1985 NAS/UWT survey said that they thought violence and disruption had become more frequent in schools over the last 10 years; 25% reported being threatened with violence and 4% said that they had actually been attacked in a six month period. 94% of those responding to the 1987 PAT survey said that they thought indiscipline was on the increase and 32% reported that they had been attacked at some time during their career. The 1988 NUT survey carried out by its school representatives found that 91% of those responding considered that discipline problems were now worse than they had been 10 years ago.

7   In its submission the NUT suggested that the results of its survey should be treated with some caution. It pointed out that, because of time constraints, the percentage of representatives responding by the deadline (the response rate, estimated at about 8%) was relatively low, and that professional researchers might criticise the design of its questionnaire. Similar difficulties arise in interpreting the results of the NAS/UWT and PAT national surveys. In both cases the response rates were very low (less than 4% of the membership of each union). We have no way of knowing how representative these self-selected samples were. It could be that only those members who felt most strongly about the issue returned the questionnaire.

8   The NUT also submitted the results of a survey it had commissioned from a professional polling organisation, National Opinion Polls (NOP). NOP interviewed a sample of just under 500 teachers selected to be reasonably representative of the profession as a whole. NOP's results are not open to the same kind of technical criticism as those of the other surveys we received. The NOP survey found that 36% of the teachers in its sample thought that there was more indiscipline in their schools than five years ago. 33% thought that there was the same amount or less. 7% of its sample reported having been threatened or physically attacked by a pupil or parent in the last year. It should be borne in mind that these figures are drawn from a relatively small sample and may be subject to considerable margins of error.

9   The NAHT survey was of headteachers of schools in 15 LEAs chosen to represent a mixture of urban and rural areas. The response rate was low

(45%) but much higher than that of the other associations' national surveys, with the exception of that carried out by NOP. The NAHT survey found that 25% of the heads who responded thought that there had been a significant increase in the amount of disruptive behaviour in their schools since 1985.

10   After considering all the evidence submitted to us by LEAs, heads' and teachers' professional associations about the incidence of bad behaviour and violence in schools we reached five conclusions. They were that:

10.1   in the absence of national statistics the problem itself could not be directly measured. Any estimate would have to be based mainly on teachers' perceptions;

10.2   while the survey results presented to us by the professional associations showed the strong concern felt by many of their members, these results could not be used as reliable estimates of the extent to which such problems affect schools across the country;

10.3   we could provide no definitive answer to the question of whether things are getting worse. To answer this question we would need a firm baseline of information about the situation at a particular point in time followed up by a further study carried out on the same basis. Clearly we could not complete such an exercise within the period of our enquiry. All we could know was that a substantial number of heads and teachers believe that the amount of bad behaviour has increased in recent years. We agreed that this belief was in itself an important consideration for our enquiry;

10.4   we should consider how an information baseline could be established for future use (see chapter 10); and

10.5   we did not know enough about the nature of the problem. The associations' surveys asked specific questions about physical aggression and verbal abuse and much more general questions about indiscipline or disruptive behaviour. We decided that we needed to look in detail at the whole range of pupils' behaviour to find out what teachers find most worrying and difficult to deal with before we made any firm recommendations for action.

11   Press attention has perhaps understandably highlighted the issue of violence in schools. Only one LEA, the Inner London Education Authority (ILEA), provided us with statistical evidence of the number of school staff involved in violent incidents. According to the report on **Preventing Violence to Staff** published in 1988 by the Health and

Safety Executive, it is the only LEA in England and Wales to keep systematic records of such incidents. ILEA figures show that, in the 1987/88 school year, 187 teachers in ordinary schools reported that they had sustained some kind of injury in incidents involving pupils, parents or other adults. This figure represents less than 1% of all the teachers working in these schools. Medical attention was recommended or received in less than 20% of these cases. 48 of these incidents can be classified as deliberate attacks by pupils on teachers. This represents about 0.2% of all teachers working in ordinary ILEA schools. Most of the other incidents involved teachers stopping fights or physically restraining pupils in some way. A more detailed breakdown of the ILEA figures is provided in chapter 10. They give a rather different picture from that which has been presented by some journalists. Figures from any single authority must, of course, be used cautiously when considering the national position. It is possible, for example, that some of the more minor incidents of physical aggression by pupils in ILEA schools were not reported by the staff involved. But in view of staff concern it seems likely that all the more serious incidents were reported. The social environment surrounding many ILEA schools should also be borne in mind. It seems likely to us that, while the ILEA figures may give some indication of the frequency of violent incidents in comparable inner city areas, such incidents may be less frequent in small town or rural settings.

12 The impression created by press reports is that the threat of violence causes teachers more concern than other types of bad behaviour. We were not satisfied that we had sufficient information about how teachers rated this problem in comparison to others they faced. The surveys provided by the professional associations gave us no guidance on this question. Our attention was drawn to a recent survey carried out by researchers from Birmingham University's Centre for Child Study (Houghton, Wheldall and Merrett 1988) which indicated a pattern of concern very different from the press picture. A representative sample of just over 250 secondary teachers in the West Midlands were asked about the types of misbehaviour they found most troublesome in their classrooms. They were given 10 categories to choose from. The behaviour that was rated most troublesome by a wide margin was 'talking out of turn'. Then came 'hindering other children' and 'calculated idleness'. Physical aggression came last in rank order. Although this survey was of a small, regional sample of teachers it provided us with a useful pointer towards a possible national approach. The main conclusion drawn by the researchers from their survey was that teachers are, in general, much more concerned about persistent minor misbehaviour than the occasional dramatic confrontation. We

decided that this proposition needed careful testing. If persistent low level classroom disruption was the central problem faced by teachers the main thrust of any action we recommended would have to be towards dealing with it.

OUR SURVEY

13 We therefore decided to commission our own research which would be designed to overcome the limitations of the other survey evidence available to us. Appendix D to our report contains a more detailed account of this project. The paragraphs that follow are a summary of its findings.

14 We asked researchers at Sheffield University's Educational Research Centre to examine teachers' perceptions and concerns about discipline. They chose to do it in two related ways. The first was to undertake a nationally representative survey of primary and secondary teachers in England and Wales. At the same time 100 teachers in 10 inner-city secondary schools not covered by the survey were interviewed. What kinds of behaviours did teachers have to deal with in the course of their classroom teaching? What kinds of problems did they encounter in the course of their duties round the school? How serious did they think discipline problems were? What, if anything, did they find difficult to deal with? What strategies and sanctions had they been using? What kinds of initiatives had they been taking? And what did they think should be done? These were the questions they explored.

15 The national survey obtained responses from over 3,500 teachers in some 220 primary and some 250 secondary schools. Of those to whom questionnaires were sent, 89% of the primary teachers and 79% of the secondary teachers returned them. These are high response rates for surveys of this kind. Well over half the respondents also wrote at length about further aspects of their experiences. In combination with the information gathered in the interviews, they provided a comprehensive picture of teachers' views on and experiences of discipline at the present time.

16 The questionnaire asked teachers to report on their experiences in the classroom and around the school during the previous week. The vast majority of primary and secondary teachers reported that, at some point, the flow of their lessons had been impeded or disrupted by having to deal with minor discipline problems. Pupils 'talking out of turn', 'hindering other pupils', 'making unnecessary (non-verbal) noise' and 'calculated idleness or work avoidance' were the most commonly reported forms of bad behaviour in class. 'Showing lack of concern for

others', 'unruliness while waiting' and 'running in the corridors' were the most frequently mentioned forms of bad behaviour encountered during the course of teachers' duties round the school. One in four teachers reported having to deal with such behaviour on a daily basis. 'Verbal abuse towards other pupils', 'general rowdiness' and 'cheeky or impertinent remarks or responses' were also encountered frequently by both primary and secondary teachers. Primary teachers made special mention of having to handle 'physical aggression towards other pupils', both in the classroom and around the school. The interviews with teachers indicated that while teachers are dealing with these problems as a matter of routine, their cumulative effects are wearing and contribute to a sense of stress and growing frustration.

17 Some teachers mentioned having to deal with problems that were more serious in themselves. More than one in 10 secondary teachers and more than one in 20 primary teachers reported that, at some point during the week of the survey, they had had verbal abuse directed towards them by pupils. Around one in 50 primary and secondary teachers also reported having to deal with some form of physical aggression directed towards them during the course of the week. Evidence obtained during the face to face interviews suggested that when teachers referred to 'physical aggression' they did not necessarily mean that they had been intentionally struck or hit by pupils. Experiences of 'physical aggression' may be by-products of other occurrences, such as interventions when pupils were fighting each other. One in 200 secondary teachers, however, indicated by their replies that their experiences had probably been more serious. The corresponding figure for primary teachers would seem to have been considerably lower than this. Hardly any of them described serious incidents.

18 About one in six secondary teachers and about one in 10 primary teachers thought that the discipline problems in their schools were 'serious'. Although the teachers who thought this way were spread across large numbers of schools and there were quite marked differences between schools, there was a noticeable tendency for teachers in particular shools to agree with one another about the seriousness of the problems. The responses of individual teachers in each school were aggregated to create an overall 'seriousness' score. In just under one in 10 secondary schools and in about one in 20 primary schools the staff as a group thought the problems were verging on the serious in that school. Teachers in schools with higher proportions of pupils from 'economically disadvantaged areas' or pupils of 'below average' attainments were more likely to think there were serious problems than teachers in other kinds of schools.

19 Six out of 10 secondary teachers reported finding one or more of their classes difficult to teach whilst eight out of 10 teachers found one or more of their pupils difficult to teach. The corresponding figures for primary teachers were rather lower than these.

20 One in three secondary teachers and one in five primary teachers reported that there were particular forms of bad behaviour by pupils which they found difficult to deal with in the classroom. 'Talking out of turn', 'hindering other pupils', 'calculated idleness or work avoidance' and 'verbal abuse towards other pupils' were among those most frequently mentioned. Among the small group of primary teachers who mentioned anything at all, 'physical aggression towards other pupils' was singled out as a particular concern. Interestingly, only a small proportion of those who reported experiencing 'physical aggression' towards themselves mentioned this as 'the most difficult' or 'next most difficult' pupil behaviour with which they had had to deal.

21 Corporal punishment was available as a deterrent in many secondary schools until fairly recently. Two out of three secondary teachers reported that it was in use in their schools, albeit occasionally, as recently as three years ago. The figures for primary schools were lower; half said it was not used at that time and most of the remainder said it was hardly used at all. Since its formal abolition, schools had developed a variety of strategies and sanctions to replace it. There were some indications, from the interviews, that the longer ago a school had dropped its use, the less likely teachers were to be concerned about its absence as a deterrent.

22 A wide variety of strategies and sanctions were reported as being in use for dealing with bad behaviour. With the exception of 'reasoning with pupils outside the classroom setting', which was generally seen as effective, none were uniformly endorsed as being highly effective or ineffective. The interviews with classroom teachers indicated a number of important areas in which schools had developed their approaches. These included: their systems of incentives, sanctions and support; the development of shared understanding and mutual support among members of staff; better ways of talking things through with pupils; the review and development of new approaches to curriculum content and teaching styles; and greater attention to the nature of home–school relationships.

23 There was broad agreement among both primary and secondary teachers that smaller classes would be beneficial in dealing with discipline problems and a variety of other factors were also identified, many of which schools could not influence. At the same time there was a

recognition, especially among secondary teachers, that more could be done within the school. Alongside 'tougher sanctions' for certain forms of indiscipline, teachers endorsed a wide variety of guidance and support systems both for teachers and pupils as well as more staff discussions and closer links with parents and the community. It was clear that, provided policies and developments were seen to be tackling discipline issues directly, there would be support from the teaching profession for a broad range of approaches.

OUR APPROACH

24   One of the most striking features of our evidence is the sheer variety of causes of, and cures for, bad behaviour in schools that was suggested to us. A few submissions fall into the single cause or single cure category, but the great majority are much more complex. Parents, teachers, heads, LEAs, teacher trainers, the Government and broadcasters are all blamed for aggravating the problem and asked to contribute towards various strategies for reducing it. We discuss a range of these suggestions in the relevant chapters of our report.

25   The variety of causes and cures suggested to us represents an important finding in itself. It is clear that most of the individuals and organisations submitting evidence consider that bad behaviour in schools is a complex problem which does not lend itself to simple solutions. Taken as a whole the evidence submitted to us indicates that any quest for a single, dramatic remedy, such as a major piece of new legislation, would be futile.

26   A few of the submissions we received took the view that bad behaviour is always entirely the fault of pupils. We reject this view. No pupil is an island. Every incident has a range of immediate and longer term causes. Events in the classroom are influenced by a complex mixture of expectations, attitudes, regulations, policies and laws which are shaped by forces at work in the classroom, the school, the local community and society as a whole. The most central of these influences is the relationship between teacher and pupils. When a teacher sees behaviour, judges it to be unacceptable and intervenes to stop it, it is the relationship between that teacher and the pupil or pupils involved which will determine the success of that intervention. Yet that relationship is itself affected by outside influences. We distinguish four levels of influence, illustrated by the diagram opposite.

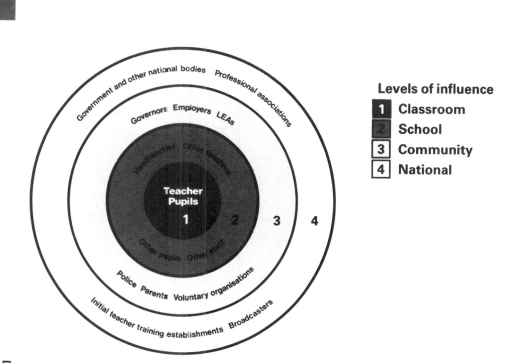

Levels of influence

1 Classroom
2 School
3 Community
4 National

27 In the chapters that follow we identify a need for action by individuals and organisations at all four levels. Many of our recommendations could be implemented within a single classroom, school or LEA. We are convinced, however, that a significant national improvement in standards of behaviour in schools can only be achieved through action by all the parties named in the diagram above.

28 Bad behaviour is not a new problem, nor is it confined to England and Wales. Teachers interviewed as part of a study of pupils' behaviour in 25 English girls schools published 50 years ago (Milner 1938) complained about the number of difficult pupils they had to deal with, about persistent noise in the classroom and about teacher 'fatigue'. Our expert witnesses from Japan and Australia talked of widespread concern about pupils' behaviour in both their countries. American evidence, such as the survey carried out the US Department of Education in 1987, indicates that many teachers there see the problem as serious. That survey found that 44% of teachers who responded considered that the amount of disruptive behaviour in schools had increased in the last five years. Teachers and other educationalists we met on our visit to the USA confirmed that there was widespread concern in American schools about pupils' behaviour.

29 Reducing bad behaviour is a realistic aim. Eliminating it completely is not. Historical and international comparisons help to illustrate this obvious but important point. Children have a need to discover where the boundaries of acceptable behaviour lie. It is natural for them to test these boundaries to confirm their location and, in some cases, for the excitement of a challenge. The proper answer to such testing is to confirm the existence of the boundaries, and to do so firmly, unequivocally and at once. This will often involve the use of an

appropriate punishment. An uncertain or delayed response invites renewed challenges which can draw children into more serious misbehaviour. They should never be left in doubt as to what is and what is not acceptable behaviour. A lack of firmness and clarity does no service to children. Our visits showed us that good schools can reduce misbehaviour to an absolute minimum. While some schools seem preoccupied with bad behaviour, others have concerted policies for raising expectations and improving standards. The schools we saw which had such positive policies seemed to be very successful in creating an orderly and purposeful atmosphere. They had marginalised bad behaviour by promoting good behaviour. The central thrust of our recommendations is towards promoting good behaviour among pupils.

30 The tone and content of many of the individual letters we received indicate that bad behaviour in schools is a particularly emotive issue. Teachers complain in the strongest terms about the lack of support that society gives them in dealing with it. We note that views on its causes and cures are often based on deeply held beliefs, such as the importance of punishment as a form of moral retribution or the need to recognise children's rights, rather than on evidence about what happens and what works in schools. Our approach has been to look for evidence of effective practice across the widest possible range of information that we could gather.

31 The Education Reform Act 1988 defines the purposes of the school curriculum as promoting *'the spiritual, moral, cultural, mental and physical development of pupils and preparing them for the opportunities, responsibilities and experiences of adult life'*. Throughout this report we emphasise the importance of this broad view of education. Co-operative behaviour makes any organisation more efficient, but in schools such behaviour is more than just useful. Schools exist to teach values as well as knowledge and skills. Educationalists call those aspects of school life which are about learning values the 'affective curriculum'. Schools teach values through specific activities such as assemblies and lessons covering religious, personal and social education. They also promote them in other equally important ways, such as through their rules and the behaviour of teachers and pupils towards one another. Promoting responsible behaviour and self-discipline, and the values on which they are based, is an essential task for schools. We consider that it cannot be separated from the practical need to maintain order.

3 Teachers

1 The classroom is the most important place in the education system. What happens there every school day decides how well the purposes of the system are being achieved.

2 In order to learn well, children need a calm and purposeful classroom atmosphere. Our terms of reference ask us to look at how this can be secured. Teachers must be able to keep order. If they cannot, all the children in their charge will suffer. They should not face this task alone. They need and deserve support from many other organisations, groups and individuals. But we start by considering teachers because they play the central role.

CLASSROOM MANAGEMENT

3 Our survey shows that teachers see talking out of turn and other forms of persistent, low-level disruption as the most frequent and wearing kinds of classroom misbehaviour. Low-level disruption is not a new feature of classroom life. All of us remember from our own school days that some teachers had problems with their classes and others did not. Those who did not were by no means always older or stricter. They were teachers we respected and very often liked. Such teachers knew how to get the best out of groups of children.

4 Our evidence shows a very broad measure of agreement across the education service (headteachers' and teachers' professional associations, training establishments, LEAs and individual teachers) that a teacher's general competence has a strong influence on his or her pupils' behaviour. There is also a broad measure of agreement on what a teacher needs to be fully effective. Knowledge of the subject to be taught is obviously crucial. So is the ability to plan and deliver a lesson which flows smoothly and holds pupils' attention. The third area of competence comprises a range of skills associated with managing groups of pupils. It includes the ability to relate to young people, to encourage them in good behaviour and learning, and to deal calmly but firmly with inappropriate or disruptive behaviour. As a useful shorthand we refer to it in our report as 'group management skills'.

5 Our evidence suggests that the importance of group management skills tends to be underestimated by teachers and by their trainers. This was confirmed by our expert witnesses. We find this worrying because it is the area of competence which relates most directly to pupil behaviour.

6 Teachers with good group management skills are able to establish positive relationships with their classes based on mutual respect. They

can create a classroom climate in which pupils lose rather than gain popularity with their classmates by causing trouble. They can also spot a disruptive incident in the making, choose an appropriate tactic to deal with it and nip it in the bud. They always seem to know what is going on behind their backs. Good group managers understand how groups of young people react to each other and to teachers. They also understand, and are in full control of, their own behaviour. They model the good behaviour they expect of pupils. All this requires an impressive range of professional skills.

7 We appreciate the difficulty of the task facing teachers, and the fact that most of them tackle it well every day. This deserves recognition and respect. We also recognise that teachers need support from a variety of sources. Many of our recommendations aim to provide or improve that support. We do not underestimate the seriousness of classroom violence. It is rare but it happens. Teachers who are attacked should have the strongest possible backing and we make recommendations to this effect in chapter 10.

8 Our evidence suggests however that there are teachers who lack confidence in their own ability to deal with disruption and who see their classes as potentially hostile. They create a negative classroom atmosphere by frequent criticism and rare praise. They make use of loud public reprimands and threats. They are sometimes sarcastic. They tend to react aggressively to minor incidents. Their methods increase the danger of a major confrontation not only with individual pupils but with the whole class.

9 Young people rightly see this kind of defensive style as a sign of weakness. Like anyone else they react badly to frequent criticism, sarcasm and aggression. A class will feel no good will towards teachers who behave in this way. Their punishments will be seen as unjust and vindictive. In this atmosphere pupils will gain status with their classmates by challenging the teacher's authority.

10 Serious classroom disruption usually comes about by a process of escalation. It is very unusual for serious trouble to start without a build-up. Escalation from minor incidents can have serious results, such as teachers being verbally abused by pupils. Several of our expert witnesses emphasised the importance of understanding escalation and avoiding it by appropriate intervention.

11 Teachers suffer from quite high levels of occupational stress, and we would expect difficulties with pupils' behaviour to contribute to these. Research evidence (Kyriacou 1986) confirms our impressions. Most

teachers work in situations where they are the only adult in a room full of children. If relationships are good the experience can be very rewarding. If not it can very stressful. The feeling that things are out of control is an important cause of stress. Teachers who lack group management skills will experience that feeling and the resulting stress will make them even less effective. Growing anxiety will also make their relationships with pupils more difficult and increase their tendency to overreact to minor incidents.

12   A few letters we received came close to saying that group management should not be part of a teacher's job. We reject this view. Teaching has never just been about the transmission of knowledge and never will be. Establishing good relationships with pupils, encouraging them to learn and to behave well have always been essential parts of a teacher's work. This cannot be achieved by talking at children, but by working with them.

13   A more common belief is that group management skills are simply a natural gift. You either have it or you don't. Our evidence does not support this belief. Its most damaging feature is that teachers who have difficulty controlling classes tend to put this down to personal inadequacy rather that to a lack of particular skills which can be acquired through training or advice from colleagues.

14   The most talented, 'natural' teachers may need little training or advice because they learn so quickly from experience. At the other extreme, there are a few teachers for whom training and advice will not be properly effective because their personalities do not match the needs of the job. It is clear, however, that the majority of teachers can become more effective classroom managers as a result of the right kinds of training, experience and support.

15   Teachers have tended to stay out of each others' classrooms and not to talk about their own discipline problems. Too often teachers do not seek help because it feels like an admission of incompetence, and they do not offer it because it feels like accusing a colleague of incompetence. As a result the tradition of classroom isolation persists in many schools.

16   The beliefs that either group management skills should not be necessary or that they cannot be learned seem to be traditional in parts of the profession. Our evidence suggests that these beliefs contribute significantly towards teacher stress. This is further increased by the more widespread tradition of classroom isolation. We see these beliefs or traditions as barriers to good teaching. They should be removed as quickly as possible.

17   In 1987 Her Majesty's Inspectors of Schools (HMI) carried out a survey of about 300 new teachers in their first year in schools. Among other things HMI asked them how well they felt their training had prepared them for classroom management. We did not find their answers reassuring. HMI say that *'most comments on education studies complained of an over-emphasis on theory ... A substantial number of new teachers felt that discipline and control had not been adequately dealt with on their courses'*.

18   HMI observed lessons taught by these teachers. In 85% of them class management was considered satisfactory, but in 15% it was not.

19   Most of these teachers were trained before the present criteria for approving teacher training courses came into effect. These criteria are set out in DES Circular 3/84 and Welsh Office Circular 21/84. They include the requirement that courses should prepare students *'to teach the full range of pupils . . . with their diversity of . . . behaviour'*.

20   We asked all 92 initial teacher training establishments in England and Wales (colleges, polytechnic and university departments) specific questions about the training they provided in the practical aspects of group management in the classroom. We received 56 replies. Many said that discipline issues 'permeated' their courses. We were however concerned to find that, despite the criteria established by Circular 3/84, few seemed to include specific units covering classroom behaviour in their courses.

21   We also wrote to all 105 LEAs in England and Wales asking them about in-service training provision for teachers on the subject of classroom behaviour. From our 67 replies we discovered that a few are developing programmes based on training packages such as **Preventative Approaches to Disruption** (PAD) or **Behavioural Approaches to Teaching Package** (BATPACK). Most do not seem to provide this kind of in-service training.

22   The general lack of initial and in-service training in group management skills was confirmed by several of our expert witnesses. It is surprising given the widespread concern felt by teachers themselves about pupils' behaviour. Three out of four teachers in our survey felt that more in-service training in this area was, or might be, needed.

23   Our evidence leads us to three important conclusions. First, that teachers' group management skills are probably the single most important factor in achieving good standards of classroom behaviour. Second, that those skills can be taught and learned. Third, that practical training provision in this area is inadequate.

24   We believe that it would be a disservice to teachers not to highlight their central role in promoting good behaviour in schools and the importance of training in helping them to carry out that role. But it is important to see our recommendations in these areas in the context of the report as a whole. Teachers are entitled to expect and receive support from heads, governors, parents, LEAs and the Government in this task. Throughout this report we stress the need for concerted action at classroom, school, community and national levels. Our emphasis on the role of the teacher and on training in classroom management should not be seen in isolation as an easy answer to indiscipline. They are simply important aspects of a wide range of recommendations for action by all those with an interest in improving standards of behaviour in schools.

25   We have identified six target areas for action to improve classroom management skills. They involve teachers, training establishments and LEAs. They are:

25.1   applying the principles of good classroom management;

25.2   careful selection of trainee teachers;

25.3   more specific initial training;

25.4   more specific in-service training;

25.5   better induction programmes for new teachers; and

25.6   the regular appraisal of teachers' classroom performance.

Applying the principles of good classroom management

26   Our purpose is not to produce a classroom management text book, nor do we need to do so. There is no shortage of good practical guides. Some are listed in our selected bibliography (Appendix E). Many teachers and their trainers will be aware of them. We commend them to those who are not.

27   Although there are some differences in detail, there is a high degree of agreement in the literature about the main features of good practice. There is also general agreement that well organised and delivered lessons help secure good standards of behaviour. Some of the clearest messages are that teachers should:

27.1   know their pupils as individuals. This means knowing their names, their personalities and interests and who their friends are;

27.2   plan and organise both the classroom and the lesson to keep pupils interested and minimise the opportunities for disruption. This requires attention to such basics as furniture layout, grouping of pupils, matching work to pupils' abilities, pacing lessons well, being enthusiastic and using humour to create a positive classroom atmosphere;

27.3   be flexible in order to take advantage of unexpected events rather than being thrown off balance by them. Examples would include the appearance of the window cleaner or a wasp in the middle of a lesson;

27.4   continually observe or 'scan' the behaviour of the class;

27.5   be aware of, and control their own behaviour, including stance and tone of voice;

27.6   model the standards of courtesy that they expect from pupils;

27.7   emphasise the positive, including praise for good behaviour as well as good work;

27.8   make the rules for classroom behaviour clear to pupils from the first lesson and explain why they are necessary;

27.9   make sparing and consistent use of reprimands. This means being firm rather than aggressive, targeting the right pupil, criticising the behaviour and not the person, using private rather than public reprimands whenever possible, being fair and consistent, and avoiding sarcasm and idle threats;

27.10   make sparing and consistent use of punishments. This includes avoiding whole group punishment which pupils see as unfair. It also means avoiding punishments which humiliate pupils by, for example, making them look ridiculous. This breeds resentment; and

27.11   analyse their own classroom management performance and learn from it. This is the most important message of all.

28   **We recommend that teachers and their trainers should recognise and apply the principles of good classroom management.**

Selecting trainee teachers

29   Stereotyping successful teachers is dangerous. There are men and women of all ages, backgrounds and ethnic origins who are good classroom managers. There is also scope for a variety of personal styles to flourish. But the range of suitable personalities is not infinite. In our view the potential ability to form good relationships with children based on mutual respect is an essential quality. It is not possessed by all adults and cannot necessarily be acquired by those who do not possess it.

30   We have been told that it has not been unknown for teacher training establishments to offer places to students without interviewing them.

Circular 3/84 requires institutions to have *'adequate procedures for assessing whether or not candidates display the personal qualities suitable for teaching'* which *'should in all cases involve a personal or group interview with each candidate being considered for admission'.* We regard an interview as essential.

31 We recognise that market forces play a part in teacher recruitment and that college admissions tutors may not always have the choice of candidates they would wish for. In our judgement, however, education is better served by not filling a place than by giving an unsuitable candidate qualified teacher status for up to 40 years.

32 **We recommend that initial teacher training establishments should give full weight to the personal qualities required for effective classroom management, particularly the potential ability to relate well to children, when selecting applicants.**

R
2

33 We believe that careers advisers working in schools, colleges and universities also have a role to play in the process of selection by guiding suitable pupils and students towards, and others away from, teaching as a career.

34 'Pupillage', which involves a student spending some time observing the work of a school before the start of initial training is a good test of their interest in, and capacity to enjoy teaching. A number of institutions recommend or require such a period of pre-course school experience and provide guidance on how to use it. Pupillage may, however, involve considerable practical difficulties. For school leavers, the time available is restricted to the gap between the end of their public examinations and the beginning of the college or university term – a few weeks in July and September. Schools may be reluctant to release or receive students at those times. We are not therefore recommending that pupillage should become a condition of entry for initial training. But we do believe that it can be used by students to test their own ability to relate to children. **We therefore recommend:**

34.1 **that initial teacher training establishments should encourage students to undertake a period of pupillage, or other work with children, before starting their courses; and**

R
3.1

34.2 **that schools should offer opportunities for intending teachers to undertake such pupillage.**

R
3.2

35 Such experience can also be gained by young people thinking of teaching as a career at an earlier stage, perhaps as part of sixth form work experience schemes. This has the advantage of taking place before any commitment to training has been made.

3

Initial
training

36 We do not pretend that better initial training offers a rapid remedy for discipline problems, but we are convinced that it can play a vital part in longer term solutions. Our evidence indicates that, for too many establishments, the general criteria set out in DES Circular 3/84 are not sufficiently detailed and specific in relation to discipline to produce the kind of systematic training in group management which is required.

37 **We therefore recommend that the Secretaries of State should, when reviewing the criteria for the approval of initial teacher training courses, incorporate the following requirements:**

R 4.1

37.1 **that all courses should contain compulsory and clearly identifiable elements dealing in specific and practical terms with group management skills;**

R 4.2

37.2 **that these elements should aim to enhance students' skills in relating to pupils by increasing their understanding of group behaviour and the techniques available to manage it;**

R 4.3

37.3 **that they should involve practical learning methods, and that the skills which effective group management is based on should be an explicit part both of college work and school experience;**

R 4.4

37.4 **that teaching practice should be systematically used to consolidate these skills; and**

R 4.5

37.5 **that the development of the ability to relate well to pupils should be a key consideration in assessing a student's overall competence to teach.**

38 Colleges providing specific training in group management will still need to ensure that discussion of these skills and their links with wider issues of classroom organisation and curriculum continues to permeate their courses. Students' de-briefing sessions with their tutors after teaching practice must, for example, cover a wide range of topics. These sessions should include detailed discussion of group management issues. We do not consider it appropriate for us to specify the amount of time that course elements covering group management skills should occupy. But it would in our view be very difficult to deliver the practical college-based training in less than 10 taught hours.

39 It may be argued that not enough course time is available to meet this requirement. This is a question of competing priorities. Classroom management and the ability to relate to pupils are central to the teacher's job. Without them, the teacher's specialist and theoretical knowledge are useless. Time must be found by a proper ordering of priorities.

40 Initial training in group management skills should not require additional resources. It may, however, have practical implications for some training establishments. They may have to bring in outside specialists, such as good classroom teachers and educational psychologists, to train the trainers. The teacher trainers themselves will need to refresh and refine their own classroom skills. Some have not taught full-time in schools for many years. Circular 3/84 recognises this problem. It states that staff who provide training in teaching skills should have had *'recent success as teachers of the age range to which their training courses are directed, and should maintain regular and frequent experience of classroom teaching. If some members of staff cannot satisfy this requirement, the . . . institution should provide them with opportunities to demonstrate their teaching effectiveness in schools, for example, by means of secondments to schools or schemes for tutor/school exchanges'.* We believe that teacher training establishments must comply closely with these requirements if they are to deliver effective training in group management skills. We consider that secondments and exchanges are particularly useful methods of updating tutors' skills, and that a minimum amount of regular classroom teaching experience should be specified for tutors. **We therefore recommend that, when reviewing the criteria for the approval of initial teacher training courses, the Secretaries of State should specify a minimum requirement for regular classroom teaching experience for staff providing training in teaching skills equivalent to one term in every five years.**

41 We believe that schools also have an important part to play in preparing trainee teachers to manage their classes effectively. Systematic consolidation of group management skills through school experience would have practical implications for schools which receive students. The role of supervising teachers, whose classes students take, will need clarifying. So in larger schools will that of a school's professional tutor, who is responsible among other things for students and probationary teachers. Headteachers will need to ensure that suitable arrangements are made and that these roles are discharged properly.

42 We have described how teachers' traditional reluctance to talk about discipline problems or to let colleagues into their classrooms feeds into a spiral of less effective group management and mounting stress. Support from colleagues as professional equals, which we call 'peer support', is a way of breaking out of that spiral. The peer support group is a valuable resource which is as yet little used in British schools. We were impressed by accounts of its effectiveness in the Australian state of Victoria and by our observation of a similar group in action in a school in North Tyneside. A peer support group is led by a 'facilitator' who is responsible for convening the group and chairing its discussions. It meets regularly

on a voluntary basis to talk about classroom management skills. The group can work on three levels. First, its discussions are a very effective form of in-service training. We were given evidence that teachers often learn more about classroom skills by talking to each other than by listening to visiting 'experts'. A peer support group provides regular opportunities for sharing experiences and skills. Second, it helps to break down the tradition of isolation by opening the classroom door. Peer support groups can develop the kind of trust and confidence which leads to mutual observation and consultancy, which involves watching and commenting on each other's teaching. This is probably the most effective method of classroom skills training available. Third, it helps to reduce occupational stress. Knowing that even the most experienced teachers can have classroom management problems and that it is acceptable to admit them is a good way of reducing stress. The feeling that it is possible to do something about those problems is even more reassuring.

R 6

43 Later in this chapter we recommend the promotion of peer support through in-service training. It would spread more quickly if new teachers arrived in schools expecting to find a peer support group. **We therefore recommend that initial teacher training establishments should introduce students to the concept of peer support and its uses.**

Induction programmes for new teachers

44 The HMI survey of new teachers in schools contains some worrying findings about the induction programmes provided for them. 37% of the new teachers in primary schools said they had not been observed teaching by colleagues during their first six months in post. Less than half the schools in the survey provided conditions which, in HMI's view, encouraged the full professional development of new teachers.

45 Induction programmes for new teachers seem to vary considerably between different LEAs and schools. In some, reduced timetables for probationary teachers and the existence of professional tutors can be taken for granted. In others, new teachers seem to be thrown in at the deep end.

R 7

46 We consider the deep end approach unacceptable. It is unreasonable to expect a new teacher to become fully effective in classroom management without guidance and support. **We therefore recommend that LEAs should ensure that their induction programmes for new teachers take full account of the need to provide on- and off-the-job training in classroom and group mangement skills.**

47 Every LEA and school should have a systematic induction programme for new teachers. In our view, the minimum requirements for such a

programme would be:

47.1   a clear statement of the school's standards or objectives for classroom behaviour and details of the support available to the new teachers to enable them to achieve these;

47.2   in schools with more that 200 pupils, a professional tutor with responsiblity for students and probationary teachers; and

47.3   reduced timetables for all first year teachers to enable them to observe lessons, visit other schools and participate in in-service training. The reduction in teaching load should be equivalent to no less than half a day per week. We recognise that this would have cost implications for LEAs in which it is not already the practice.

48   The proposals set out in the Qualified Teacher Status consultative document issued by the DES in May 1988 aim to tidy up the 'non-standard' routes into teaching (ie other than through college training). A new category of 'licensed teacher' would be established. Licensed teachers would be mature entrants to the profession with, for example, industrial or commercial experience. Their employer (usually an LEA) would ask the Secretary of State to grant them a licence to teach for a probationary period of two years. If their performance was satisfactory their employer would recommend that they be granted qualified teacher status. Like other school staff licensed teachers would be appointed by governing bodies. **If the proposals in the consultative document on qualified teacher status are implemented, we recommend:**

48.1   **that governing bodies should take full account of the personal qualities of candidates when appointing or recommending the appointment of licensed teachers; and**

48.2   **that induction programmes for such teachers should be strongly reinforced with tailored in-service training, particularly in the area of classroom management.**

R
8.1

R
8.2

In-service training

49   We have commented earlier in this chapter on the general lack of in-service training in classroom management which seems to be available. Most in-service training is funded by the Local Education Authority Training Grants Scheme (LEATGS). Total expenditure for 1989/90 is planned at £214 million. The priorities for spending most of this money (£130 million in 1989/90) are decided by LEAs. Expenditure on local priorities is 50% grant-aided by the DES or Welsh Office. Other priorities (worth £84 million in 1989/90) are decided by the Secretaries of State. These national priorities are grant-aided at 70%. We consider that providing in-service training in classroom management is of such

importance to the effectiveness of schools that is should become a national priority for at least five years.

50 **We therefore recommend that the management of pupil behaviour should become a national priority for funding under the Local Education Authority Training Grants Scheme from 1990/91 until at least 1994/95.**

51 The main aim of this programme should be to set up in-service training groups to discuss classroom skills in schools. Its first phase should involve training school facilitators to establish such groups. These facilitators would not be trainers or instructors. They would convene and chair meetings. Training would be delivered through the groups' use of relevant materials, such as videos of typical classroom incidents, and through mutual observation and consultancy.

52 Such groups can only work properly on the basis of mutual trust. It is therefore important that they should be voluntary, and that they should be seen as genuine peer support groups. Telling a teacher in difficulty to join for 'remedial' training would damage both the individual and the group. The presence of heads and deputies could, in some schools, be inhibiting. However, if they volunteer to join after the group has become well established it could help teachers to realise that even their most senior colleagues can admit to problems and benefit from in-service training.

53 Facilitators should be experienced teachers who are able to relate well to a wide range of colleagues. The smallest primary schools may not need such structured arrangements but the majority of schools should have at least one facilitator. The programme should aim to achieve this objective in five years.

54 LEAs employ many excellent teachers who can act as trainers or facilitators. They also employ other staff who can offer valuable insights into pupil behaviour. In some authorities, educational psychologists are active in classroom management training. Education welfare officers are in a good position to see schooling from the pupil's point of view. This is an important perspective for classroom managers. Youth workers have a range of social skills for relating to young people informally, and their knowledge of rapidly changing youth sub-cultures is a valuable resource. LEAs should ensure that opportunities for joint training exist and are used.

55 Our recommendation for establishing a national in-service training programme covering the management of pupil behaviour need not

require any additional expenditure by the Government or LEAs. It is however open to at least two other objections.

55.1 The first is that there are other pressing needs for LEATGS spending. Why should behaviour management become a national priority? We believe that the widespread concern expressed by teachers themselves about managing pupil behaviour establishes its priority as a training target. The main LEATGS national priority for the immediate future is preparation for the introduction of the National Curriculum. We do not dispute this priority. However, the National Curriculum will not be delivered properly in disorderly classrooms.

55.2 The second is that in-service training can itself cause disruption, because it pulls teachers out of their classrooms. We discuss this problem in chapter 10. School facilitators would certainly need to be taken out of school for intensive training. However, this would only involve providing cover for one or two teachers per school for a few days. If the group itself were to be successful it would involve a high proportion of the school's staff. It is therefore impractical for it to be run on a day release basis. In the few schools where such groups exist they meet at the end of the day. The teacher's working year can now be five days longer than the pupil's. Schools may also wish to use some of the time available in these non-teaching days for this purpose.

Teacher appraisal

56 Teachers need, and in good schools receive, support from senior managers (heads and deputies) and in secondary schools middle managers (heads of year or department), as well as peer support. The tradition of classroom isolation makes this difficult in two ways. Good teachers may get little or no recognition from senior staff for their achievements. This is demotivating. Professional etiquette may also leave teachers who are having difficulty to suffer regular humiliation in the classroom. Teacher appraisal is another way of opening the classroom door. Supportive appraisal schemes should improve standards of classroom management.

57 Guidance on appraisal, issued by the DES in 1988, suggests that it should help individual teachers with their professional development and career planning. More specifically it can give teachers a regular opportunity to discuss their performance with those who have management responsibility for them (eg a head of department in a secondary school), to set objectives and to identify training needs. It involves regular classroom observation, interviews and reports and covers all areas of professional competence including classroom management. Six LEAs are currently running pilot appraisal schemes

funded by Education Support Grant. Evidence from the pilot schemes suggests that appraisal can encourage greater openness among teachers, which includes talking about discipline problems.

58 We therefore welcome the Government's intention to require LEAs to introduce appraisal schemes covering all their teachers within a period of three or four years from September 1989. We consider that the ability to relate to pupils and the standard of classroom management should be important elements of any appraisal system. Because of the critical part played by a teacher's confidence in classroom control, we would emphasise the need for appraisal to be supportive rather than threatening.

59 Some people are less well suited to teaching than others. It would be surprising if a few of these had not found their way into a workforce of over 400,000, particularly during periods of teacher shortage. The education service and individual schools continue to change. Some teachers adapt better to these changes than others. There is evidence that a small number of teachers consistently fail to achieve any degree of effective control in the classroom. This is damaging to the pupils, to their colleagues and, perhaps most of all, to themselves. Appraisal may be able to help such teachers by providing a mechanism for identifying their problems and producing plans of action to deal with them. These plans may, for example, involve training or redeployment within the school or outside it.

60 Such plans will not always succeed. There will be cases in which a teacher's performance in classroom management cannot be raised to acceptable standards. In these circumstances some teachers may choose to leave the profession. Early retirement in the interests of the service may be appropriate for some older teachers. We would encourage LEAs to make such schemes available. In the last resort, and only when it is clear that attempts to help a teacher have failed, heads and governors should recommend dismissal on the grounds of incompetence. We make a recommendation relating to this in chapter nine.

AUTHORITY AND STATUS

61 Teachers need authority to be successful classroom managers. They use three kinds of authority in differing combinations. First there is the authority that all teachers have from their status in society. This is sometimes called traditional authority. Then there is the authority that is based on personality and skills rather than official position. Finally there is the authority that goes with the job and is conferred by the law.

62 Some of our evidence suggests that the teacher's traditional authority has become less effective in recent years. This does not surprise us. Attitudes to authority generally have changed in the post-war years. This change has affected the professions, and public attitudes to them, generally. Professional status no longer inhibits complaints against those who hold it. Between 1981/2 and 1985/6 the number of consumer complaints registered against professional services more than doubled (**Social Trends** 1988). This change of attitude has not by-passed the consumers of education. The latest British **Social Attitudes Survey** (1988) found that nine out of 10 people in its national sample thought that parents and pupils respected teachers less now than 10 years ago. We conclude that the authority conferred on teachers by their position in society is significantly less than it used to be. A teacher who relies too heavily upon status to deal with challenges from pupils may therefore face particular difficulties.

63 The teaching profession's relationship with its clients has also been changed by recent history. This may in part result, as some of our expert witnesses suggested, from some of the more alarmist press reports suggesting widespread classroom chaos. But we attach much more importance to the fact that between 1985 and 1987 a total of 910,000 working days were lost as a result of the industrial dispute involving teachers, LEAs and the Government.

64 We do not seek to allocate responsibility for these events. Nor do we think that the parties involved should do so. We merely observe that they occurred. We believe, however, that this period of disruption has resulted in significant damage to the status of teachers in the eyes both of parents and of pupils. Over 60% of those responding to the latest British **Social Attitudes Survey** thought teachers were now less dedicated to their jobs than they had been 10 years ago.

65 The damage has been greatest where the interests of pupils have been most clearly seen to suffer; where, for instance, their career prospects have been diminished by disruption of the preparation for, or administration of, examinations. Reports of school inspections carried out by HMI during this period comment on some of the damaging effects of industrial action. These include a lack of staff meetings and in-service training, uncompleted pupil records and reports, loss of contact with parent where parents' evenings were stopped, and higher absence rates for pupils. The more effective industrial action is in disrupting the education of pupils in any way, the more clearly does it fall within our terms of reference.

R

10

66   We are concerned that such events should not recur. It is not for us to decide whether the use of industrial action would or would not be in the interests of either teachers or employers at some future time. That question lies beyond our remit and must be for them to decide in the circumstances that then apply. What concerns us is that no such action shall be taken which damages the education of pupils or puts their safety or well being at risk. Such action would, we believe, reduce the standards of behaviour in schools into which we were appointed to enquire. We believe that those who teach children cannot properly take action which harms those children's interests. Such conditions have meant that teachers have had to make difficult and stressful decisions as to whether they should take industrial action or not. We recognise that this places strict limits on the forms of industrial action which should be available to those who may wish to use them. We believe that those restrictions flow naturally from the responsibilities accepted by both teachers and administrators of education. **We therefore recommend that urgent consideration should be given, by all the interested parties, to establishing a framework of relationships between teachers and their employers which will reduce the risk of future industrial action to a minimum.**

67   If the first source of a teacher's authority is the general one of status, the second is the particular one of his or her own personality and skills. To ensure that the right kind of people become teachers, the education service must have suitably discriminating selection procedures and an adequate supply of candidates. We discuss appointments in chapter nine and teacher supply later in this chapter.

68   We have suggested that changes in the public perception of teachers' status have had an influence both upon their authority and on their morale. Although teachers' recourse to industrial action has had a major influence on that perception, there have been other influences. Great concern has, in particular, been expressed to us about the effects of adverse publicity on both the status and the morale of teachers. It has been suggested to us that this treatment of the profession has reduced its members' authority and that it is likely to affect recruitment.

69   We share this concern. We therefore urge all those parties with a role in maintaining an effective education service to bear in mind the need to enhance the public image of the profession when making public statements about or on behalf of teachers.

70   Other positive steps should be taken. The publicity campaign mounted by the Teaching as a Career task force (TASC), which stresses the economic and social value of the work done by teachers, provides some

useful examples of how the Government, LEAs and teachers' professional associations can generate constructive publicity.

71   The third basis of a teacher's authority is that which is conferred by the law. This authority can be tested and challenged in the courts. For some time this has not been of critical importance, presumably because there was general agreement about the nature and validity of that authority. However, we have already noted that attitudes to professional providers of services seem to be changing. Such changes in this country often follow similar changes in the USA. We were therefore disturbed to learn that legal action by parents against the disciplining of their children is now a regular feature of the US education system and is seen by teachers there as a factor which significantly limits their authority. We also note with concern the steady increase in this country of litigation in many fields. Between 1981 and 1986 the number of civil actions started for breach of contract, for instance, increased by 50% and for negligence by 80% (**Social Trends** 1988).

72   We therefore thought it prudent to enquire into the basis in law of teachers' authority over their pupils. We expected to find this simply and clearly stated in an Act of Parliament. We were concerned to discover that it is not The basis for the teachers' authority is commonly understood to be the *in loco parentis*' principle, which gives teachers the same authority over their pupils as parents have over their children. But most of the legal judgements which support this principle (eg Fitzgerald v Northcote 1865) were delivered before the introduction of compulsory education. If teachers' authority over pupils was delegated to them by parents, it would follow that parents would be able to withdraw part or all of that authority. We were advised that this question had been considered in depth after the European Court of Human Rights ruling on corporal punishment (1982). The conclusion was that the relevant case law did not support the right of parents to revoke any part of a teacher's authority. It was also concluded that the teacher's authority derives from his or her position as a teacher. The accumulation of case law is probably sufficient to inhibit litigation by parents opposed to particular actions, such as putting a child in detention, but the present legal position does not offer teachers the explicit support which we consider they should have.

73   Having taken advice, we remain uncertain that the legal basis of teachers' authority over their pupils is beyond challenge. If, as we believe, society wants teachers to have effective authority over pupils, it should make the basis and nature of that authority clear in statute.

74 The effects which a successful challenge would have on the proper conduct of schools could be very damaging until a new basis of teachers' authority had been established. **We therefore recommend that the Secretaries of State should consider introducing legislation to clarify the legal basis of teachers' authority.** They would need to consult widely before doing so. We consider that any such legislation could usefully establish that:

74.1 the teacher has general authority over pupils for the purpose of securing their education and well being and that of other pupils in the school and ensuring that they abide by the rules of conduct set by the school;

74.2 this authority is not delegated by the parent, but derives from the teacher's position as a teacher. In matters relating to the school, this authority overrides that of the pupil's parent;

74.3 the teacher's authority includes the right to set homework and to impose punishments for conduct contrary to the school rules which should be made known to parents and pupils. Such punishments must be reasonable and proportionate to the breach. They may include extra academic work to be completed in or out of school, tasks to assist the school in any reasonable way (including repairing damage), a requirement to stay in school beyond normal school hours (detention), withdrawal of privileges or any other reasonable punishments consistent with the school's discipline policy and the law. This authority is not intended to override the provisions of the Education (No. 2) Act 1986 covering corporal punishment. Parents must be given adequate notice of any punishment which obliges a pupil to remain in school for longer than a few minutes outside normal hours, or to take part in an activity off school premises; and

74.4 the teacher's authority extends beyond the school to any off-site activity which is a continuation or extension of schooling such as a field trip or a school journey. It also applies to other situations, such as bullying out of school, where pupils' conduct impinges on the school.

75 While the 'in loco parentis' principle may no longer be a satisfactory basis for teachers' authority we believe that the duty of care which it implies should remain central to a teacher's responsibilities towards pupils. Nothing should be done to diminish or obscure that duty.

76 The proposals set out above do not represent any substantial change in the existing law. But we consider that to have these matters clearly established by statute, rather than having to be deduced from decisions of courts going back many years, would be of substantial benefit in clarifying the authority of the teacher and setting it beyond argument.

MORALE AND RECRUITMENT

77   The Interim Advisory Committee on Teachers' Pay and Conditions (IAC), reporting in March 1988, concluded that teachers' morale was low. It commented that this '. . . *is not only – perhaps not principally – a matter of pay . . . Many teachers complain of a lack of public appreciation and recognition; they feel that they have been blamed for all the faults of the education system, and expected to implement a succession of initiatives, for which resources and training are limited'.*

78   We received a large number of submissions making the same points. No-one suggested to us that teachers' morale had improved since the publication of the IAC report. Our evidence of difficulties with pupil behaviour simply adds to the list of reasons for demoralisation.

79   Low morale, combined with the reduced status considered earlier in this chapter, seem likely to result in reduced motivation and consequent recruitment difficulties. In any job, morale and motivation affect confidence in dealing with people and problems. We emphasise the importance of confidence for effective classroom management earlier in this chapter.

80   The recruitment of teachers to schools has less immediate effects, but its long term importance can hardly be underestimated. Earlier in this chapter we urge initial teacher training establishments to look for particular personal characteristics in aspiring teachers. In chapter nine we recommend that governing bodies look for these qualities when appointing qualified teachers. A shortage faces recruiters with the choice of leaving places unfilled or filling them with people who are below the desired standard in some respect. If the teaching force falls significantly below its planned level, those who serve in it will be placed under additional stress which may add to the difficulty of dealing with behaviour problems. If, on the other hand, the places are filled by lowering the admission standard, the quality of teaching will be reduced. This amounts to a hidden shortage, and is likely to be more damaging than lower levels of recruitment because problems will persist for as long as the unsuitable entrants continue their teaching careers. We consider it important to maintain the quality of the teaching force even at the cost of occasional under-recruitment.

81   There are at least four ways of covering unfilled posts without actually sending pupils home. These are: using supply teachers; making classes larger; using teachers outside their normal specialisms; and cutting subjects out of the curriculum. All four have serious drawbacks which may affect standards of behaviour. Supply teachers face particular difficulties because they may not know the school or the pupils. The risks of using the wrong materials or methods are greater when teaching an unfamiliar subject or age group. It is therefore very important to ensure that the supply of new teachers is adequate both generally and in specific subjects to maintain the size and quality of the teaching force at the proper levels.

82   Levels of teacher recruitment are influenced by a variety of factors including professional status, morale and pay. Able young people are unlikely to leave school wanting to be teachers if they see the job as having low status and being unrewarding. They are more likely to take this view if some of their career advice comes from demoralised teachers.

83   The IAC concluded that the number of teachers recruited in 1987 was 'just about adequate', but that there were signs that recruitment was generally becoming more difficult. One indicator of teacher supply is vacancy data. The number of secondary vacancies in January 1988, which stood at just over 2,000 posts, was equivalent to about 1% of the secondary teaching force in England and Wales. Primary vacancies were about 1.5% of the primary teaching force, or just over 2,500 posts. Our impression is that recruitment problems in certain subjects and regions are acute.

84   Longer term prospects are more worrying. Most teachers enter the profession in their early twenties. The size of this age group will decline progressively throughout the next decade. If general prospects for graduate recruitment continue to be good, the education service will face increasingly stiff competition in the labour market.

85   Status and morale are related issues. We believe that the action we suggest earlier in this chapter to improve the public image of teachers and clarify the legal basis of their authority would also improve the morale of the profession.

86   Morale and recruitment cannot be separated from pay and conditions of service. We welcome the Government's view, expressed in the Secretary of State's letter to Lord Chilver of 14 September 1988, 'that school teachers' pay and conditions of service should be such as to enable the maintained school system to recruit, retain and motivate sufficient teachers of

the required quality both nationally and at a local level within what can be afforded'. The letter also asked the IAC to advise on modifications *'needed to deal with subject shortages'.* **We recommend that the Secretaries of State and LEAs should give due weight to the serious implications of any actual or predicted teacher shortages (whether specialist, regional or general) when considering future pay levels and conditions of service for the profession.**

87 Teachers are much less likely to come from minority ethnic backgrounds than their pupils. It has been suggested to us that increased recruitment from these groups could improve standards of behaviour in schools. This will not happen unless they perceive teaching as an attractive career. There are at least two good reasons for encouraging the recruitment of teachers from such backgrounds. They can provide positive role models for pupils from similar backgrounds, and reduce the risks of cultural misunderstandings between other teachers and these pupils. We consider that particular emphasis should be given to increasing minority ethnic representation in the teaching force. **We therefore recommend that the Secretaries of State, LEAs, governors and headteachers should encourage the recruitment of teachers from minority ethnic backgrounds.**

SCHOOLS MAKE A DIFFERENCE

1   When we visited schools we were struck by the differences in their 'feel' or atmosphere. Our conversations with teachers left us convinced that some schools have a more positive atmosphere than others. It was in these positive schools that we tended to see the work and behaviour which impressed us most. We found that we could not explain these different school atmospheres by saying that the pupils came from different home backgrounds. Almost all the schools we visited were in what many teachers would describe as difficult urban areas. We had to conclude that these differences had something to do with what went on in the schools themselves.

2   The findings of recent studies support this view. Research published in the last 10 years shows quite clearly that schools do make a difference. The most influential work in this field is the study of 12 London secondary schools by the team led by Rutter, published as **Fifteen Thousand Hours** in 1979. A more recent study of 50 London junior schools by the team led by Mortimore, published as **School Matters** in 1988, confirms many of Rutter's findings. These studies were commended to us in a considerable number of submissions we received from LEAs, teacher training establishments and teachers' professional associations. Other important studies of school effectiveness include work led by Reynolds in Wales and Gray in Scotland.

3   Most researchers now agree that some schools are much more effective than others in promoting good work and behaviour. This does not mean that schools can eliminate the effects of social differences between pupils. A child from a disadvantaged background is still likely on average to do less well than a child from an advantaged home when they attend the same school. But if the disadvantaged child attends an effective school he may well do better than a more advantaged child attending an ineffective school.

4   The message to heads and teachers is clear. It is that they have the power, through their own efforts, to improve standards of work and behaviour and the life chances of their pupils.

5   Looking at school timetables, we were impressed by their sheer complexity. A secondary school may contain well over 1,000 children and adults. Even the smallest primary school is in some ways more complicated than a small company because it has a greater variety of aims. The reasons why some schools are better than others have not been explained in every detail by researchers. Nor do all their findings confirm that good schools are good at everything they set out to do. We

cannot therefore offer a standard formula for success in every school. But much of our evidence, together with recent research findings, can be used to identify useful signposts towards improving standards of behaviour.

6   Visiting different schools left us with the strong impression that the attitudes and motivation of their headteachers and staff were decisive influences on their atmosphere. This impression is confirmed by research evidence. Heads manage schools in different ways. Teachers use different classroom styles. Schools have different discipline codes and different timetables. Research shows that differences in the ways in which schools and classrooms are run are associated with different standards of work, behaviour and attendance among their pupils. Rutter suggests that the school atmosphere, which is produced by all these routines or processes working together, also has an effect on pupils' behaviour which is stronger than the sum of individual processes. This idea must be used with caution, but we found it useful in explaining what we saw and heard in schools.

SCHOOL ATMOSPHERE

7   In chapter three we consider the ways in which an effective teacher can create a positive, encouraging atmosphere in the classroom and an ineffective teacher can create a negative, demotivating one. Schools can have a positive or negative atmosphere. Our evidence from visits, confirmed by research findings, suggests that schools with a negative atmosphere will suffer more from bad bahaviour than those with a positive one.

8   We supplemented our first hand experience with evidence from reports by HMI and from research in order to identify some symptoms of a negative atmosphere in a school. They include widespread litter and graffiti, teachers starting lessons late and finishing them early, teachers ignoring bad behaviour in corridors and playgrounds, pupils regularly skipping lessons and getting away with it, pupils' work not displayed and the regular use of inappropriate punishments.

9   Our evidence suggests that these symptons indicate a school's failure to achieve a sense of community. Neither staff nor pupils feel valued or respected. Teachers expect pupils to behave badly. More often than not their expectations are fulfilled.

10   Research evidence suggests that pupils' behaviour can be influenced by all the major features and processes of a school. These include the

4

quality of its leadership, classroom management, behaviour policy, curriculum, pastoral care, buildings and physical environment, organisation and timetable and relationships with parents.

11   The way in which a school is run can be changed. We know that this is not easy. Changing the nature of an institution can be a long, complicated and uncomfortable process. We recognise that the difficulties involved in breaking into the vicious circle of ineffective performance and low morale can be very great, and that some schools may need a great deal of help in achieving this breakthrough. We are convinced however from what we have seen in schools, from research evidence, and from experiences described to us in other countries that successful change can be achieved. The first and most important requirement is a positive commitment to change by the headteacher and other senior staff. The second is for them to carry as many of the rest of the staff as possible with them and to be open to their suggestions. To see the need for change, heads and teachers need to recognise the school's present atmosphere, particularly from the pupils' point of view. This is not always easy for an insider. They need to recognise their power to create a different atmosphere, and to be convinced that the changes they make will produce positive responses from the pupils. They then need to work out what practical steps they intend to take and how they are to be taken. For most schools, effective action starts with the recognition that behaviour problems cannot simply be attributed to factors outside the institution, such as pupils' home backgrounds.

12   Heads should keep up to date with the research evidence on school effectiveness. This evidence currently suggests:

12.1   that school processes and the atmosphere which they produce can have a substantial influence on pupils' behaviour;

12.2   that in schools where standards of behaviour are considered unsatisfactory by staff, significant improvements can be achieved through institutional change; and

12.3   that perhaps the most important characteristic of schools with a positive atmosphere is that pupils, teachers and other staff feel that they are known and valued members of the school community.

LEADERSHIP AND MANAGEMENT

13   Our evidence indicates universal agreement that the quality of leadership provided by the headteacher and the senior management

team (deputies, senior teachers etc) is crucial to a school's success in promoting good behaviour. Mortimore's study of junior schools found that good work and behaviour were not only linked with purposeful leadership by the headteacher but with the active involvement of the deputy head in managing the school. We are aware of many examples, both here and in the USA, of schools in difficulty which have been 'turned around' by energetic heads and senior management teams. The concept of teachers as a team of managers even in a small primary school can be a powerful starting point for improvement.

14 Our visits to schools convinced us that, while good heads can have different personal styles, consistent themes run through effective school management. These include clear aims for teachers and pupils and good staff morale and teamwork. Effective leadership tends to produce a positive atmosphere and a general sense of security.

15 We consider that quality of leadership has two distinct but related aspects. The first is personality. Just as not all adults can become good teachers not all teachers can become good heads. The personal qualities needed to manage adults are similar but not identical to those needed for managing children. Selecting senior managers is therefore a key task for governing bodies. We discuss this in chapter nine. The second is management style. This can be acquired through experience and training.

16 We have identified seven aspects of school management which seem to be particularly important for pupils' behaviour. The head's role is central to them all. They are: staff management; establishing and maintaining internal and external communication systems; fostering a sense of community; taking the lead in setting aims and standards; encouraging collective responsibility; supporting staff; and directing overall curriculum and organisational planning. There is scope for positive action in each of these areas, but effective staff management is the key to success in them all.

**Staff
management**

17 A high proportion of our letters from teachers emphasise the importance of team work in schools. Our survey confirms this desire for discussion and consultation. Managing professionals presents special challenges. A headteacher must be both line manager and first among equals. We believe that getting the best out of professional staff means combining positive leadership with a consultative management style. Teachers need to feel that their school has a sense of direction. They also need to feel that it can be influenced by their views. Some headteachers find this balance difficult to strike.

4

18   At one extreme is the permissive management style. This allows a school to become a mere collection of classrooms. Contrasting disciplinary regimes operate. Corridors and playgrounds become a no man's land. The fragmented atmosphere which this style produces is confusing and demoralising both to teachers and to pupils. There is no sense of direction, no sense that someone is 'in charge', and no sense of collective responsibility for good behaviour. Consistent standards cannot be maintained in a school like this.

19   At the other extreme is the autocratic style, in which decisions are made without consultation with staff. This demoralises teachers by denying their professional competence. It produces a similar lack of collective responsibility. It can also have more specific effects on standards of behaviour. For example, our evidence indicates that schools which achieve good standards tend to deal with disciplinary problems where they happen, and at the lowest possible level. The active involvement of class teachers and form tutors is a vital factor. In autocratic regimes problems tend to be quickly referred up to senior management level. This reduces the authority of class teachers and gives status to misbehaviour. Such systems also tend to become overloaded because senior staff are dealing with an endless stream of minor offenders.

20   We consider that the existence of such ineffective management styles should not be blamed entirely on headteachers and their senior colleagues. Our impression is that few senior managers in schools have had any systematic management training. Traditionally it has been assumed that training in, and experience of dealing with children provides sufficient preparation for managing adults. This is a false assumption.

21   The Secretary of State has set up a task force for the management training of heads and other senior managers in schools. Its aims are to review existing arrangements, to identify training needs and to recommend patterns of training for the future. We welcome this development. We recognise that the task force's terms of reference include the full range of management skills required by senior school staff. We have two concerns. The first is the impression that, in some LEAs at least, courses which have the word 'management' in their title are actually about other issues. They are, for example, about the content of the curriculum rather than about how to manage curriculum change. The second is the possible impact of the local management of schools (LMS) initiative on headteachers' training. Under LMS, heads will be responsible for managing school budgets. This will generate considerable demand for training in financial management. Our

concern is that personnel management in its broadest sense, which includes leadership and team building, should not be neglected as a result of this demand. We also believe that the introduction and implementation of whole school approaches to behaviour should be a feature of future management training programmes. This would cover how to analyse the problems, how to draw up a behaviour policy, how to establish priorities within that policy, how to make sure that it is being applied and how to ensure that staff have the motivation to apply it consistently. **We therefore recommend that the school management task force should ensure that management training programmes for headteachers and other senior staff give specific emphasis to personnel management in its broadest sense and to the management of institutional change.**

R
14

Communication systems

22 Poor communication is generally recognised as a feature of bad management. Our evidence suggests that communication with and between staff is particularly important for maintaining the kind of morale and atmosphere necessary to promote good behaviour. Controlling the volume of communication is also important in any busy organisation. Staff want to be kept informed of and, where appropriate, consulted about significant developments. They do not want to be swamped with low grade information. In a large secondary school communication systems will tend to be fairly formal. In smaller schools more informal systems may be appropriate.

23 Throughout this report we emphasise the importance of mutual expectations as an influence on behaviour, and the need for consistency and fairness in relations between staff and pupils. Appropriate expectations and consistency depend to a large extent on staff and pupils having a clear understanding of their roles in the school. An effective communication system helps to clarify these roles and produces the necessary sense of coherence within the institution.

24 Heads also represent their schools when dealing with parents and governors. We discuss the importance of effective communication with parents later in this chapter, and the head's role in relation to the governing body in chapter nine. Heads are often in a better position than other members of staff to pick up messages about how the school is perceived by the community that it serves. They should ensure that the staff as a whole are aware of the school's public image and, where necessary, work to improve it.

25 The local press provides one effective way of communicating with parents and the wider community. Schools can get a lot of bad publicity. We have read many lurid accounts of bad behaviour in local

4

papers. But we know that local papers will also print good news about schools if they are given the right kind of material. It does not seem unreasonable to us for headteachers to set targets for positive publicity in order to promote the public image of their schools. **We recommend that headteachers should review and, wherever necessary, improve channels of communication within the school and between the school and parents, governors, the community and outside agencies.**

R 15

Sense of community

26   At the beginning of this chapter we identify a sense of community as an important factor in promoting good behaviour. This involves a feeling of commitment to the school by staff, governors, pupils and parents. Heads should take the lead in communicating that sense of commitment.

27   Assemblies provide a regular opportunity to transmit this message. Researchers have found positive links between features of school assemblies and pupils' behaviour. Heads can use assemblies to communicate their own enthusiasm and expectations directly to staff and pupils. In primary schools it is not uncommon for parents to attend assemblies. We consider that this adds to their potential value.

28   Heads can promote a sense of commitment in a variety of other ways. They can, for example, encourage staff through private and public recognition of their efforts and achievements. They can ensure that open evenings are organised in ways that make them as rewarding as possible to the parents and staff involved. They can encourage pupils to identify with the school by emphasising the value of wearing its uniform and supporting the development of clubs and other extra-curricular activities. **We recommend that headteachers use all the means available to them to build up a sense of community in their schools and to encourage staff, governors, parents and pupils to play an active part in that community.**

R 16

Aims and standards

29   We have emphasised the need for heads to combine purposeful leadership with maintaining the professional involvement of their staff in decision making. This is not always easy. The balancing act becomes even more complicated when governors and parents are brought into the picture. The ideal would be universal agreement about the standards of behaviour that the school is aiming for. In practice complete consensus is impossible, not least because of the turnover of staff and parents from year to year.

30   It is the head's statutory duty under section 22 of the Education (No. 2) Act 1986 to decide how acceptable standards of behaviour are going to

be achieved. We believe that it is also the head's responsibility as a manager to take the lead in defining these standards.

31 We consider it unlikely that they will be achieved without a wide measure of agreement among staff, governors and parents. We believe that it is also the head's job to ensure that the communication systems needed to achieve this agreement exist and are used. In chapter nine we emphasise the need for governors to take account of the head's professional advice if they decide to draw up general guidelines for the school's behaviour policy. We emphasise later in this chapter the need to involve staff in working out the details of the policy and the need to communicate it clearly to parents. The head's role is crucial to all these processes.

32 Once standards have been set, it is the job of the headteacher and other senior managers to ensure that they are consistently applied by teachers and other staff. Pupils will quickly spot any inconsistency between public statements and what staff actually do. This will undermine the effectiveness of any policy. **We therefore recommend that headteachers should:**

32.1 **take the lead in defining the aims of the school in relation to standards of behaviour;**

32.2 **create the conditions for establishing the widest possible measure of agreement on these standards and how they will be achieved; and**

32.3 **ensure that these standards are consistently applied throughout the school.**

Collective responsibility

33 Teachers have a general responsibility for encouraging pupils to behave well at all times, but different management styles will make them more or less willing to translate that responsibility into action. We have suggested that permissive or autocratic management styles are likely to diminish teachers' sense of collective responsibility. We believe that the right balance between leadership and consultation will increase it.

34 In chapter three we stress the need for teachers in their classrooms to model the kinds of behaviour they wish to see in pupils. This is equally important for the school as a whole. The maxim 'don't do as I do, do as I tell you' convinces no one. In this as in many other areas, heads should lead by example. **We recommend that headteachers should ensure, by consistent policy-making and encouragement, that all teachers accept responsibility for maintaining good behaviour throughout the school and that they model the types of behaviour encouraged by school policy.**

In the right margin beside paragraph 32: R 17.1, R 17.2, R 17.3

In the right margin beside paragraph 34: R 18

Support for staff

35 We highlight the need for management support for teachers in our discussion of appraisal in chapter three. Some of our evidence from individual teachers complains of a lack of support from senior colleagues and particularly from the headteacher. It has been suggested to us that some heads are more concerned about protecting the public image of the school than with supporting staff in disciplinary matters. We have no objective evidence to confirm this, but the fact that some teachers believe it is worrying in itself. Teachers need to feel that they are supported by senior management when they are facing difficulties in the classroom, but it must be the right kind of support. We have suggested that taking responsibility for discipline away from classroom teachers is the wrong kind. It simply undermines their authority and confidence. The primary aim of management support should be to increase teachers' capability to solve their own classroom problems.

36 It is good practice for heads and other senior staff to visit classes taught by their colleagues. This is not necessarily to 'inspect' but to be seen, both by staff and pupils, to be interested in and to value their work. With proper planning, these visits can be very supportive and encouraging. Headteachers should also create opportunities for regular one-to-one discussions with teachers. These discussions should give teachers the opportunity, in a relaxed way, of voicing any concerns they may have, of proposing improvements which could be made in their working environment and of exploring their professional and career development, including training needs. We believe that teacher appraisal will help in this. Heads should encourage the development of peer support groups in their schools (see chapter three). They should also ensure that when their staff take part in in-service training courses they are able to apply and pass on what they have learned, and also that the extent to which any training has achieved its objectives for those taking part is monitored. **We therefore recommend that headteachers should promote the development of both management support and peer support within the staff team, and the professional development of its members.**

Curriculum and organisation

37 The headteacher has overall responsibility for the school's internal organisation. This includes such major features as management structure, staff deployment, timetabling and supervision. The introduction of LMS, giving heads and governors control over school budgets, will increase heads' scope for decision making. The theme of this chapter is that all the major features and processes of a school can influence pupils' behaviour. They also affect staff morale. The rest of this chapter deals with these processes in more detail. We feel it important, however, to emphasise the key role of the head in shaping

them. **We therefore recommend that, in making all major management decisions, headteachers should consider their likely effects upon the commitment and morale of teachers and pupils.**

APPRAISAL OF HEADTEACHERS

38   The pilot teacher appraisal schemes discussed in chapter three also include arrangements for the appraisal of headteachers. Their performance is appraised by an appropriate person with relevant experience as a head. We welcome this development and look forward to the introduction of headteacher appraisal schemes nationally in the near future. We consider that a school's success in promoting good behaviour among its pupils should be an important factor in headteacher appraisal. We recognise that the part played by the headteacher cannot be evaluated as directly as the effectiveness of individual teachers in classroom management. We would, however, expect appraisers to consider the headteacher's effectiveness in developing the structures and promoting the atmosphere in which good behaviour is most likely to occur.

CLASSROOM MANAGEMENT

39   We discuss classroom management in chapter three. The classroom management styles of individual teachers play an important part in creating a positive or negative atmosphere in a school. Complete uniformity is impossible and undesirable, but styles which do not take account of the principles of good practice that we identify are likely to have a negative influence.

BEHAVIOUR POLICIES

40   We have referred in chapter two to the need for clearly identified boundaries of acceptable behaviour, and for teachers to respond promptly and firmly (with punishment if necessary) to pupils testing these boundaries. These boundaries and responses are sometimes regarded as a self-sufficient system of discipline. They are not.

41   All schools have rules. Some of those we visited also had behaviour policies. Rules may be no more than a list of prohibitions. Behaviour policies underlie the rules and affect the whole conduct of the school. They ensure that a whole range of important school processes are consistent with one another. In particular they establish:

   41.1   the reasons for rules. It may be clear to teachers why particular rules are necessary. It is not always clear to pupils or parents.

Rational authority depends on understanding. Any rule for which no rational explanation can be provided is suspect;

41.2 the affective curriculum (see chapter two). Schools teach values as well as knowledge and skills. Some of this teaching is done in lessons. Most is through the way in which teachers and pupils behave to each other, including how rules are applied. A set of written rules does not mean that they will always be applied by all teachers in the same way. There must be a consensus among staff on the aims of the affective curriculum;

41.3 models of behaviour. Most sets of rules are written for pupils. The behaviour of teachers must be consistent with them. If pupils are told, for example, to be polite and respectful to others, teachers must provide good examples of such behaviour in their dealings with adults and children; and

41.4 consistency with religious education and personal and social education. Tolerance and self-discipline are common themes in these areas. The values which underlie the rules must be consistent with them.

42 We consider that schools which simply have long lists of prohibitions and no consistent behaviour policy are more likely to be troubled by bad behaviour than those which have harmonised all the features of the institution concerned with behaviour.

43 Our evidence suggests that schools which put too much faith in punishments to deter bad behaviour are also likely to be disappointed. This is confirmed by research findings. Rutter found that different forms or frequencies of punishment bore little or no relationship to standards of behaviour in secondary schools. Mortimore found that behaviour tended to be worse in junior schools which emphasised punishments more than rewards. The more punishments listed, the more negative the effect seemed to be.

44 The use of corporal punishment illustrates these points. We received few submissions recommending its reintroduction which is not, in any case, in prospect. We are, however, aware that strong feelings still surround this issue.

45 The corporal punishment argument has two strands. One is about principles, the other about effectiveness. The issue of principle is about whether corporal punishment is right or wrong. We decided that this question was outside our terms of reference, which were to look at what works. We therefore commissioned a brief review of research findings on the effectiveness of corporal punishment.

46 Its conclusions will be surprising to some. They are that there is little evidence that corporal punishment was in general an effective deterrent either to the pupils punished or to other pupils. There is also some evidence that standards of behaviour tended to be worse in schools which made more frequent use of corporal punishment when differences in the nature of their catchment areas had been taken into account. The argument that corporal punishment reduced the need for other sanctions is also not supported by the evidence. One study found that schools which used corporal punishment more frequently also tended to exclude pupils more frequently. This seemed to be the case irrespective of catchment area differences.

47 The general conclusion which seems most relevant to our work is that some schools appear to have more punitive regimes than others, and that punitive regimes seem to be associated with worse rather than better standards of behaviour. This does not mean that punishments are not necessary. All the effective schools in the studies we refer to, as well as those we saw in action, had punishments and used them. The message seems to be that, in order to create a positive atmosphere, schools need to establish a healthy balance between punishments and rewards.

48 Several of our witnesses commented on the lack of praise for good behaviour in many schools and emphasised its importance. Most schools have a range of rewards for good academic work or effort such as good marks, good reports, prizes etc, but they tend to benefit a limited group of children. We are left with the disturbing impression that in some schools a pupil can only get attention in one or other of two ways – by working well or by behaving badly.

49 We received a number of submissions suggesting that more and/or tougher punishments provided by schools would by themselves be the answer to indiscipline. Our evidence does not bear this out.

50 We consider that the best way to encourage good standards of behaviour in a school is a clear code of conduct backed by a balanced combination of rewards and punishments within a positive community atmosphere. Establishing a whole school behaviour policy is an important step in that direction.

51 Appendix F to this report offers examples of guidance given by three schools to pupils and staff derived from such policies. They are not blueprints. We consider that the process of developing a whole school behaviour policy which is owned and valued by the staff as a whole is

R 21

just as important as its content. **We therefore recommend that headteachers and teachers should, in consultation with governors, develop whole school behaviour policies which are clearly understood by pupils, parents and other school staff.**

52 We believe that successful policies are likely to have the following characteristics.

Clear principles and rationale

53 The policy should be based on a clear and defensible set of principles or values. Our suggestion is that mutual respect is a useful starting point for policy building. These principles should be consistent with the school's overall aims and its affective curriculum. The need for punishment will not disappear but it should be clear that the central purpose of the policy is to encourage good behaviour rather than simply to punish bad behaviour.

Professional agreement

54 Behaviour policies should be specific to each school. The head should take the lead in proposing principles and standards, but the policy should be worked out co-operatively by the whole of the teaching staff in consultation with non-teaching staff. The commitment of governors is also vital (see chapter nine).

Rules

55 The number of rules should be kept to an essential minimum, and only include ones which the school will enforce. The reasons for each rule should be obvious. Obscure, arbitrary or petty rules discredit the whole code. The distinction between rules which are a direct application of fundamental principles, such as an absolute ban on physical violence, and administrative regulations, such as the name tagging of clothes, should be made quite clear. Wherever possible rules should be expressed in positive terms: for example 'take care of the building' rather than 'don't write graffiti'. **We recommend that schools should ensure that their rules are derived from the principles underlying their behaviour policies and are consistent with them.**

R 22

Rewards and punishments

56 Rewards for pupils may include such things as commendations, merit marks and letters home. We believe that they should cover the broadest possible range of academic and non-academic achievements, for example group projects and community service. Telling parents about their children's achievements, as well as any behaviour problems, should be an important part of this system. **We recommend that schools should strike a healthy balance between rewards and punishments and that both should be clearly specified.**

R 23

57 We do not suggest that schools should have a rigid scale of punishments covering every conceivable offence. However, the system of

punishments should be designed to signal the degree of disapproval involved. This should mean for example that the most severe punishments, such as exclusion from school, should be reserved for the most serious offences such as violent behaviour. **We recommend that pupils should learn from experience to expect fair and consistently applied punishments for bad behaviour which make the distinction between serious and minor offences apparent.**

R
24

58   Our evidence suggests that pupils expect and respond well to fair play and an ordered atmosphere. If a pupil is late, for example, it should always be made clear that a rule has been broken. Pupils are, however, sometimes late because their home circumstances are extremely difficult. They may, for example, be responsible for looking after younger brothers or sisters. We are not suggesting that schools should turn a blind eye to lateness in such cases. It should be made clear to pupils that they are expected to be on time. But punishment in these circumstances is not seen as fair by the pupils involved or by their friends. Teachers will have to make judgements about whether punishment is appropriate in such cases. We do not pretend that judgements like this are easy to make. But we are aware of evidence suggesting that inflexible punishment systems are associated with worse rather than better standards of behaviour. **We recommend that headteachers and teachers should ensure that rules are applied consistently by all members of staff, but that there is flexibility in the use of punishments to take account of individual circumstances.**

R
25

59   Punishing the innocent with the guilty is always seen as unfair by pupils and their sense of grievance damages the school's atmosphere. In their recent survey report on secondary schools (1988) HMI comment that the use of whole group punishments seemed to be a feature of the schools they described as too permissive. In one school it was used as a last resort when things got completely out of hand. **We recommend that headteachers and teachers should avoid the punishment of whole groups.**

R
26

60   We comment on the use of humiliating punishments in chapter three in relation to classroom management. Humiliating young people in front of their friends by, for example, public ridicule makes good relationships impossible. It breeds deep resentments which can poison the school's atmosphere. Punishments do not need to be humiliating to be effective. **We recommend that headteachers and teachers should avoid punishments which humiliate pupils.**

R
27

Guidance to staff

61 The principles of good group management outlined in chapter three apply just as strongly throughout the school. 'Succeeding' rather than 'winning' should be the aim when dealing with conflict situations in school. Success is more likely to result from de-escalation than from confrontation. We consider that an important feature of any whole school behaviour policy should be written guidelines for staff based on these principles.

Support from non-teaching staff, governors and parents

62 Our visits convinced us that non-teaching staff and, in particular, midday supervisors play an important part in promoting good behaviour. They need to be recognised as an important part of the school community. The school's behaviour policy needs to be made clear to them. So should the action they can take to support it. Governors should support the policy in principle and in detail. We discuss their role in chapter nine. Parents have a very important part to play in encouraging their children to behave well in school. We discuss this later in this chapter and in chapter five. Where they have not been involved in developing it, the school's behaviour policy, and the principles and reasons behind it, should be communicated to them as clearly as possible.

Where the policy applies

63 It should be clear that the principles of the behaviour policy apply to all school activities on- or off-site. We recognise that the detailed requirements of some off-site activities may be different. Uniform, for example, may not be appropriate for field trips. But the policy must contain the message that the school is a community of people, not just a physical space, and that consistent standards of behaviour are expected in all school activities.

Monitoring and review

64 We have said that it is the job of the headteacher and the senior management team of a school to monitor the way in which the behaviour policy is working. They must see that it is being applied consistently and consider whether it is achieving the right results. It is equally important to keep the whole staff involved. We consider that the best way of doing this is by a regular review of the policy's effectiveness to which all staff should be invited to contribute. The policy will not be fully effective unless non-teaching staff are involved in this process.

Bullying and racial harassment

65 Misbehaviour is usually defined as behaviour which causes concern to teachers. But there are also some serious forms of bad behaviour which only or mainly affect pupils. Bullying and racial harassment are cases in point. Bullying includes both physical and psychological intimidation. Recent studies of bullying in schools suggest that the problem is widespread and tends to be ignored by teachers (Tattum and Lane

1989). In Norway our attention was drawn to the work of Olweus and other Scandinavian researchers which analyses similar problems there. Research suggests that bullying not only causes considerable suffering to individual pupils but also has a damaging effect on school atmosphere. This is perhaps even more true of racial harassment. The Commission for Racial Equality expressed concern to us about accounts of racist name calling, graffiti and physical attacks in schools. We consider that sexual harassment is also an aspect of bullying, and are concerned that this was given very little attention in the evidence put before us. It is hard to see how a school can win the confidence of its pupils if it fails to deal with behaviour which so seriously damages the quality of their lives.

66 A positive school atmosphere involves a sense of community. This sense of community cannot be achieved if a school does not take seriously bad behaviour which mainly affects pupils rather than teachers. It should be clear to pupils that such behaviour is a serious offence against the school community which will be punished. **We therefore recommend that headteachers and staff should:**

66.1 **be alert to signs of bullying and racial harassment;**

66.2 **deal firmly with all such behaviour; and**

66.3 **take action based on clear rules which are backed by appropriate sanctions and systems to protect and support victims.**

R 28.1

R 28.2

R 28.3

67 Pupils will often be aware of serious bullying and racial harassment which are unknown to staff. The school's behaviour policy should make it clear that they have a responsibility to share this knowledge with staff in confidence. **We recommend that pupils should tell staff about serious cases of bullying and racial harassment of which they are aware.**

R 29

CURRICULUM

68 On the curriculum there are issues at three levels. First, the National Curriculum. Second, the curricula offered by individual schools. Third, the curricula pursued by individual pupils.

The National Curriculum

69 The Education Reform Act 1988 established a National Curriculum. The National Curriculum aims to ensure that all pupils can receive a broad and balanced education which is relevant to their needs. Its requirements will be introduced gradually from 1989. It will consist of either three or four core subjects (mathematics, science and English plus

Welsh in Welsh medium schools) and between six and eight other foundation subjects (history, geography, technology, art, music and physical education, plus a modern language in secondary schools and Welsh in those schools in Wales where the teaching medium is English). Religious education also forms part of the basic curriculum. Attainment targets will establish what children should be expected to know and to be able to do at around the ages of seven, 11, 14 and 16. There will be a system of national assessment at these ages to show what pupils have learned in comparison with these attainment targets. The National Curriculum will, with very few exceptions, be followed by all pupils aged five to 16. Formal assessment will be a new experience for many pupils, particularly in primary schools. In some secondary schools, the National Curriculum will mean that less able and lower achieving pupils will have to study a wider range of subjects than at present.

70   Strong concerns have been expressed to us that the National Curriculum will make things worse for low achievers and will therefore lead to more disruption. We hope that these concerns will prove to be ill-founded. They do, however, highlight two important general points. The first is that good behaviour has a lot to do with pupils' motivation to learn. The second is that motivation can be increased or reduced by the content of the curriculum and the methods used to deliver it. Children who feel that they are failing at school, or who see what it has to offer as boring or irrelevant, are those most likely to behave badly. Links between pupils' behaviour and detailed aspects of the curriculum, such as particular subjects or teaching methods, are not well understood. Research has tended to concentrate on other issues. Our present state of knowledge does not allow us to make recommendations in precise detail. It seems clear, however, that the curriculum and the way in which it is delivered are significant factors.

R
30

71   **We therefore recommend that all parties involved in the planning, delivery and evaluation of the curriculum should recognise that the quality of its content and the teaching and learning methods through which it is delivered are important influences on pupils' behaviour.** Interest, relevance, breadth, balance and accessibility to pupils of differing abilities, are all important considerations. The parties involved include the Government, the National Curriculum Council, the Curriculum Council for Wales, the School Examinations and Assessment Council, LEAs, school governors, heads and teachers.

72   The focus of concern in our evidence is on the implications of a National Curriculum for low achieving pupils. Particular anxieties are

expressed about provision for such pupils in their fourth and fifth years of secondary education. It is clear from our survey that, for teachers, this is the most difficult group of pupils to deal with. In some secondary schools low achieving fourth and fifth year pupils are provided with an 'alternative curriculum'. This often means studying a more limited range of subjects than other pupils. It may also mean more active learning involving practical and problem-solving methods and project work. It has been suggested to us that the need to provide these pupils with the full range of subjects required by the National Curriculum will mean the end of 'alternative' provision, including 'vocational' activities like office skills or motor vehicle maintenance, and that this will result in an increase in disruptive behaviour and truancy.

73   Some pupils are low achievers because they lack the motivation to work in school, others because they lack intellectual ability. For many both factors are at work. We have evidence that a significant number of pupils involved in persistent and serious disruption, resulting in their exclusion from school, may be much less able as well as less well motivated than other pupils. In some cases they may have special educational needs which have not been identified. We discuss this issue in more detail in chapter six. The National Curriculum can be modified for individual pupils with special educational needs.

74   The National Curriculum is intended to cater for pupils of all abilities. If this aim is achieved, we believe that it may help to promote better behaviour. 'Non-examination' fourth or fifth year groups are notorious among teachers for being difficult to manage. An important reason for this seems to be the pupils' feeling that their chances of any academic success have been written off by the school. They may see their alternative curriculum as confirming that judgement. We believe that giving such pupils access to all areas of the National Curriculum and to a system of assessment which records their achievements may reduce their sense of rejection by the system. Their need for stimulating learning methods and opportunities to succeed will not however diminish. If the introduction of the National Curriculum were to mean a worse match between the abilities and interests of lower achieving pupils and the work that they are asked to do in school the result would be more bad behaviour. We understand that one of the intentions of the National Curriculum is to identify achievements and goals more clearly for pupils of all abilities. It is important that this intention is realised.

75   We do not underestimate the problems of giving all fourth and fifth year pupils access to the mainstream curriculum. In some schools they will be considerable. We believe that it is important to preserve the most

successful features of alternative approaches within the National Curriculum. These seem to relate to learning methods rather than to content. Clear links with the 'real' world outside school, an emphasis on solving practical problems, work experience and link courses with colleges of further education all appear to improve pupils' motivation and performance. It is important to find means of reconciling them with the requirements of the National Curriculum.

76   By stressing the importance of meeting the needs of lower achieving pupils we are not in any way suggesting that those of average or high achievers should be neglected. They too can become bored and disaffected as a result of inappropriate curriculum content and teaching methods. Our emphasis on low achievers simply reflects the balance of concern expressed in our evidence.

77   Section 2 of the Education Reform Act 1988 makes it clear that the content of the National Curriculum and the processes through which it is to be delivered should be matched to the different abilities and maturities of pupils. We welcome this commitment and look forward to its implementation. **We recommend that the Secretaries of State should ensure that the National Curriculum offers stimulating programmes of study suitable for the full ability range.**

Testing and assessment

78   Our evidence suggests that many children who behave badly in school are those whose self-esteem is threatened by failure. They see academic work as competitive and the competition as unwinnable. They soon realise that the best way to avoid losing in such a competition is not to enter it. Testing is an essential school process. However, the use of test results often gives the test itself the characteristics of a competition. Among high achievers this can actually encourage better work. But for low achievers it can involve regular public failure. This can be very threatening to their self-esteem and lead to disaffection, bad behaviour and truancy. Where the test is a part of a national rather than an internal system its importance, and hence the threat it poses, will be increased.

79   The Task Group on Assessment and Testing (TGAT), set up by the Secretary of State to consider assessment within the National Curriculum, was fully aware of this problem. It therefore recommended that the national system of testing at seven, 11, 14 and 16 should be criterion-referenced, that test results for individual pupils should be confidential and that, up to the age of 16, its primary purpose should be formative. This means that testing should provide information about a pupil's achievements in relation to specific learning objectives rather than to the performance of other pupils; that individual pupils' results should only be available to themselves, their parents and teachers, and

others who need to know; and that the results should inform decisions about pupils' future learning needs. Ranked class lists should not be produced. We consider it essential for assessment systems to be supportive rather than threatening to pupils. We support the TGAT principles of criterion-referencing, formative assessment and confidentiality. We believe that they can form the basis for a supportive system, which is particularly important for younger pupils. We therefore welcome the acceptance by the Secretaries of States of these principles.

80   We have mentioned the need for schools to recognise non-academic as well as academic achievements in order to improve pupils' motivation. We consider that this has important implications for the development of records of achievement for secondary pupils. We discuss these implications in chapter six.

Curricula for individual schools and pupils

81   We identified six possible problem areas. They are: emphasis on academic achievement; grouping pupils by ability; teaching and learning methods; relevance to the outside world; cultural messages; and messages about values.

Emphasis on academic achievement

82   Our evidence suggests that an emphasis on academic achievement is likely to promote good behaviour as long as it is not the school's only emphasis. Rutter found that regular setting, checking and marking of homework in secondary schools were associated with better pupil behaviour. Mortimore found that a work-centred atmosphere was important in encouraging good behaviour in junior schools. But both studies also found that good behaviour was associated with praise and rewards. A school in which academic achievement is the only source of positive encouragement is likely to experience more difficulties with low achieving pupils.

Grouping pupils by ability

83   These difficulties may be increased if academic emphasis is translated into the rigid streaming of pupils by ability. Streaming is now relatively rare, but it still exists. About 5% of the secondary schools covered by the recent HMI survey report were streamed. Streaming means that a pupil is in the same class for all subjects even though his level of ability in, say, art may be substantially different from that in maths. A pupil in the seventh stream of a seven form entry secondary school knows exactly where the system places him – at the bottom. It is therefore not surprising that lower stream classes have a reputation for bad behaviour. Setting is a more common system of grouping pupils. It involves placing them in different 'sets' for different subjects according to their differing abilities. Careful setting and the recognition of a wide range of non-academic achievements can help to restore to low academic achievers a

proper sense of self-respect, and avoid generating the feelings of rejection and hostility that often give rise to bad behaviour.

84 Most primary schools have mixed ability classes throughout. In secondary schools this is hardly ever done but the extent to which pupils are separated by ability into streams, bands or sets varies considerably. Mixed ability teaching can be demanding. Matching learning materials to a wide variety of abilities can be difficult, but it probably reduces the feeling of rejection which seems to be common among low achieving pupils. There is a balance of advantage to be struck. In the case of banding, which consists of grouping pupils into two or three broader ability ranges, and setting, which consists of ability grouping for particular subjects, the balance is finer. **We therefore recommend that schools should not use rigid streaming arrangements to group their pupils by ability and that they should take full account of the implications for pupil behaviour when reviewing their arrangements for grouping pupils.** The probability of improving general standards of behaviour through dispersing lower achieving pupils needs to be balanced against the demands imposed by mixed ability grouping on teacher skills and resources.

85 It is not unknown for lower bands or sets to be given the least effective teachers and the worst rooms. This is clearly bad practice. We consider it essential for lower achieving pupils to have a fair allocation of the school's resources. It is, for example, important that heads of department should teach pupils across the full range of ability. Pupils should also have equal access to a range of rewards, such as commendations and merit marks, both for academic and non-academic achievements. **We recommend:**

85.1 **that schools should distribute their teaching and other resources equitably across the ability range; and**

85.2 **that they should provide a range of rewards accessible to pupils of all abilities.**

Teaching and learning methods

86 Even in schools that value non-academic ability, academic achievement remains a principal goal for all pupils and they are encouraged to value it. If the school itself places obstacles in the path to this achievement it is understandable if they become frustrated and angry. We emphasise the importance of lesson planning as an aspect of effective classroom management in chapter three. Bad lesson planning and delivery, which includes failure to match learning tasks to abilities, therefore makes disruptive behaviour by bored or frustrated pupils more likely. It is the lot of the inefficient teacher.

87   Our recommendations on teaching methods in the classroom are to be found in chapter three. Pupils also learn in a variety of other settings. We consider that educational visits, residential education, work experience and other forms of 'off-site' learning are important in motivating pupils generally and providing alternative opportunities for achievement for less academic pupils. **We therefore recommend that schools should make full use of off-site learning as a means of motivating their pupils.**

R
34

Relevance

88   Our impression is that a significant number of pupils see part or all of the conventional curriculum as irrelevant to the 'real' world outside school. By no means all of them are low achievers. However, the prospect of rewards such as good examination grades, college places and white collar jobs at the end of the process helps pupils who rate their chances of academic success as reasonable to resist the temptation to 'muck about' in lessons or play truant. Low academic achievers looking towards an unskilled job or unemployment lack this incentive to co-operate.

89   Our evidence suggests that an important factor in promoting good behaviour among pupils is a curriculum which they see as being relevant to their needs. The Technical and Vocational Education Initiative (TVEI) is making a positive contribution in this area by developing technical, practical and work-related elements in the curricula provided for 14 to 18 year olds. There is evidence, both from the national evaluation of TVEI and from evaluation at local levels, that it has improved the motivation of the pupils involved. Its practical emphasis and relevance to the real world seem to be important factors in achieving this improvement. We hope that the momentum of TVEI development can be maintained in the context of the National Curriculum. We have emphasised the need for a practical and relevant curriculum in particular for low achieving pupils earlier in this chapter. Our evidence suggests that initiatives such as TVEI are also likely to improve the motivation and behaviour of a much wider range of pupils. Work-related activities, work experience and compacts between pupils and employers are also important aspects of curriculum relevance. We look at them in more detail in chapter six.

Cultural messages

90   We have argued that good schools give pupils a sense of community. Many schools contain pupils from a variety of cultural and ethnic backgrounds. It seems to us unlikely that a school will be able to create this sense of community if its curriculum does not convey the message that all cultures are of equal value. This includes that of the majority of pupils as well as those of minorities. Our attention was drawn to a study of primary schools serving multi-ethnic areas in New Zealand (Ramsay

1983). This found that the most effective schools in terms of both work and behaviour were those which built on the pupils' own cultural backgrounds. In less effective schools teachers tended to think that cultural background was irrelevant to the curriculum. This confirms our own impressions. The curriculum becomes more meaningful in schools where the cultural realities of young peoples' lives are taken seriously. This applies equally to children from minority ethnic and white working class backgrounds.

91   We refer to evidence of racial harassment in schools earlier in this chapter. It seems clear that racist attitudes among pupils can lead to anything from name-calling to assaults resulting in serious injury or even death. Schools must counter these attitudes. Head-on confrontation is likely to be counter-productive. It may alienate as many pupils as it wins over. We believe that using the curriculum to emphasise the importance of tolerance and respect for other cultures is a more productive approach. A variety of subjects can be used to point out the achievements of different cultures. Where possible these achievements should be linked to cultures represented in the school as well as to the principle of mutual respect in the school's behaviour policy.

92   Testing which is culturally biased will not help schools to build a sense of community. TGAT recommended that assessment tasks should be reviewed regularly for evidence of such bias. We welcome and support that recommendation.

93   **We recommend that the Secretaries of State should ensure that multi-cultural awareness and equal opportunities become indentifiable cross-curricular themes and are used to promote the attitudes on which respectful and tolerant behaviour are based.**

Messages about values

94   There is more to behaviour than impulse. It springs from attitudes and moral values. Our impression is that many schools are not making explicit use of the formal part of their affective curriculum which covers religious education and personal and social education to establish and reinforce their behaviour policies. This is a lost opportunity.

95   We received a considerable number of submissions expressing concern about personal and social education (PSE) being 'squeezed out' by the National Curriculum. PSE is not one of the National Curriculum's core or other foundation subjects.

96   PSE is an important part of the affective curriculum of many schools. It covers such areas as moral education. It deals explicitly with issues like

social responsibility and tolerance and coming to terms with adolescence. It can be used to discuss the way in which the school works as a community with pupils, and to help them to understand their role and behaviour in school. Throughout this report we emphasise its importance in reinforcing schools' behaviour policies. We also consider that it has a part to play in educating pupils to be responsible adults and good parents. This is discussed in chapter five. We would therefore be very concerned if we thought that PSE was about to disappear or be reduced. We believe that it should be strengthened, and that it should be provided by all schools.

97   We do not consider that the National Curriculum need pose any threat to PSE. If the right action is taken it could encourage its development. PSE should be delivered in two ways. Some elements can form a cross-curricular theme, dealt with in a number of different subjects, within the National Curriculum. It can also be provided as a course in the time available outside that taken up by the foundation subjects of the National Curriculum. Our primary concern is not how it is delivered but that it is delivered effectively. The Secretaries of State have specifically asked the National Curriculum Council and the Curriculum Council for Wales to advise them on the place and content of PSE in the curriculum. We welcome this recognition of its importance. We recommend:

R
36.1

R
36.2

97.1   that the Secretaries of State should ensure that personal and social education is effectively covered as a cross-curricular theme within the National Curriculum; and

97.2   that schools should also provide personal and social education programmes outside the National Curriculum.

PASTORAL CARE

98   The tradition in British schools is for teachers to combine academic, disciplinary and welfare functions. Its strength is its integration. It makes knowing and educating the 'whole' pupil possible. Some other education systems do not have this pastoral tradition. Some teachers in this country look wistfully at such systems. But they are not always so highly regarded in their home countries. Deep concern was expressed to us in the USA about the effects on pupils' behaviour of high schools described as impersonal 'education factories'. The concept of the tutor group was a revelation to one very eminent American educationalist. If, as we have argued, a pupil's sense of being known and valued by the school is an important factor in ensuring good behaviour, the pastoral system has a vital role to play.

111

99 The primary class teacher and secondary form tutor are key figures. Their active involvement in both welfare and disciplinary functions is crucial to the success of a pastoral system. Secondary schools also have senior pastoral staff, including heads of year or house as well as deputy heads who exercise oversight of all systems in the school.

100 The existence of such senior staff may tempt teachers to refer welfare or discipline problems to them. Some systems seem to encourage rapid referral in all cases. This is unwise. Our evidence suggests that schools in which form tutors carry out mainly administrative functions, such as taking registers and reading notices, tend to suffer from more disruptive behaviour than schools in which they are actively involved in disciplinary, counselling and guidance activities, monitoring academic progress and other pastoral work. Disciplinary systems which result in streams of minor offenders being sent out of class by teachers to be dealt with by senior staff seem to be particularly ineffective.

101 Heads of department in secondary schools are potentially valuable sources of disciplinary as well as academic support for their teams. A drawback of splitting academic and pastoral functions too sharply is that it denies them a disciplinary or welfare role.

102 Secondary schools should have a structured referral system which involves all teachers. Behaviour problems in class should always be dealt with in the first instance by the class teacher. When more serious problems arise the form tutor should be brought in. Form tutors should only refer the pupil involved to a more senior level if they consider that the problem is too serious or too persistent to be dealt with at the first level of referral.

103 **We recommend that secondary headteachers and teachers should base pastoral systems on the strengths of the traditional integrated academic, welfare and disciplinary role of the teacher.** They should expect their senior pastoral staff to give priority to advising, supporting and encouraging colleagues carrying out pastoral functions rather than dealing with a large number of pupils directly.

104 In their recent survey report on secondary schools, HMI comment that there are still too many schools which are not making good use of tutorial time. Tutor periods are usually at the beginning of the school day. A session which just consists of taking the register and killing time before the bell goes gets the day off to a bad start for a number of reasons. First, the opportunity to foster commitment to the school has been lost. Second, the pupil is not taken seriously. Third, there is no crossing of a psychological frontier which helps young people take up

the role of pupil, rather than son or daughter, and which demonstrates that adults have taken up the role of teachers rather than parents or child-minders. The quality of this opening session of the school day is, we believe, crucial for creating a climate of mutual expectations which lead on to purposeful behaviour during the day.

105 Tutor periods are valuable opportunities to carry out pastoral work. They can be used to teach study skills or to deliver part of the school's PSE programme. We have emphasised form tutors' central role in effective pastoral systems earlier in this chapter. A structured programme of activities should help to develop the relationship between tutors and their groups. **We recommend that secondary headteachers and teachers should identify clear aims for the use of tutorial time, and that these aims should include reinforcing the school's behaviour policy.**

R 38

106 The tutor group system can also provide valuable information from pupils on the problems that they see around the school. Seeing the school from the pupils' point of view is important for heads and teachers. Knowing what pupils see as positive helps them improve the atmosphere. Although they may not realise it, schools that do not use their pastoral systems in this way to provide them with feedback receive it nonetheless through bad behaviour. Primary class teachers are well placed to gather this kind of information from pupils. In larger secondary schools a more formal system is needed. Form tutors and other pastoral staff should provide channels of communication through which the senior management team and the staff as a whole can pick up the feelings of pupils about their school. This is a valuable source of management information. Where they exist, school councils on which pupils are represented can also provide a forum for constructive discussion. We consider school councils in chapter six. PSE programmes can also provide opportunities for exploring pupils' perceptions of the school. **We recommend that headteachers and teachers should:**

106.1 **recognise the importance of ascertaining pupils' views; and**

106.2 **organise systems for doing so and for taking the information gathered into account in the management of the school.**

R 39.1 R 39.2

107 Pastoral staff are important points of contact for support services outside the school, for example education welfare officers, educational psychologists, health and social services personnel, and for parents. Our evidence suggests that when persistent behaviour problems arise with a pupil, some schools do not call in the support services or parents until a point of crisis has been reached. The pupil may for example be on the brink of exclusion. This is usually too late. By then so much bad feeling has been generated that the situation may be very difficult to retrieve.

R
40

108   In some of the schools we visited, pastoral staff were clearly in close and regular contact with both parents and LEA support staff such as education welfare officers and educational psychologists. Written evidence and statements from expert witnesses suggest to us that this is by no means universal. **We recommend that headteachers should ensure that there is regular and effective communication between their staff and support services, and that these services are given early warning of developing problems.**

109   Timetabling senior pastoral staff for regular meetings with education welfare officers and educational psychologists is a practical method of ensuring regular contact in secondary schools. This can be easier if educational welfare officers are based in schools. We consider this possibility and other ways in which educational welfare officers and psychologists can be used to support the work of schools in chapters six, seven and 10.

R
41

110   Effective schools seem to be able to combine high expectations with a sympathetic atmosphere. Teachers are not social workers or psychotherapists. They cannot solve a pupil's home problems however much they may sympathise with them. Rutter found that schools in which teachers saw misbehaviour as a disciplinary rather than a welfare problem tended to achieve better standards of behaviour. He also found better behaviour in schools where teachers made themselves available to be consulted by children about their problems. These findings are not inconsistent with one another. They illustrate the need to strike this balance. **We therefore recommend that headteachers and teachers should ensure that pastoral care in schools is characterised by a healthy balance between challenge and support for pupils.**

R
42

111   We are convinced that there are skills, which all teachers need, involved in listening to young people and encouraging them to talk about their hopes and concerns before coming to a judgement about their behaviour. We consider that these basic counselling skills are particularly valuable for creating a supportive school atmosphere. The skills needed to work effectively with adults, whether teachers or parents, are equally crucial. **We therefore recommend that initial teacher training establishments should introduce all their students to basic counselling skills and their value.** We regard such skills as particularly important for all senior pastoral staff (deputy heads, heads

of house and year). **We recommend that LEAs should provide in-service training in basic counselling skills for senior pastoral staff at least.**

112   A few secondary schools have specialist counsellors on their staff. The school counsellor is a senior member of the pastoral staff, usually with extensive training, whose job is to provide guidance and support for both pupils and colleagues. We visited one school with a counsellor. Our impression is that, where they exist, school counsellors are well used. They can themselves, for example, provide in-service training in basic counselling skills for their colleagues. A recommendation for their general use would, however, need to be based on convincing evidence of their effectiveness. We do not have such evidence.

113   Maintaining regular contact with parents is an important function not only of pastoral staff but of the staff as a whole. We consider this in detail in the last section of this chapter.

BUILDINGS AND ENVIRONMENT

114   We noticed considerable differences in the appearance of the schools that we visited. It seemed to us that there was a connection between their appearance and the behaviour of their pupils. In some we were impressed by the obvious care and effort which had gone into producing an attractive environment. Classrooms and corridors were well decorated. There were no signs of litter or graffiti. In primary schools particularly there were colourful displays of pupils' work on the walls. Staff commented to us about the benefits to the school's general atmosphere of a welcoming environment. The appearance of other schools was bleaker and less well cared for. The lack of display of pupils' work in some of the secondary schools was particularly noticeable.

115   We recognised that the pupils themselves had a considerable effect upon the appearance of the accommodation, for good or ill, but we felt that the resulting conditions also had an effect, for good or ill, upon the pupils as well as upon visitors and staff. We were therefore interested to note that, while there is no evidence that the age or size of school buildings have any effect on pupils' behaviour, there is much clearer evidence of a link between shabby, untidy classrooms without posters, plants or displays of pupils' work and poorer standards of behaviour. The converse also seems to be true.

116   It was brought home to us on many occasions, both at home and abroad, that where pupils are provided with a pleasant environment they respect it, and where they have contributed to it they treat it as

their own. This applies to buildings, grounds and equipment. We believe that this sense of participating in the ownership of a school plays an important part in the way pupils behave.

R 44

117 Staff and pupils can do a great deal themselves to improve and maintain the quality of their school's environment. We were impressed by the concerted efforts being made in some of the schools we visited. **We recommend that headteachers and staff should adopt comprehensive policies for the care of premises, with responsibilities allocated to specific people, including pupils.** Such policies should cover:

R 45

117.1 damage and graffiti control. Staff and pupils should be encouraged to notice and to report damage and graffiti as quickly as possible. The school's behaviour policy should make it clear that intentional damage to premises and equipment, including graffiti, is considered a serious offence against the community which will result in appropriate punishment. Ideally, graffiti should be removed immediately and minor damage repaired in a day or two. If possible, pupils responsible for damage should be involved in repair work as part of their punishment. Where work cannot be done by pupils, rapid repairs would be made much easier by employing caretakers whose contracts include such duties. **We therefore recommend that LEAs and governing bodies which employ school staff should include the repair of minor damage and the removal of graffiti in the duties of caretaking staff where such arrangements do not already exist and can be negotiated;**

117.2 litter control. The first and most obvious steps are to ensure that there is an adequate supply of sensibly designed and placed litter bins around the school, and that they are regularly emptied. Headteachers should make clear to staff and pupils that keeping the school litter-free is the responsibility of the whole community. Punishments for dropping litter should involve picking up litter; and

R 46

117.3 display of pupils' work. We believe that more secondary schools would do well to follow the good example set by many primary schools in this area. **We recommend that headteachers and teachers should recognise the importance of displaying pupils' work in creating an attractive environment, increasing pupils' self-esteem and fostering a sense of ownership of the premises.**

118 While the age of buildings does not seem to be particularly important, their state of repair does. There is nothing that staff or pupils can do about the results of seriously neglected maintenance. The daily sight of

defaced or damaged accommodation suggests to all that those who own the buildings do not care for them. Where the damage or defacement has been done by pupils the message is doubly regrettable because it also advertises their misdeeds. In either case the effect is depressing and ought not to be allowed to persist.

119   We are not qualified, nor would we wish, to provide guidelines for the construction of new school buildings. But we have seen the effects upon users of many school buildings put up in the past. We therefore feel that we should emphasise that the cost of maintenance, and therefore the probability of its being done, is affected by the design standards set and the materials used at the time of construction. DES Building Bulletin 67, **Crime prevention in schools – practical guidance** (1987), contains a number of useful suggestions about careful design reducing the risk of intentional and unintentional damage to school buildings.

120   While considering the influence of buildings upon those within them we noticed that their design, as well as their maintenance, is of importance. We found that in a number of schools, even of recent design, quite elementary requirements had been overlooked. In particular we would emphasise the need for adequate space for circulation between rooms and the need for staff to have a good view at all times of the pupils in their charge. Neglect of either point results in difficulty of supervision.

121   We recommend that the Secretaries of State, LEAs and governing bodies with responsibility for buildings should ensure that school buildings are designed with durability (consistent with attractiveness), ease of maintenance, avoidance of circulation bottlenecks and good sightlines for the supervision of pupils in mind.

R
47

122   The impact of major maintenance work, such as re-wiring, can clearly be very disruptive if undertaken in term time. It can not only disrupt school routines but also have a disturbing effect on pupils' behaviour.

123   Headteachers should always be consulted about the phasing and timing of such work. This may appear too obvious to be worth saying, but we know that extensive works are sometimes carried out in term time and without any consultation with the headteacher. The result is severe disruption and damage to staff morale. We therefore recommend that LEAs and governing bodies with responsibility for buildings should ensure that large scale maintenance and other building work are carried out only with due notice after consulting the headteacher and, whenever possible, in the school holidays.

R
48

124 Maintenance is a key issue. For the majority of schools this is currently an LEA responsibility. As LMS schemes are phased in from 1990 heads and governing bodies will take over responsibility for day to day maintenance and internal decoration. LEAs will retain responsibility for structural maintenance. Delegating part of the maintenance budget to schools in this way may encourage them to care for their buildings. It may also result in a more flexible and effective use of maintenance funds by, for example, combining self-help with the use of local contractors. But it may mean that maintenance is neglected because other priorities seem to be more pressing. LMS will not change the essential nature of the maintenance problem. Our impression is that, in some LEAs at least, there has been for whatever reasons a history of substantial underinvestment in maintenance. The result is some rather shabby, depressing school buildings. LEAs have argued that their budgets are restricted and that building maintenance cannot be given the same priority as, for example, maintaining the pupil–teacher ratio (see chapter 11). Under LMS, governors will be faced with equally difficult choices. We consider it essential that building maintenance should be given adequate priority. It seems clear from our evidence that inadequate maintenance is likely to lead to progressive deterioration in the quality of a school's environment. This will have a damaging effect on its atmosphere. It may lead to a downward spiral with pupils doing further damage to the building and equipment because they see that it is not cared for. Regular structural maintenance and redecoration and the prompt repair of minor damage can reverse this downward spiral. **We recommend that the Government, in its expenditure plans, should give explicit encouragement to LEAs and governing bodies with responsibility for buildings to ensure that adequate funds are made available for the maintenance of school premises.**

125 We were impressed by the effect on school atmosphere of areas with carpets. Such areas are commonplace in primary schools. Expert witnesses mentioned the effect of carpeting in improving pupils' regard for their schools. Soft floor coverings not only produce a pleasanter environment. They also significantly reduce noise from the scraping of chairs, the pounding of feet and the echoing of voices. This can make school life noticeably less stressful for teachers and pupils. In general, carpets are to be found in domestic settings. Hard floors belong more in public and institutional buildings. It may be for this reason that pupils appear to treat carpeted areas with more care than uncarpeted ones. An increasing number of LEAs are finding that the use of carpeting now compares economically with that of vinyl flooring. **We therefore recommend that LEAs and governing bodies with responsibility for buildings should help schools to create a better environment for both**

staff and pupils by providing soft floor coverings and other noise reducing features wherever possible.

TIMETABLING, CIRCULATION AND SUPERVISION

126 Some of our evidence suggests that the organisation of the school day can increase or reduce the chances of pupils misbehaving, particularly in the secondary sector. Certain aspects of primary school timetabling and organisation, such as the withdrawal of small groups of pupils receiving specialist support from their classes for part of the day, can cause difficulties if they are badly arranged. But the greater size and complexity of secondary schools increases the risk of disruption as a result of organisational defects. Most of the comments in this section are therefore about secondary schools.

127 We identified five issues related to the pattern of the school day which can affect a school's atmosphere and the behaviour of its pupils. They are: the use of assemblies and tutorial time; the structure of the timetable; circulation between lessons; the general supervision of pupils outside lessons; and lunchtime supervision.

128 We have commented on the use of assemblies by headteachers. We consider them to be an important feature of school life. An assembly which consists of nothing but a token prayer and a string of notices is more that just a wasted opportunity. It gives a negative message to pupils about the nature of the school community. So does wasted tutorial time.

129 We believe that the timetable is an important management tool which may be undervalued by some schools. Timetabling is a complex process. Structuring the school day and matching teachers to classes is complicated enough in a primary school. The number of variables involved in constructing a secondary school timetable is very great, and the task is highly complex. We recognise that there is no standard formula for success. Each school has a different mixture of people and buildings, so timetables have to be individually tailored. Each school has its own priorities. Our evidence suggests, however, that some arrangements are more likely to produce behaviour problems than others. These include:

129.1 excessive movement between classrooms. Movement from classroom to classroom can be stressful for both pupils and teachers. The more there is, the greater the chance of misbehaviour in corridors. In primary schools pupils are taught by one teacher in one room for most of the week. This tends to produce a more stable atmosphere. We know that secondary schools cannot adopt this model, although we are aware of some which use a 'transitional' timetable, with more time spent with one teacher, for their first and sometimes their second year classes. We consider that the principle of keeping movement between classrooms down to a necessary minimum is valid for all schools;

129.2 movement in 'nil time'. Some timetables allow no time for movement between lessons. This means that everybody is always late. In schools with large sites and scattered buildings, both pupils and teachers may be several minutes late. Research evidence suggests that late starts to lessons are associated with worse standards of behaviour. Lesson time should be set to allow for movement, and to make a punctual start possible;

129.3 bunching of activities. Good teachers know that they can keep pupils' attention by varying activities in lessons. We consider that the same principle should apply to timetabling. If, for example, a group gets nearly all its practical and activity lessons on a Monday it is likely to become rather restive by the end of the week;

129.4 mismatches between teachers and groups. We know that primary heads spend a great deal of time thinking about matching teachers to classes. We recognise that this is more difficult in secondary schools, but the same principles apply. If, for example, an inexperienced teacher is given a particularly difficult fourth year group behaviour problems are likely to arise, especially if they have a lesson in a hut at the end of the playground on a Friday afternoon;

129.5 lack of consultation with staff. We comment earlier in this chapter on the weaknesses of autocratic management styles and on teachers' proper desire to be involved in decision making processes. The staff represent an invaluable source of information and professional advice. We believe that failure to use that source of advice is likely to produce a less effective timetable. It will also be resented by teachers because of the lack of consultation involved in constructing it; and

129.6 teacher stress. Timetable features can generate or reduce stress. In one school we visited year groups had, until recently, had breaks and lunches at different times in order to reduce congestion in the playground and dining hall. This meant that teachers' breaks were also staggered. The difficulties involved in arranging lunchtime meetings and loss of informal staff room contacts increased stress among teachers. A new timetabler identified the problem from staff comments and changed the practice. This example also illustrates the danger of suggesting standard solutions. We know of other schools that have found staggering the lunch break helpful in improving behaviour. What matters is that headteachers and timetablers are fully aware of the effects of the timetable on behaviour, and its importance as a management tool, and are prepared to use it as such.

130   Timetables should be constructed with pupils' behaviour in mind. **We recommend that headteachers and their senior management teams should recognise the importance of efficient and sensitive timetabling as a management tool which can be used to reduce problems of circulation, supervision and classroom management, and that the annual timetabling cycle should involve thorough consultation with staff.** This may mean that, in some secondary schools, the timetable planning cycle will need to be changed and perhaps extended.

131   We observed pupils circulating between lessons in all the schools we visited and were, in general, favourably impressed by what we saw. We are, however, aware of schools where circulation is a much less orderly affair. In a large school, circulation can involve over 1,000 people moving simultaneously. Bottlenecks in narrow corridors or stair wells and badly placed queues can lead to pushing, jostling and other behaviour problems which damage the atmosphere and sometimes the fabric of the school. They can also escalate into more serious problems such as fights. A high proportion of teachers in our survey reported that physical aggression between pupils was a frequent problem around the school. Building design and layout impose constraints upon any school, but circulation problems can be exacerbated by bad timetabling and bad flow management.

132   Standard solutions to circulation problems are also of very limited value. Some schools operate 'one way' systems to relieve bottlenecks. These need to be carefully signposted and supervised. Unorthodox solutions may work. One school we visited had abandoned the use of bells. It had a very concentrated pattern of circulation with large numbers of classrooms off a long, central corridor, and this caused difficulties when every class emerged simultaneously. Abandoning bells had the effect of slightly staggering the beginning and end of lessons which alleviated congestion. The solution was successfully tailored to solve the school's particular problem.

133   We emphasise earlier in this chapter the collective responsibility of staff for promoting good behaviour throughout the school. Schools in which senior teachers are 'visible' during lesson breaks are less likely to suffer

from bad behaviour in circulation areas. Schools in which teachers tend to ignore bad behaviour when they are not inside their own classrooms are much more likely to suffer from it. To ignore bad behaviour in these circumstances is to condone it, and to encourage its spread to the classroom. Regarding general supervision, **We recommend:**

R 52.1

133.1 **that senior staff should be visible and strategically placed during mass circulation periods between lessons; and**

R 52.2

133.2 **that headteachers and teachers, when moving about the school, should be aware of and take responsibility for pupils' behaviour.**

134 Although we recognise that allowing pupils into school buildings during breaks may present supervision problems, locking them out is likely to have a negative effect on a school's atmosphere. It generates resentment among pupils, indicates a lack of trust and prevents any sense of ownership of the buildings. Admitting them may seem a bold step to take in a school where there is no sense of community, a tradition of vandalism and no effective or rapid means of repairing damage. Our recommendations, however, are meant to be taken as a whole. In this context, heads and their staff should recognise that the gains derived from greater pupil commitment to the institution and the elimination of feelings of resentment caused by 'lockouts' are likely to outweigh the extra effort involved in supervising such arrangements. We were very disturbed to learn that some schools keep toilets locked for most of the day. In our view this is never justified. **We recommend that headteachers should ensure that pupils have access to school buildings outside lesson times.**

R 53

LUNCHTIME SUPERVISION

135 We were told at several schools that the supervision of pupils at lunchtime is the biggest single behaviour-related problem that they face. This was confirmed by a number of expert witnesses. We also note that the analysis of injuries to school staff sustained as a result of violent incidents provided by the Inner London Education Authority (ILEA – see chapter 10) suggests that the risk to midday supervisors is significantly greater than to other staff, particularly when breaking up playground fights. We observed lunchtime supervision arrangements at most of the schools we visited. It seemed clear to us that they were a source of difficulty even in the best ordered schools we saw. We concluded that this is an issue which needs to be taken very seriously.

136 We believe that the most effective lunchtime supervision is provided by teachers. It is also clear to us that teachers need lunch breaks. The debate about whether lunchtime supervision is a normal part of a teacher's duties ran on for many years. The agreement that it is not a contractual obligation dates back to 1968. Between 1968 and 1985 many teachers continued to volunteer for lunchtime duties in exchange for free meals. However some LEAs had to bring in midday supervisors, who are not teachers, to make up numbers. Industrial action by teachers in 1985 ended voluntary lunchtime supervision in many schools. Many teachers are no longer prepared to do it. Although some LEAs employ teachers under separate contracts for this purpose, the use of midday supervisors in schools is now more or less universal.

137 Headteachers are formally responsible for lunchtime arrangements. We were told by the National Association of Head Teachers (NAHT) that, in a few schools, the head alone provides supervision. We believe that this is unacceptable. Employing adequate numbers of midday supervisors will not, however, in itself result in acceptable standards of behaviour at lunchtime. In many of the schools we visited, we were told that some midday supervisors may actually provoke a certain amount of bad behaviour unintentionally while trying to maintain order. We have emphasised the importance of effective authority for teachers. Midday supervisors do not have the same status as teachers. Nor in general are they likely to have been trained in group management skills. Some midday supervisors seem to rely entirely on their status as adults as a source of authority. They may, for example, refuse to listen to, shout at, or threaten pupils. We were given numerous accounts of situations, and witnessed one, in which this kind of approach escalated a minor incident into a major confrontation involving intervention by the headteacher. In most schools, midday supervisors who are not teachers will continue to be employed. **We recommend that LEAs and governing bodies which employ school staff should ensure that midday supervisors are given adequate training in the management of pupils' behaviour.** Training programmes should take account of the findings of the ILEA analysis referred to above.

138 In 1985 the Government made an Education Support Grant (ESG) available to supplement the funding already provided by LEAs for midday supervision. Its current (1988/89) value is about £40 million. This grant was always intended to be a temporary measure. The Government has announced that it will be discontinued from April 1989. The money will not be lost to LEAs, since it will be redeployed within the ESG pool, but will no longer be available to help fund midday supervision. LEAs will have to find the whole cost of midday supervision from other sources of revenue as they did before this ESG

R
54

was introduced. It has been suggested to us that, in the light of concern about pupils' behaviour in general and behaviour at lunchtime in particular, the timing of this change is unfortunate.

139   We accept that ESG funding is temporary or 'pump priming' in nature, and that priorities change. We are not, therefore, recommending the restoration of this ESG. Taking account of the strong concerns expressed to us about this issue, however, **We recommend that the Government, in its expenditure plans, should give explicit encouragement to LEAs to ensure that adequate funds are made available for lunchtime supervision.**

140   LEAs will be able to devolve the funding of lunchtime supervision to schools as LMS is phased in from 1990. We consider that such devolution would be consistent with the headteacher's overall responsibilities. It would make possible the negotiation of local arrangements, which could result in different combinations of teachers and midday supervisors being deployed according to schools' circumstances and needs. We believe that it is important for some teachers to be employed for lunchtime supervision, perhaps as leaders of supervisory teams. We recognise that the present rates of pay received by midday supervisors would not be sufficient to attract many teachers. Headteachers will need to bear this in mind when making their arrangements. It is important that the schools make adequate financial provision for lunchtime supervision. **We recommend:**

140.1   **that LEAs should devolve the funding of lunchtime supervision to schools; and**

140.2   **that headteachers should use these funds to devise schemes which meet the needs of their schools and encourage participation by teachers.**

PARTNERSHIP WITH PARENTS

141   The majority of individual teachers who wrote to us suggested that the attitudes and behaviour of some parents were major causes of bad behaviour by their children in school. We were told that the factors involved ranged from family instability, conflict and poverty to parental indifference or hostility to school. We consider the role of family conflict and poverty in chapter five. This section deals with teachers' perceptions of parental indifference and hostility and what schools can do to improve matters.

142   Teachers' attitudes towards parents seemed to differ in the schools we visited. Some of the schools clearly gave high priority to promoting the active involvement of parents in as many aspects of school life as possible. Others generally saw parents as a source of difficulty, and appeared reluctant to involve them in disciplinary matters because of a feeling that they would not support the school. Most fell between these two extremes. We could not explain different attitudes to parents by differences in the schools' catchment areas.

143   We know that there is a minority of parents who seem to be actively hostile to schooling. There are even a few who assault teachers. Our evidence suggests, however, that the hostile minority is very small. We are convinced that the vast majority of parents, regardless of social class, ethnic or cultural origin, want their children to work hard and behave well at school. We do not perceive any major divergence of interest between schools and parents at this fundamental level. But we do perceive a range of practical problems which can prevent active partnership developing.

Talking about behaviour

144   We believe that parents have a vital role to play in promoting good behaviour in schools. There is much that they can do on their own initiative, but they also need help and encouragement from schools. We felt that two research findings were particularly interesting in this connection. About 900 secondary pupils in the West Midlands were asked in a survey which reward for good work or behaviour in school they valued most, and which punishment for bad behaviour they feared most (Wheldall and Merrett 1988). A positive letter home was one of the two rewards most valued. The punishments most feared were also those involving parents – a letter home or being put 'on report' (a system in which teachers write comments on a pupil at the end of every lesson, a summary of which can be made available to parents). Wheldall and Merrett suggest that, while schools often use letters of complaint, positive letters home are very rarely used. This must mean that some parents get nothing but negative messages about their children from school. Parents most likely to find themselves in this position are those of lower achieving pupils whose own memories of school may be bad. It seems likely to us that they will become hostile to the school rather than being prepared to work with teachers to improve matters. **We recommend that headteachers and teachers should ensure that parents receive positive and constructive comments on their children's work and behaviour as a matter of course.**

R
57

145   Good communications with parents are made more important by the home–school 'perception gap'. Researchers have consistently found that when parents and teachers are asked to identify children with behaviour

South East Essex College
of Arts and Technology, Southend

problems in a class they identify roughly the same number, but they are largely different children. The overlap is small. Parents who tell the headteacher that their child 'doesn't behave like that at home' are likely to be telling the truth. Our evidence suggests that many heads and teachers tend to underestimate or even ignore the school-based factors involved in disruptive behaviour. We have also been told that some schools only involve parents in behaviour problems as a last resort. Again, demanding that parents 'deal' with behaviour which they do not recognise seems likely to us to provoke a negative or even hostile reaction. **We recommend that, when disciplinary problems arise, headteachers and teachers should involve parents at an early stage rather than as a last resort.**

R 58

R 59

146   **We recommend that teachers should recognise that pupils' behaviour at home may differ markedly from their behaviour at school, and that they should take this into account when discussing pupils with their parents.** This helps to encourage co-operation and reduce the risk of confrontation with parents. In this, as in other contexts, it is very important for teachers to listen to what parents have to say. The aim should be to reach agreement about the nature of the problem and what needs to be done about it. If such agreement is reached it may even be possible for parents to use home-based strategies, such as the removal of televisions from bedrooms, to reinforce school behaviour policies. We heard of examples where such steps had proved effective.

147   One method for bridging the gap, which was illustrated by our visit to schools in Norway and has also been suggested in this country (Hargreaves 1984), is an association of the parents of pupils in one tutor group or class. Meetings between this small group of parents and the form tutor or class teacher help to establish closer understanding between them. They also provide opportunities for parents to compare notes on children's claims about what other parents permit. This will often come as a surprise to them and help them considerably in controlling their children's behaviour.

Involving parents

148   Schools are not always welcoming places for parents to visit. We know that many parents themselves have bad memories of failure at school. They may find schools intimidating. If heads and teachers do not open the door to parents and create a welcoming atmosphere for them, they should not be surprised if some parents appear to be indifferent or even hostile when contacts are made.

149   One of the most important findings of the **School Matters** study of junior schools was that school effectiveness is related to parental involvement. The most effective junior schools in the sample, in terms

of work, behaviour and attendance, were those which had the best informal relationships with parents. These schools encouraged parental involvement in a variety of ways. Parents were to be found in classrooms using their talents and experience to work with individual pupils or groups. Parents were also encouraged to involve themselves in their own children's learning out of school through home reading and other similar schemes. The research team found that formal links with parents such as parent–teacher associations (PTAs) were not a substitute for other kinds of parental involvement. The most effective junior schools in their sample seemed to have been successful in breaking down the barriers between home and school. This is not just true of the primary sector. The recent national survey of parental involvement in schools carried out by the National Foundation for Educational Research, and the 'Parents and the Community as Educators' project have identified numerous examples of good practice. These range from the use of parent volunteers in primary classrooms to parental contributions to careers education and work experience in the secondary sector. Schools involved in these kinds of initiatives see parents as a valuable resource for educating children, rather than as a hindrance.

150   We discuss the role of PTAs and parents' evenings in chapter five. Schools can involve parents in their work in at least five other ways, by;

    150.1   maintaining good channels of communication. This includes both written information and regular opportunities for parents to meet teachers;

    150.2   providing a welcoming environment for parents visiting the school which may include social facilities such as a parents' room;

    150.3   ensuring effective liaison with individual families. This is sometimes called home–school liaison and may involve education welfare officers as well as teachers;

    150.4   using parents as helpers in the classroom to work with individuals and small groups of pupils; and

    150.5   encouraging parents to take part in home learning schemes, which may involve them reading or watching particular television programmes with their children as an extension of work in school.

151   Good communication systems, a welcoming environment and effective home–school liaison are important for all schools. We were impressed by the use of parents' rooms (usually a spare classroom equipped with a

kettle) in some of the primary and one of the secondary schools we visited, though this facility can only be set up when a spare room of some sort is available. Any arrangements which make parents feel welcome are helpful as, especially, is a friendly attitude on the part of staff.

152 We recognise that active parental involvement in schools poses practical problems. Liaison with parents takes time which teachers may have difficulty in finding. In schools where there has been a tradition of keeping parents at a distance, teachers may be apprehensive about the possible threat to their professional status posed by bringing them into the classroom. Our evidence suggests, however, that the benefits which can flow from collaboration with parents can be substantial and make it worthwhile for schools to overcome these difficulties and make the experiment. The scope for using parents as classroom helpers and in home learning schemes is probably much greater in primary than in secondary schools. **We recommend:**

> 152.1 **that headteachers and teachers should develop an active partnership with parents as an aid to promoting good behaviour;**
>
> 152.2 **that they should ensure that their schools provide a welcoming environment for parents; and**
>
> 152.3 **that, particularly in primary schools, they should encourage parental involvement in the classroom and in home learning schemes.**

R
60.1

R
60.2

R
60.3

153 Parents should have direct access to their child's class teacher or form tutor outside formal parents' evenings. Schools may also wish to hold regular 'open door' evenings at which senior staff make themselves available on a regular basis, for example once a month, to discuss issues which parents wish to raise in order to promote a sense of partnership. **We recommend that headteachers and teachers should develop policies to secure easy access to them by parents and good communications between them and parents, which go beyond the provision of formal parents' evenings.**

R
61

154 Good written communications are important. They can take a number of forms including information booklets, news sheets and letters home. They should always be expressed in terms which are easily understood by all parents. This generally means no more than using plain English, but schools serving areas in which there may be parents who are not fluent in English should also produce information in other community languages. In many parts of Wales, of course, information should be

provided in both Welsh and English. **We recommend:**

154.1   **that schools should ensure that written communications to parents are in language easily understood by them; and**

154.2   **that, where significant numbers of parents use first languages other than English, communications are available in these languages as well as in English.**

155   Parents should be given a clear statement of what they can expect from the school and what the school expects from them and their children. Opportunities should be available to discuss these expectations. We consider that clear communication of expectations is essential in relation to pupils' behaviour. This is particularly important for nursery and primary schools because they provide the first school contact for parents. Induction arrangements are important for all schools, but they need to be particularly thorough for the parents of children entering nursery and reception classes. **We recommend:**

155.1   **that headteachers should ensure that their schools have effective induction arrangements for parents of new pupils; and**

155.2   **that they should ensure that their schools' behaviour policies are communicated fully and clearly to parents, who should be reminded of them regularly and informed of any major changes to them throughout their child's school career.**

Home-school agreements

156   The NAHT suggested to us that the most effective way of doing this would be through a home–school 'contract' or agreement. This agreement would be a document setting out what the school will provide for the pupil and the parent, and what it expects from the pupil, in the way of effort and good behaviour, and the parent, in the way of support, in return. It would be signed by parents when their children entered a school and could, in secondary schools at least, also be signed by pupils. We were told that a number of schools already use such agreements and are satisfied with them.

157   The NAHT's representatives told us that, at this stage, they were recommending the use of home–school agreements by schools on a voluntary rather than a statutory basis. They did not, however, dismiss the idea that signing such an agreement should become a legal condition of entry to school in the future. We decided to explore the possibility of a legal entry 'contract'.

158   Our first conclusion was that it would be inappropriate to borrow the contract concept from civil law for this purpose. Contracts are usually

entered into voluntarily by both parties. A breach on either side can involve legal action for damages. If all schools used contracts but parents were still legally obliged to see that their children were educated, it could hardly be argued that a parent's agreement to sign was voluntary. We found the concept of damages even more difficult to envisage in the school context. Damages need to be proved. In chapter five we suggest that there may be other means of making parents accountable for physical injury or damage done by their children in school. When it comes to breaches of school rules which do not involve injury to people or property, it is difficult to see what measure of damages could be specified. The 'contract' model could also expose schools to litigation from parents as a result of the school's failure to deliver its side of the bargain, which might be because of staff vacancies or other factors beyond its control. We therefore rejected the notion of a contract enforceable in civil law.

159 We went on to consider the possibility of making it a condition of entry that parents should sign an undertaking to make every effort to ensure that their child conformed with the school's behaviour policy. If any such requirement were to be imposed by law, it would have to be reconciled with the provisions of section 6 of the Education Act 1980, which require LEAs and governors to comply with any preference expressed by parents as to the school to which their child should be admitted. Making parents sign such undertakings would be a very forceful method of communicating a school's behaviour policy to them. Its advantages would, however, stop there. If a pupil's parents refused to sign and did not send him to school, they would be served with an attendance order. The pupil would then be required to attend a school to which the missing signature was a condition for entry. If he was excluded, no educational advantage would have been secured. If he was admitted without a signature the system would be seen to be unworkable. Moreover, breach of the undertaking would not involve any penalties for child or parent which are not currently available. The NAHT's representatives suggested that a significant minority of parents would refuse to sign. This would undermine such a system. We concluded that the balance of advantage lay with schools making use of non-statutory agreements rather than with our recommending changes in the law.

160 We consider that all schools should formally specify conditions for the readmission of pupils who have been excluded for an indefinite period. Pupils should only be indefinitely excluded for serious and persistent misbehaviour. They should only be allowed to re-enter a school on the basis of a clear and specific understanding about how they will behave. We consider it essential for parents to be asked to sign an undertaking

that they will make every effort to ensure that their child complies with the terms specified in this re-entry agreement. Pupils themselves should also be asked to sign the agreement. If parents or pupils refuse to sign, exclusions should be made permanent. **We recommend that headteachers should use re-entry agreements, specifying the conditions under which an excluded pupil can be re-admitted to school, as a means of ending indefinite exclusions.**

R
65

Home visits

161 We emphasise the value of education welfare officers as channels of communication between parents and schools earlier in this chapter, and recommend that schools make full use of them. Education welfare officers spend a considerable amount of their time talking to parents and children in their homes. Home visiting can be an effective method of breaking down barriers, but it requires time and skills which are more likely to be possessed by education welfare officers than teachers. Senior pastoral staff in some schools make regular home visits. Teachers we spoke to in the Netherlands regarded home visiting as a normal part of their duties. The introduction of home visiting as a normal part of a teacher's duties in this country would have major resource and training implications. A recommendation on these lines would need to be supported by strong evidence of significant benefits in terms of pupils' behaviour. We do not at present have such evidence. It seems clear to us, however, that there are occasions on which home visits by teachers are appropriate, necessary and beneficial. **We therefore recommend that, in appropriate cases, LEAs and headteachers should make time available for home visits by teachers, who should consult with the education welfare service and other agencies where necessary.**

R
66

162 Some LEAs employ teachers whose job is to develop links between schools and parents. They can do this by home visiting, by encouraging parental involvement in schools, by developing materials such as home reading schemes for home–school learning and by advising colleagues. In Wales a number of these home–school liaison teachers have been funded by an Education Support Grant (ESG) since 1985. We were given a preliminary LEA evaluation of the Welsh project. This concluded that some useful results had been achieved but problems had also been encountered, including significant cost in terms of staff time and other resources. In one English school we visited, we met a teacher whose post was funded through arrangements established by section 11 of the Local Government Act 1966 (covering provision for Commonwealth immigrants). Although she was not called a home–school liaison teacher and had other duties, she seemed to have been successful in creating links between the school and Asian parents. We do not doubt the value of effective home–school liaison. We are

not, however, convinced that the appointment of specialist teachers is, in general, the best way forward in this area. It may, however, be appropriate to create such posts in particular schools for various reasons, some of which have little to do with pupils' behaviour. Where this is done, home–school liaison teachers should be aware of the implications of their work for pupils' behaviour.

163

Links with the community

Parents are part of the wider community in which schools are set. Primary schools usually serve a fairly small geographical catchment area. Secondary schools may have much larger and more scattered catchment areas, taking in a number of neighbourhood communities. A number of LEAs have set up community schools which may provide facilities for adult education classes, youth centres, pre-school playgroups, pensioners' groups and even social facilities such as bars. We visited one purpose-built community school and were impressed by the enthusiasm of staff for the concept. They were convinced that community use of the premises during the school day improved standards of behaviour because it gave the local community, which includes parents and pupils, a sense of ownership of the school. It has also been suggested to us that the presence of more adults in school encourages better behaviour by pupils, that community schools provide opportunities for pupils to behave responsibly on the premises by helping the very young and the very old, and that community schools make it easier for teachers and parents to meet informally on a more equal footing.

164

Standards of behaviour in the community school we visited appeared to be very good. We do not, however, have research or other evidence indicating that behaviour in community schools is generally better than in other secondary schools. Thus we cannot recommend community use as a way of improving behaviour problems. **We do, however, recommend that LEAs, headteachers and governing bodies should give serious consideration to providing community access to school facilities, where it does not already exist, as a means of fostering good relations with parents and the wider community.**

1   We recognise that educationalists are more likely to read this report than parents. We have therefore considered whether it would be sensible to direct any or our recommendations towards parents. We concluded that not to do so would suggest that parents have no independent power to influence their children's behaviour. This is cleary absurd. Parents are the first educators. They play a crucial part in shaping their children's personalities and attitudes. They continue to have a powerful influence over them throughout their school years.

2   Parents are not the only influences in these years. We highlight the importance of classroom and school factors in chapters three and four. Other children are also an important influence on behaviour. But an essential ingredient is the establishment of an effective working partnership between parents and schools. This point is emphasised in evidence sent to us by the National Confederation of Parent–Teacher Associations (NCPTA). The partnership can only become real if parents accept that they have a duty not only to send their children to school but also to encourage them to behave well when they get there.

3   Our evidence suggests that teachers' picture of parents is generally very negative. Many teachers feel that parents are to blame for much misbehaviour in schools. We consider that, while this picture contains an element of truth, it is distorted. We note in chapter four that there is considerable scope for misunderstanding between teachers and parents. It also seems clear that there is a small minority of parents who cannot or will not provide appropriate guidance for their children and who are positively hostile to schooling. We are convinced, however, that the vast majority of parents share and support the aims and values of the schools to which they send their children. In this chapter we suggest ways in which that support can be realised.

RESPONSIBLE PARENTHOOD

4   We believe that socially responsible parenthood is particularly crucial in the first five years of a child's life. Parents must do everything they can to help their children relate co-operatively to adults and to other children. They must also do their best to encourage their children to develop the attitudes and values on which both school and society are based. These include self-respect, respect and concern for others, self-discipline and moral qualities such as truthfulness and honesty. Some aspects of bringing up children may be instinctive. Others must be learned. Our impression is that, whereas many parents are highly skilled in guiding their children towards adulthood, others are less so. A few seem not even to recognise the need for such skills at all.

5 Our evidence indicates that many teachers are experiencing problems with children who have great difficulty in relating to each other or to adults in a co-operative way. Most of these pupils are boys, but the number of girls in this category is not insignificant. These children seem to use verbal and even physical aggression as a substitute for other forms of communication. A number of submissions to us suggest that this kind of behaviour is becoming more common among young children. We have been told that some of the children now entering nursery and reception classes lack the basic social skills needed to talk to and play with other children. A recent study of disruptive behaviour in primary schools has drawn attention to the use of aggressive behaviour as a means of getting the teacher's attention, particularly by boys (Steed and Lawrence 1988). Our survey also highlights the concern felt by many primary teachers about aggression by pupils towards one another.

6 We are aware of research findings which link anti-social and aggressive behaviour to the quality of children's upbringing and family relationships (eg West 1982). Research evidence also suggests that children who present serious behaviour problems in school are likely to have experienced either neglect or rejection or a combination of both. It also suggests that children's capacity to feel and show concern for others is influenced by the degree of concern shown by their parents for them. Guidance and support in the home seem to be key factors. One study found that the most violent boys were likely to be those whose parents' response to their behaviour was one of two extremes, either permissive or punitive (Lefkowitz 1977). Neglect can be expressed through permissiveness, and rejection through physical punishment. We were told by teachers at schools we visited of parents who seemed to ignore or even encourage their sons' aggressive behaviour towards other children. We were also told of parents whom schools were reluctant to contact when their children misbehaved. Teachers knew that a complaint to these parents would lead to a severe beating for the child and probably result in more bad behaviour in school. Other parents were reported to treat their children in unpredictable and inconsistent ways – sometimes kind, sometimes cruel, sometimes indifferent.

7 We have emphasised the importance of teachers modelling the behaviour they expect to see in children. This is even more important for parents who are presenting models of behaviour to children from their earliest years. Many of our correspondents commented on the poor models of behaviour presented by some parents, including verbal and even physical aggression towards each other.

8 When it comes to the reasons suggested for irresponsible parenthood, our individual correspondents can be very roughly divided into two

groups. The 'tough' group belive that the parents of pupils who behave badly tend to be irresponsible, immoral and hostile to the values represented by schools. The 'tender' group believe that these parents tend to be so distressed by factors such as marital breakdown and poverty that they bring up emotionally disturbed children who behave badly in school.

9   We believe that, while both views contain valuable insights, each has serious limitations. The 'tough' view rightly emphasises parents' resonsibilities for bringing up their children properly, and the need for them to make conscious decisions to do so. We consider that it overestimates the extent to which parents and schools disagree over fundamental values, and underestimates the effects of family stress. The 'tender' view highlights the real problem of family stress, but comes dangerously close to absolving parents from any responsibility for their children's behaviour by suggesting that some have been rendered incapable of positive action.

10 We use the term 'family stress' to cover both the emotional and material problems from which families can suffer. Such problems can interact with one another. They include marital discord, poverty and bad housing. We are concerned in this report with the effects of these problems, not their causes. The Government Statistical Service's publication **Social Trends** (1988) includes figures which suggest that the incidence of family stress has increased over the last two decades. The increase in the divorce rate is well known. The 1985 rate was more than double that in 1971. The number of single parent families has also increased from about 3% of all households in 1971 to about 5% in 1985. Child poverty also seems to have increased. In 1971 22% of the poorest households contained children. In 1985 this proportion had risen to 30%. The increase in the number of new clients registered by the Samaritans is an indicator of distress which we found particularly striking; it rose from about 90,000 in 1971 to just under 400,000 in 1985. The largest single group of clients were women aged 25 to 39.

11 Research evidence seems to show that the majority of persistent absentees from school live in very poor material conditions. We discuss this further in chapter seven. The material circumstances of pupils involved in seriously disruptive behaviour seems to be more varied. A detailed study of pupils who had been excluded from secondary schools in Sheffield found that, while half of them lived in council accommodation, just under a third came from owner-occupied homes (Galloway 1982). Emotional tensions within the family seemed to be a more important factor. The mothers of excluded pupils were

interviewed. Nearly half had symptons associated with depression or anxiety.

12 We do not believe that family stress absolves parents from their responsibilities for bringing up their children properly. But it would be unrealistic to assume that all families are equally well placed to discharge those responsibilities. Some need more help that others.

13 Schooling is disrupted by selfish and aggressive behaviour. We have suggested that the kinds of bad parenting which encourage such behaviour are characterised by permissiveness (neglect), harsh punishment (rejection) or inconsistency (a combination of both). We have also suggested that children are more likely to behave in this way if their parents do.

14 Our evidence suggests that the way in which some boys are brought up causes particular problems in schools. Some parents tolerate or even encourage aggressive behaviour. In some cases, parents telling boys to 'stick up for themselves' seems to mean that they should attack other children and defy teachers. We were concerned by the extent of this behaviour brought to our notice in the primary sector. This kind of aggressiveness should have no place in schools. Our evidence also suggests that parents who respond aggressively to their children's aggressive behaviour are likely to aggravate rather than reduce the problem.

15 **We recommend that the Government, LEAs, governors and headteachers should consider means of impressing on parents that the way in which they bring up their children is likely to have a significant influence on their behaviour in school. Parents should recognise the need to:**

15.1 **provide firm but affectionate guidance in the home, which is most likely to produce the attitudes on which good behaviour in school can be based;**

15.2 **ensure that they set a good and consistent example to their children by their own behaviour; and**

15.3 **avoid permissive or harshly punitive responses to aggressive behaviour, particularly by boys, which can encourage attitudes which are incompatible with schooling.**

16 These proposals are well established and of great importance. They need to be understood and acted upon by each generation in turn. They cannot be implemented by any single agency. We hope that all agencies

that have an influence on family life, from the Government to social services departments and from the churches to the courts will make it their business to bring them home to young parents whenever it is appropriate.

17   It seems clear from our evidence that some parents lack the skills necessary to bring up children in a socially responsible way, and that this is affecting standards of behaviour in schools. But parenting skills can be learned. We believe that the education system can help to reduce this problem by providing systematic preparation for adult life including parenthood. We believe that pupils of both sexes should be introduced to the values and skills involved in good parenting, and that schools should aim to identify and cultivate the adult attitudes which form the basis of responsible parenthood. **We recommend:**

17.1   **that the Secretaries of State should ensure that education for parenthood is fully covered as a cross-curricular theme in the National Curriculum; and**

R
69.1

17.2   **that governors and headteachers should ensure that education for parenthood is fully covered in school personal and social education programmes.**

R
69.2

18   We believe that there is also a need for education for parenthood for some of those who have left school. The objective should be to promote responsible attitudes to bringing up children. We are aware of the difficulties of identifying and then reaching the priority target group of potentially irresponsible parents. The means by which such education could be delivered to this group would need to be considered very carefully. Colleges of futher education, adult education centres, voluntary organisations, ante-natal and other health clinics, health visitors, broadcasters, the Open University and Open College might be able to play some part in such an initiative. **We recommend that the Government should develop a post-school education strategy aimed at promoting socially responsible parenthood.**

R
70

LONE PARENTS

19   It has been suggested to us that the increase in the number of single parent families has in itself caused standards of behaviour in schools to deteriorate. The wide variety of causes for lone parenthood, and the differing ages of the children involved, makes it difficult to generalise. However, the quality of family relationships seems to be a more important influence on children's behaviour than the number of parents. The poverty factor cannot, however, be discounted. Single

parent families are much more likely to be poor than families with two parents.

20   We are aware of evidence from the USA that vocational training packages which provide for childcare can be successful in lifting lone parents out of poverty. The Government's scheme of Employment Training (ET) for the unemployed provides a childcare allowance for lone parents. Applicants for the scheme need to be registered as unemployed for at least six months to be eligible. When planning ET the Government recognised that this was difficult for many lone parents because without childcare they were not available for work, which is a condition of registration. It relaxed this restriction for lone parents with children of school age. We welcome this development and urge lone parents to take up the training opportunities offered by ET.

BREAKING DOWN BARRIERS BETWEEN HOME AND SCHOOL

21   In chapter four we discuss the barriers that exist between schools and parents, and some of the ways in which they can be broken down. We emphasise the importance of good informal relationships between teachers and parents and discuss what schools can do. Good relationships will not, of course, develop if parents do not take up the opportunities for contact and co-operation offered by schools. **We therefore recommend that parents should take full advantage of all channels of communication made available by schools and develop good working relationships with teachers in order to help their children to become constructive members of the school community.**

22   Formal links between schools and parents also exist. Others could be created. In this chapter we consider three types of link. They are: PTAs, parents' evenings and annual parents' meetings. We also consider the question of parental accountability for their children's behaviour in school.

23   PTAs aim to bring staff and parents together for regular meetings, social

Parent–teacher associations

events and collaborative projects such as school fairs. The NCPTA, in its evidence to us, describe how such events and functions can also help to develop a sense of community and encourage parents to take a greater interest in the education of their children. But they also note that many associations still limit their activities to fund-raising. Although many schools have PTAs, some do not. The **School Matters** study found that having a PTA was no guarantee of good relations with parents. The existence of PTAs in the sample schools was actually associated with lower standards of work and behaviour. There seem to be two reasons for this. First, PTAs can be used by schools as a substitute for good relations with parents. Second, they may be dominated by a small group of enthusiasts who are not typical of the parent body as a whole. They may, for example, have more time to spare or be more articulate. The result often seems to be that staff spend a considerable amount of time talking to this small and unrepresentative group while the majority of parents feel excluded.

24 These findings do not, however, lead us to conclude that PTAs should be discontinued. On the contrary, they are potentially useful organisations which should be improved. We consider that parents themselves must take action to improve them. Activities should, for example, be planned to happen at times and in places convenient to most parents. Particular efforts may need to be made in schools serving communities which are mixed in terms of social class, ethnic or cultural origins. We believe that more representative PTAs, whether operating at school, class or tutor group level, would provide better informal opportunities for staff and parents to discuss pupils' behaviour. **We therefore recommend that parent–teacher associations should ensure that their activities are accessible and rewarding to as many parents as possible.**

R
72

Parents' evenings and meetings

25 Attendance at parents' evenings varies greatly from school to school. Although they are traditional in all schools they often do not attract the parents that teachers most want to see. There is much that schools can do to maximise attendance but parents must respond positively to these opportunities to discuss their children's progress.

26 Annual parents' meetings, at which the governing body presents its annual report to parents, were introduced very recently (1987). Traditions of attendance have yet to be established. In chapter nine we recommend that the governors' annual report should cover pupils' behaviour and attendance. We believe that regular discussion of these issues at annual parents' meetings should be helpful to schools, but only if that discussion is responsible and constructive. References to individual teachers and pupils should be avoided. Alarmist statements can have a very damaging effect on the morale of staff, pupils and other parents.

27 We believe that parents' evenings and meetings are important channels of communication between schools and parents, and that high turn-outs for such events can contribute towards realising the ideal of partnership. **We therefore recommend that parents should make every effort to attend parents' evenings and annual parents' meetings.**

R
73

PARENTAL ACCOUNTABILITY

28 In chapter four we suggest that schools should consider the use of written agreements with parents to reinforce their behaviour policies. We have received a number of submissions suggesting that, in cases of the most serious misbehaviour such as major damage to school property or violence towards staff, parents should be made legally liable for their children's acts. We consider the question of attacks on school staff in chapter 10. Our survey indicates that teachers do not see damage to school buildings or equipment as a particularly widespread or a serious problem. We are, however, impressed by the strength of feeling behind calls for greater parental accountability.

29 We consider that there is a need to increase parental accountability for their children's behaviour. Scope exists within the present law. It could be extended by new legislation. The issues involved are complex and need careful consideration.

30 The law covering damage to school property by pupils can be summarised as follows. Causing such damage may be an offence under criminal law, a 'wrong' under civil law, or both. It is a fundamental principle of English law that a person can only be held liable for his own criminal acts. The minimum age of criminal responsibility is set at 10. Most primary pupils cannot therefore be prosecuted for a criminal offence. Almost all secondary pupils can. If they are, section 55 of the Children and Young Persons Act 1933 (as substituted by section 26 of the Criminal Justice Act 1982) places a duty on courts to order parents to pay any fines, costs or compensation imposed, unless the parents cannot be found or this would be unreasonable in the circumstances. The courts also have power to order the payment of compensation to the victim of a crime, either instead of or in addition to imposing a fine.

31 The two possibilities for change would be lowering the age of criminal responsibility and making parents liable for the criminal acts of their children. Our evidence suggests that, while there is some concern about destructive behaviour in primary schools, the majority of incidents which might warrant criminal prosecution occur in the secondary sector. Lowering the age of criminal responsibility would have implications far beyond schools. We are not convinced that the severity of this particular problem in the primary sector justifies such major change and we do not recommend it.

32 We consider that the indirect penalties which can be imposed under section 55 of the Children and Young Persons Act 1933 provide adequate parental accountability for criminal offences committed in

school by children aged 10 to 16. Headteachers and LEAs will need to consider whether to press for criminal prosecution in particular cases. We discuss this further in relation to attacks on staff in chapter 10.

33 There is no minimum age of civil responsibility. A child of any age can be sued for damages. However, the child will not normally have the means to pay damages and the parents will not be liable for them, since the normal rule is that a person cannot be held liable for a civil wrong committed by somebody else. The major exception to this rule is the liability that employers have for the wrongful acts or omissions of their employees, committed in the course of their employment. This is called vicarious liability.

34 As regards civil wrongs, we consider that there may be a case for extending the principle of vicarious liability to make parents liable for any injury or damage caused by their children's wrongful actions in school. There is no civil law equivalent to the provisions of the criminal law which relate to parents, and the change suggested would be a development from an existing legal principle. We do not underestimate the difficulties involved in doing this. Vicarious liability is not a simple concept which can be easily applied in a new context. Legislation would be required to introduce it, and its implications, particularly those which extend beyond education, would need to be studied very carefully. The economic viability of civil actions in this context would also be an important consideration. If the claim made by LEAs or governors against parents was less than the limit of the small claims court, which currently stands at £500, costs would not be awarded. Such action might only be worthwhile in cases involving much larger sums. A more economical approach to less serious damage would be to act through the criminal law by prosecuting the child in the juvenile court and seeking a compensation order against the parents. Bearing in mind these complications, **we recommend that the Government should explore the possibilities for imposing on parents civil liability for their children's acts in school.**

R
74

35 In some cases punishment may not be the most constructive response. We would encourage the Government to consider how, in suitable cases, the courts could provide for family counselling as an alternative to damages, fines or other punitive measures.

6 Pupils

1 Pupils are not passive receivers of education. They have to participate in their own learning. In the schools we visited we were impressed by the pupils we met. With few exceptions their behaviour was admirable. Its quality was not always recognised by some of the teachers. We formed the strong impression that there was more scope for pupils to take responsibility for their work and for the standards of their behaviour than was given them in many of the schools.

2 Pupils do not appear in our terms of reference among those to whom we are asked to direct recommendations. But we consider that they have a full part to play in achieving and maintaining high standards of behaviour.

RESPONSIBLE PUPILS

3 We have suggested that pupils learn more in school than they are taught. They also learn from messages carried by the way in which the school is run and the relationships between people in it. Our impression is that, in schools with a negative atmosphere, pupils learn to see themselves as irresponsible beings who must be contained and controlled at all times. Our evidence suggests that pupils tend to live up, or down, to teachers' expectations.

4 Both Rutter and Mortimore found that schools which gave pupils positive responsibilities tended to achieve better standards of behaviour. Rutter found better behaviour in secondary schools in which higher proportions of pupils held positions of responsibility such as form captain. He also found better behaviour in schools where pupils were responsible for caring for their own learning materials, such as books and folders. Mortimore found better behaviour in junior schools where pupils were responsible for managing their own work within clear guidelines set by the teachers. These findings suggest that pupils are likely to react to being given responsibilities by behaving more responsibly.

5 Parents know that there are considerable differences between the ways in which five and 10 year olds see themselves. The differences in self-image between 11 and 15 year olds is even greater. Many older secondary pupils are very conscious of their developing adult status. They may even be regarded as 'adults' by their families because of out-of-school responsibilities such as looking after younger brothers and sisters. This does not always sit easily with their subordinate status in school. It is clear from our survey that secondary teachers consider that 14 and 15 year old pupils are the most difficult to deal with. There are a variety of

reasons for this. It has been suggested to us that one may be the failure of some schools to link responsibilities and privileges with pupils' ages and developing maturity.

6   In chapters three, four and five we emphasise the need for adults to model responsible behaviour for children. The models of behaviour provided by older pupils to younger ones may well be as powerful an influence. We believe that schools should encourage older pupils to take up the responsibility of setting a good example for the rest of the school. In the secondary sector this has traditionally been seen as the function of sixth forms. They have been given duties and privileges to go with their responsibilities. Where sixth forms exist, we believe that they should continue to be encouraged to play the part of pupil leaders. We also consider that, in every secondary school, fourth and fifth year pupils should be expected and encouraged to take on more adult and responsible roles. Similarly in primary schools, every opportunity should be given for older children to set a good example to younger ones and to look after new entrants.

7   Our evidence suggests that schools can promote better behaviour among their pupils by giving them more responsibilities. We consider that these responsibilities extend beyond pupils' own learning to active participation in managing the school community. We believe that schools would find it particularly beneficial to match levels of responsibility and privilege to the ages of their pupils.

8   **We therefore recommend that headteachers and teachers should give pupils every opportunity to take responsibilities and to make a full contribution to improving behaviour in schools.**

School councils

9   In chapter four we emphasise the importance of giving pupils a clear understanding of the institution's behaviour policy. There is also scope for pupil participation in this area. We visited a number of secondary schools which had school councils. School councils are forums for discussion between teachers and pupils, or sometimes between pupils with teachers' participation being introduced at a later stage. The normal arrangement is for each tutor group to elect a council representative. It was clear from the schools we visited which had such councils that rules and behaviour were among the issues regularly discussed. We consider that the main advantage of school councils is that pupils are able to discuss school policies openly and make positive suggestions. This encourages a sense of collective responsibility. Our impression is that, where they exist, pupils are likely to make responsible use of them. We would, however, discourage the creation of token councils. If it becomes clear to pupils that staff are taking no

notice of their views, the council is likely to become a liability rather than an asset. Setting up a council that works involves a commitment by staff to listen to what pupils are saying and to take their views seriously. We believe that commitment is worth making. **We therefore recommend that headteachers and teachers should encourage the active participation of pupils in shaping and reviewing the school's behaviour policy in order to foster a sense of collective commitment to it.** This may be achieved in secondary schools by, for example, the use of school councils.

Mediation

10 We were interested to hear from some of our expert witnesses about mediation schemes which have been introduced in some high schools in the United States and to meet those involved in a scheme of this kind in one New York school. Under these schemes, pupils of secondary age are invited to volunteer for training as mediators. Fellow pupils can ask their trained mediators to help resolve disputes which arise between them. Headteachers of schools with mediation schemes have reported that they have led to lower exclusion rates for fighting, lower drop-out and truancy rates and an improved school atmosphere. As yet little work has been done here in developing such schemes, although we heard of some training which aims to help teachers to resolve classroom conflicts. At this early stage it is not clear how mediation techniques can best be applied in this country to help promote good discipline. However, we believe they could be valuable.

MOTIVATING PUPILS

11 Our survey indicates that older boys of below average ability are the pupils whom teachers find most difficult. This confirms the picture presented by our other evidence and by research. In chapter four we discuss the effects of academic failure on pupils' self-esteem. Research suggests that boys and girls are likely to respond differently to such failure. Girls tend to blame themselves. Boys are more likely to blame or reject the system. Some researchers identify 'anti-school' groups which attract lower achieving boys. Our expert witness from Japan described a broadly similar phenomenon in schools there. One explanation offered by researchers is that many boys counter the threat that academic failure poses to their self-esteem by looking for alternative sources of status. This may mean trying to impress their friends, whose attitude to school is likely to be similar, by work avoidance or disruptive behaviour.

12 Schools can counteract the development of these disaffected groups in several ways. They can try to deter their bad behaviour simply by punishing it. Although punishment will be necessary in many cases, it is

unlikely to reduce the problem by itself. In chapter four we suggest that schools which rely too heavily on punishments to deter bad behaviour are likely to experience more of it. This is particularly true when dealing with 'anti-school' groups whose members gain status by being punished. A second approach is to improve the motivation of such pupils by increasing the scope for non-academic achievement in school and for its recognition. We consider that this, combined with a clear school behaviour policy, is likely to be much more effective.

13   In chapter four we suggest various ways in which non-academic achievement can be recognised. We believe that four national initiatives are likely to be particularly helpful in extending opportunities for such recognition. They are: the development of records of achievement (ROA); the promotion of work experience; the development of compacts between pupils and employers; and voluntary community service as part of the school curriculum.

Records of achievement

14   The aim of ROA is to give credit to pupils for the full range of their achievements in school, academic and otherwise. Education Support Grants (ESGs) are currently funding development work on ROA pilot schemes involving 22 LEAs. These schemes have been looking at ways of recording achievements in areas such as working with others (eg group projects, working with old people or young children), reliability (eg attendance, punctuality) and personal commitment (eg persistence). ROA will enable young people to present employers with a document which gives a much fuller picture of their personal qualities than that provided by examination grades alone. Employers in the pilot schemes have expressed enthusiasm for the concept since they recognise the importance of non-academic achievement and personal qualities. We welcome the Government's support and urge all LEAs to work towards establishing ROA systems for all secondary pupils by 1990. **We recommend:**

14.1   **that the Secretaries of State, LEAs and schools should ensure that records of achievement give due weight to a wide range of achievements and personal qualities; and**

14.2   **that employers should give balanced consideration to the full range of a young person's achievements when appointing school leavers.** This will maximise the credibility of the ROA with pupils.

Work experience

15   The Government's aim is for all pupils to have had at least two weeks work experience by the time they leave school. We believe that work experience is an important part of education for the responsibilities of adulthood. Our impression is that pupils respond well to it. For some

R 77

R 78

145

lower achieving pupils their work experience report may be the best that they ever receive during their school career. It can change their view of themselves, and their teachers' view of them. In the future, work experience reports will probably contribute to pupils' ROA. This is likely to be a part of the ROA that potential employers will take particularly seriously. Work experience must, of course, be used properly by schools. We have some evidence that a few difficult fifth year pupils are sent out for 'extended' work experience which has limited educational value. This is bad practice which discredits work experience schemes. We believe that this is rare and that the vast majority of work experience schemes, whether they are run by individual schools or by LEAs or voluntary organisations such as the Trident Trust, are based on sound principles. We welcome the Government's initiative and urge LEAs and employers to continue to work together to develop the range and quality of work experience.

Compacts

16   Compacts provide individual pupils with clear performance targets. Ideally pupils should be guaranteed a job, or training leading to a job, if they are able to achieve agreed standards of work, behaviour and attendance. Alternatively, employers may only offer a priority interview. The first compact scheme in Britain was set up in East London in 1987. The Government has recently provided development funding for 30 more inner city compact proposals in England and Scotland through the Department of Employment's Training Agency, with a view to funding successful development projects from early 1989. The preliminary evaluation reported by Her Majesty's Inspectorate of Schools (HMI) on the first year of the East London compact suggests that some real improvements in pupil motivation are being achieved. HMI point to improvements in pupils' attendance and punctuality in the schools involved in compacts. The ILEA reports an increase in the number of pupils from these schools continuing their education beyond the age of 16. We welcome the compact initiative and the Government's support for it. Although the full value of compacts has yet to be proved, we believe that they have real potential for improving standards of behaviour and attendance. We consider that compacts may be particularly useful for schools in the most economically disadvantaged areas of the country. Pupils need to be assured that employers will deliver their end of the bargain or compacts will be discredited. The reduction in the number of school leavers in the near future will increase employers' incentive to do so. **We recommend that schools, LEAs and employers should increase their co-operation in developing means of increasing pupils' motivation, such as compacts.**

PUPILS AT RISK

17 Our evidence indicates that certain pupils are more likely to present behaviour or attendance problems than others. In the case of attendance, the picture of the pupil most at risk seems fairly clear – a low achiever from a severely disadvantaged home background. In the case of seriously disruptive behaviour, the picture of the pupil most likely to be involved seems less clear in terms of his or her material circumstances, such as quality of housing and family income. Some other characteristics can, however, be identified. Our survey and other evidence, such as LEA exclusion statistics, indicate that boys are about four times more likely to be involved than girls. They are likely to be rated as of below average ability by their teachers and to have a history of low achievement at school. They are also likely to come from highly stressed family backgrounds.

18 Such 'risk profiles' must be treated with great caution. We emphasise the importance of teachers' expectations as an influence on pupils' behaviour throughout this report. Low expectations as an influence can be self-fulfilling prophecies. We believe that it is crucial for teachers and other readers of this report to be wary of stereotypes. The statistical associations between, say, particular types of family background and ways of behaving cannot and should not be used to predict the behaviour of any individual pupil. Even where the 'risk profile' is fairly clear, as it is with non-attenders, it must be remembered that it is only a minority of pupils from such backgrounds who will become persistent absentees. Teachers should always expect the best of their pupils.

19 'Risk profiles' are dangerous tools, but they help to sharpen teachers' awareness of potential problems. Waiting until patterns of bad behaviour or non-attendance are well established before taking any kind of remedial action may be too late. Our evidence suggests possibilities for preventive action early in children's educational careers before such patterns are set.

20 In chapter four we suggest that some pupils may be behaving badly because they have particular needs such as learning difficulties, which are not being met. Schools and individual teachers also need early warning and guidance on the nature of potential learning and behaviour problems which new pupils are likely to present. We consider it essential for a record of pupils' progress, and learning and pastoral needs, to be established from their first days in school and to be transferred with them when they change schools. It is not unusual for pupils to change from one LEA to another during their school careers. We therefore welcome the recent DES consultative document

Regulations on the Keeping and Disclosure of Pupil Records which proposed that schools should be required to keep records of the educational progress of their pupils, and transfer such records on request when a pupil moves to another school. **We recommend that pupil records should cover their pastoral as well as their learning needs and that they should be in a format which could be adopted by schools and LEAs throughout England and Wales.**

21 In its evidence to us the Association of Chief Education Social Workers, representing principal education welfare officers, included a request to primary heads to give education welfare officers early warning of persistent behaviour or attendance problems developing in younger pupils. We support this request. We emphasise the importance of education welfare officers in establishing links between home and school in chapter four. They maintain long term contacts with families in difficulty. The earlier in a child's school career that these contacts can be established the better.

22 It has been suggested to us that providing more pre-school or nursery education might help to improve children's behaviour in school. There is no conclusive evidence to show that an overall expansion in this kind of provision would produce general improvements in behaviour. There is, however, evidence from the USA suggesting that it can improve the behaviour of certain children who are 'at risk'. Large scale evaluations of pre-school education programmes for children from severely disadvantaged backgrounds indicate that such children are more likely to develop a positive self-image and to succeed at school if they have pre-school education than if they do not. Local authorities should therefore ensure that enough provision is available to meet the needs of such children. DES and Welsh Office statistics for 1988 show large variations between LEAs in the provision that they make for pupils under five in nursery and primary schools, ranging from 8% to 89% of the relevant population. We are aware that there are other ways of providing pre-school education such as day nurseries or playgroups, but almost all require some kind of local authority support. **We therefore recommend that all local authorities should ensure that adequate provision for pre-school education for severely disadvantaged children is available in their areas.**

23 We were particularly interested in two voluntary projects dealing with children 'at risk' in primary schools. **Catch 'em Young** is a scheme which concentrates on pupils who behave badly in their final year of primary school. It aims to improve their ability to co-operate with other children and adults and their sense of social responsibility by providing them with a series of closely supervised 'outward bound' experiences in

which senior secondary pupils play an important role. Courses are held at an outdoor education centre in North Yorkshire. The project started in 1986 and is currently being evaluated for the DES.

24 The **Muppet Club** based in Hounslow, West London, also aims to promote children's readiness for secondary school by developing their ability to relate to others. The project deals with eight and nine year old children – a younger age group than the 'Catch 'em Young' scheme. Its methods are based on group therapy. Children 'at risk' are identified by primary teachers. They are invited to join a group or 'Muppet Club' led by trained volunteers which carries out co-operative projects and activities such as crafts, drama or games. The project started in 1978. The progress of Muppet Club 'graduates' has been monitored and compared with a control group of children with similar risk profiles. Results seem to show that the incidence of behaviour and attendance problems was much lower among the 'graduates' than among the control group.

25 These projects sound promising. There may well be other organisations of this kind which have not submitted evidence to us. **We recommend that the Government should evaluate preventive schemes aimed at primary age children with a view to encouraging the development of such schemes if they are found to be effective.**

R 82

PUPILS WITH SPECIAL EDUCATIONAL NEEDS

26 The Education Act 1981 defines special educational needs as learning difficulties or disabilities which require special educational provision to be made. LEAs are required to assess such children's needs, taking educational, psychological and medical advice and evidence from parents and other sources into account. The purpose of assessment under the 1981 Act is to identify a child's special educational needs and any educational provision which may be required to meet them. Where, following such an assessment, the LEA decides to determine the special educational provision that should be made for a child, it is required to make and maintain a statement of the child's special educational needs specifying those needs and the educational provision to be made to meet them. Such provision can be made in ordinary schools or in units, for example through additional staff or equipment, or by transferring the child to a special school. It is estimated that, at any given time, about 20% of the pupil population have special educational needs and about 2% have statements.

27 Our interpretation of the Enquiry's terms of reference was that it should concentrate on mainstream schools. We have not therefore considered

the question of pupils' behaviour in special schools. Our terms of reference do however include the relationship between pupils' behaviour in mainstream schools and provision for special educational needs.

28   Our evidence draws attention to two issues in this area. The first relates to the assessment of pupils with emotional and behavioural difficulties. The second is about pupils whose disruptive behaviour may be a response to their own learning difficulties.

29   A small minority of pupils have such severe and persistent behaviour problems as a result of emotional, psychological or neurological disturbance that their needs cannot be met in mainstream schools. In such cases the way forward is for the LEA to assess the pupil's needs and produce a statement which confirms that the pupil has emotional and behavioural difficulties and specifies the alternative provision to be made for that pupil elsewhere.

30   We recognise that it is sometimes difficult to distinguish between 'ordinary' bad behaviour and disturbed behaviour, but the distinction has to be made. Children with emotional and behavioural difficulties tend to present behaviour problems earlier in their school careers than other 'difficult' pupils, and to behave in a disturbed and disturbing way regardless of which class or teacher they are with. The problems they present also tend to be more severe. Judgements must be made by teachers, educational psychologists and other professionals in individual cases. This is one of the purposes of the assessment process.

31   We have been alerted to two problems relating to assessments involving emotional and behavioural difficulties. First, provision in special schools for pupils with special needs tends to be expensive. LEAs have many competing priorities for expenditure. We have been told that at least one LEA does not recognise emotional and behavioural difficulties as a reason for making special provision because it is not considered to be specifically a learning difficulty. We consider this to be unacceptable, not least because we regard social learning, as well as academic learning, to be a necessary concern of schools. It is clear from our evidence that some children exhibit such disturbed patterns of behaviour that they cannot benefit properly from mainstream schooling. It is also clear that they can disrupt the education of other children.

32   The second problem seems more widespread. Evidence presented to the House of Commons Education, Science and Arts Committee (ESAC), in the course of a review it undertook in 1986/87 of the workings of the Education Act 1981, registered strong concern about the length of time

involved in the assessment and statementing process for pupils with emotional and behavioural difficulties in some LEAs. Our impression is that there has been no significant improvement since the ESAC report. We have been told that it is not uncommon for the process to take a year or more. The effects of such delays, in causing 'anxiety and paranoid feelings' among the individual pupils and the schools involved, were graphically described to ESAC. A similar experience was described to us by the headteacher of one of the schools we visited. We recognise that the rapid assessment of special needs is generally desirable. We consider that the need for prompt action is particularly pressing in cases involving emotional and behavioural difficulties. We also recognise, however, that placing a child on a waiting list for assessment of emotional and behavioural difficulties does not relieve the school of the responsibility of acting as constructively as it can while it awaits advice from outside. LEAs must take account of the effect on other pupils and staff of the continuing presence in school of a child who may be both profoundly disturbed and profoundly disturbing.

33 The role of educational psychologists is central to assessment and statementing. We have been told that their availability is a key factor in determining the time taken by these processes in different LEAs. The statistics for 1987/88 published by the Chartered Institute of Public Finance and Accountancy (CIPFA) show large variations in the number of educational psychologists employed by different LEAs. The ratio of educational psychologists to pupils aged five to 16 ranges from about 1:2500 to about 1:8000. The average is about 1:4500. CIPFA figures do not, of course, show how effectively staff are used, but it seems probable to us that schools in LEAs towards the bottom of the range are more likely to experience delays in the statementing process than those in LEAs with average provision.

34 We discuss the well established link between disruptive behaviour and low academic achievement in chapter four. We have pointed out that some pupils are lower achievers because they lack the motivation to work and others because they lack the ability to make progress. In many cases both factors apply and may reinforce one another. Our evidence suggests that more attention should be given to the educational needs of pupils who behave badly. We visited two secondary schools with support teachers whose jobs include working with such pupils. One of these teachers commented to us that he spent a high proportion of his time helping pupils with academic work rather than managing their behaviour. It was clear to him that some at least of these pupils had real learning difficulties and that their disruptive behaviour was partly provoked by the frustration these caused. This impression is supported by studies of pupils excluded from secondary schools which have found

that a significant proportion of them are of well below average ability. It has been suggested to us that some of these pupils may have special educational needs, other than emotional and behavioural difficulties, which have not been identified because teachers have explained their lack of progress in terms of laziness or bad behaviour rather than learning difficulties. The danger of neglecting learning needs is particularly acute if a pupil has been stereotyped as 'disruptive'.

35   The draft circular issued recently by the DES, Department of Health and Welsh Office to replace DES Circular 1/83 and Welsh Office Circular 5/83 gave new advice to LEAs on the implementation of the Education Act 1981. The draft circulars say that each Secretary of State *'expects that statements should be processed within six months and that only in exceptional circumstances should it take longer than this'*. We fully endorse the six month target for cases involving emotional and behavioural difficulties.

R 83

36   **We recommend that all LEAs and schools should ensure that the special educational needs of pupils with emotional and behavioural difficulties are assessed and met.**

R 84

37   **We recommend that LEAs should set and maintain an establishment of educational psychologists adequate to achieve the target of six months for the processing of statements of special educational needs specified in the draft circulars recently issued by the DES, Department of Health and Welsh Office to replace DES Circular 1/83 and Welsh Office Circular 5/83.**

R 85

38   **We recommend that LEAs and schools should ensure that the learning needs of pupils involved in disruptive behaviour who may not be suffering from emotional and behavioural difficulties are properly identified as part of any plan for remedial action.** This may involve assessment of special educational needs in some cases.

PROVISION FOR THE MOST DIFFICULT PUPILS

39   We suggest throughout this report that ordinary schools should do all in their power to retain and educate all the pupils on their roll on-site. However, we recognise that in the case of a small number of pupils this may be difficult, and in some cases impossible. Mainstream teachers may not be able to find the time, if unassisted, to handle the frequent disruption such pupils may cause; and in some cases may not have the skill to do this. The behaviour of these difficult pupils can also have a serious effect on the progress of other pupils. Even the most skilled

teachers may find themselves having to spend most of a lesson trying to maintain order.

40 We asked every LEA about the provision it made for those pupils whose behaviour teachers found most difficult to manage and for their schools. Most of the LEAs submitting evidence outlined their provision. Many pointed out that their education welfare officers and educational psychologists had an important role to play in supporting teachers, pupils and parents. All have some form of special provision for such pupils which consists of two or more of the following resources:

40.1 special schools catering for children with emotional and behavioural difficulties, access to places in special schools run by other LEAs, or access to places in independent special schools;

40.2 units which are not part of mainstream schools for pupils who may or may not have statements of special needs. These are called off-site units. Pupils are transferred to them on either a temporary or a permanent basis;

40.3 units which are part of mainstream schools. These are called on-site units. Pupils are transferred to them on a temporary basis usually, and sometimes for part of their timetable only; and

40.4 support teams of specialist teachers working with such pupils in mainstream schools.

41 The pattern of provision varies considerably from authority to authority. There are also variations between different areas within a single LEA. A few LEAs appear to have a coherent support system which combines most if not all of the four elements identified above. In others, provision seems to have been made as a more or less improvised response to needs and opportunities. A number of LEAs told us that they are currently reviewing their arrangements with the aim of providing a more coherent and effective pattern of support for schools and pupils. A few LEAs seem to be expanding the amount of alternative provision available. Others are moving towards more flexible patterns combining support teams with unit places.

42 Although no national figures are available, our evidence suggests that the quantity of provision, in terms of the number of pupils supported in the mainstream or placed in special units or schools, is fairly consistent between different LEAs. The range seems to be from about 0.2% to about 0.5% of the mainstream school population, with 0.3% as the most commonly occurring figure.

43 The case for particular types of alternative provision for most children with statements of special educational needs specifying emotional and

behavioural difficulties is clear. The rest of this section deals only with those pupils who do not fall within this category. We need to consider what can be done to help these pupils and their schools.

44 A number of submissions that we received suggest that one answer to the problem of disruptive behaviour would be to increase the number of places in units. We are cautious about this suggestion. We recognise the argument that units, by removing difficult pupils from general circulation in school, may be able to help other pupils to make progress without constant disruption. But in fact the relationship between the availability of unit places and general standards of behaviour in schools is obscure. Since the 1970s the number of special units has increased dramatically. It has been estimated that their number has more than quadrupled since 1977 (Graham 1988). Our evidence does not suggest that this has been accompanied by any noticeable improvement in standards of behaviour. A study of exclusions from schools in Sheffield found that setting up on-site units had no significant effect on the exclusion rates of the schools at which they were established (Galloway 1982). This does not suggest that general standards of behaviour in the schools with units had been improved. The Sheffield sample was small, and the study looked at exclusions and the units themselves rather than behaviour in ordinary classrooms. We would not wish to put too much weight on it. But it is a useful warning against seeing units as offering a simple solution in themselves.

45 The evidence presented to us on the quality of special units was conflicting. Some on-site units are well integrated with the schools to which they belong, while others have little contact with the mainstream. We visited two off-site units which were known to be making good provision for the pupils placed there. Others were represented to us as being much less satisfactory. We are concerned to find that both on-site and off-site units are often working under great difficulties. The pupils who come to them often believe that they have been treated badly by ordinary schools, and they feel rejected and resentful. Their educational needs and their degree of maturity are often very different. They stay in the units for different lengths of time. Some of these pupils never return to ordinary schools, but remain in limbo until the end of compulsory schooling. We consider that the aim in almost every case should be to return the pupil to a mainstream school as soon as possible. We recognise, however, that this can be very difficult in practice, partiularly in the case of pupils in off-site units.

46 We realise that there will always be a need for some forms of alternative provision for pupils who reach a stage at which they cannot constructively be educated in ordinary schools, either because of their

own difficulties or the difficulties they cause for other pupils. LEAs have, for example, to provide education for pupils who have been permanently excluded from schools. Reintegration into the mainstream may not always be a practical possibility, particularly in the case of older secondary pupils.

47 The main advantage of units is that the small numbers of pupils in them can get close attention from teachers, and time can be spent in improving their attitudes and motivation. But there are disadvantages in terms of the curriculum. Although pupils in on-site units may in theory have access to a full curriculum, this is seldom so in practice. Off-site units are usually far too small to provide a full curriculum. To do so, they would need extra resources on a very large scale. These curricular disadvantages will become more serious when the National Curriculum is introduced, and will increase the difficulty of achieving a return to mainstream schooling. The future prospects of pupils remaining in units are often limited. Some units nevertheless manage to work successfully with the pupils who are sent to them but it seems to require very great skills on the part of the teachers in them. Because these units are isolated from the system as a whole, those skills are seldom passed on to other teachers.

48 Almost all the alternative provision made by LEAs is very expensive in terms of cost per pupil. There was little indication from our evidence that the balance between the costs and benefits of various forms of provision are being analysed. We consider that LEAs should carry out such analysis which should take account of educational as well as financial considerations. These would include the needs of schools, teachers and the majority of pupils, those of the minority for whom alternative provision is made and the quality of the system as a whole.

49 We consider that the balance of advantage lies with the development of LEA support teams. We envisage such teams helping teachers in ordinary schools in a variety of ways to improve their skills in dealing with pupils who present them with difficulties. Such help might take the form of individual discussions with teachers and with pupils to provide diagnosis of specific difficulties and suggest action; 'support teaching', where a teacher from the support team teaches a group together with a teacher from the school; mobilising other agencies such as the education welfare officer and the educational psychologist; helping pastoral staff, for example with case conferences; facilitating peer support groups; providing other forms of in-service training, such as training in developing teachers' group management skills; and acting as consultants on matters related to behaviour and discipline.

50 We saw one support team in action which had been recently set up. It was already doing good work with some pupils, but needed more status to have more than a marginal influence on the schools it served.

51 Where schools have, or wish to set up, on-site units, a support team of the kind we envisage would be a particularly valuable resource. Such units need a clear rationale, clear criteria for referral, accurate diagnosis of the learning and behavioural difficulties of each pupil, a programme devised to meet these difficulties, and clear targets for the early reintegration of each pupil into mainstream classes. Above all, their quality and success rates need close and careful monitoring by the headteacher and the governors. Support teams would be well placed to help with all these matters.

52 Where LEAs have support teams, or decide to set them up, it is essential that the team leader should have sufficient status to work effectively with the heads of large secondary schools. The teachers staffing such teams will need to be of appropriate calibre and capable of dealing tactfully and effectively with children in difficulties and also with teachers in ordinary schools who need their help but may feel defensive about seeking it. They will need very considerable skills, not least those of counselling, negotiation and in-service training. Team leaders and members should expect to be seconded from ordinary schools for a period and to return with enhanced career prospects. The work of such teams will also have to be rigorously and regularly reviewed and evaluated.

53 Alternative provision has often been developed piecemeal by LEAs as needs have been perceived. A number of LEAs are currently reviewing their pattern of provision with the aim of making it more coherent. We commend such reviews, especially if they give proper consideration to the balance of advantage involved in different forms and combinations of alternative provision. **We recommend that all LEAs should review the alternative provision that they make for the most difficult pupils and that, in determining future patterns of provision, they should take full account of:**

53.1 **the need to provide adequate, appropriate and cost-effective support for schools and individual pupils;**

53.2 **the importance of keeping pupils in and, if they are removed, returning them to mainstream schools wherever possible;**

53.3   the balance between the inherent disadvantages of off-site units and the need to maintain a minimum number of off-site places;

53.4   the benefits that can accrue from the work of support teams in mainstream schools with access to on-site units; and

53.5   the need to ensure that support teams are adequately resourced to carry out their work effectively.

54   The introduction of the National Curriculum will in itself require LEAs to review their provision of off-site units. At present, headteachers can transfer a pupil to such a unit provided that a place is available and the governors and the LEA are in agreement. When the necessary regulations have been made under section 19 of the Education Reform Act 1988, headteachers will be able to give directions temporarily modifying or disapplying the National Curriculum for a pupil who is transferred to a unit unless the unit can offer the full curriculum, which is unlikely. This will entail informing the parents as well as the governing body of the reasons for such temporary modification or disapplication and of the plans for readmitting the pupil to the National Curriculum. It will also entail specifying a maximum period for the disapplication, after which the headteacher should either give a fresh direction, reapply the National Curriculum or take steps towards a statement of special educational needs.

55   In these circumstances we envisage off-site units providing specialist help for those pupils who can, at least temporarily, no longer be constructively educated in ordinary schools. Their main purpose should be to reintegrate pupils into the mainstream at the earliest possible stage or to begin procedures for statementing. They would be run by members of the support team, an arrangement which would prevent the isolation which we describe above, and would improve communication and procedures for referral. They would offer a breathing space, specialist diagnosis and an individually tailored programme aimed at reintegration. In certain cases, pupils might be prepared for entry to a different school from the one they had previously attended. While they were attending an off-site unit, they would remain on the roll of the school which had referred them there.

56   We have commented on the piecemeal development of alternative provision over the last 10 to 15 years, and on the new context which is being established for it by the National Curriculum. Work remains to be done that is innovative and experimental. There is also a need to help LEAs to convert their often improvised provision into integrated and

coherent support services. Although such services will give better value for money in the long term we recognise that setting them up can be expensive. We consider that the Secretaries of State could assist LEAs in improving their provision for those pupils who present the greatest difficulties to schools by making ESG funding available to stimulate developments in this area. **We therefore recommend that the Secretaries of State should establish an Education Support Grant to encourage innovative projects aimed at providing comprehensive yet flexible support for the most difficult pupils and their schools. All LEAs should be eligible to bid for this grant for three years.**

R 87

57   It is important that children in a unit should benefit from the other recommendations of our report. We have in mind such matters as quality of environment, challenge and support, respect for individuality, codes of behaviour, rewards and sanctions, and particularly the quality of relationships. **We therefore recommend that on- and off-site units should take full account of the recommendations in this report wherever they are appropriate.**

R 88

GROUP DIFFERENCES

58   There are group differences between pupils as well as individual ones. Pupils come from a variety of cultural and ethnic backgrounds. We believe that, while schools should aim to become harmonious communities with a common core of shared values, they will not achieve this by pretending that these group differences do not exist. 'We treat them all the same' sounds like an excuse for not tackling some of the more awkward issues involved.

59   It is quite clear from our evidence that the great majority of pupils involved in disruptive behaviour are male. Boys are also far more likely to be involved in physical aggression than girls. Research evidence suggests not only that boys behave in a more attention-seeking way than girls in class but also that they also get much more attention from teachers (eg Morgan and Dunn 1988). This is not to say that girls do not sometimes behave badly. The difference is that the incidence of misbehaviour is much lower, and that some of the anti-social activities typical of girls are much less noticeable than boys' aggression. Bullying illustrates this point. Research shows that both boys and girls are involved in bullying (see chapter four). The difference is that, while boys are likely to use physical intimidation and violence, girls make use of more subtle techniques.

60   Exclusion statistics from schools in inner London suggest that pupils of Afro-Caribbean origin are proportionately more likely to be excluded

than whites or Asians. A study of exclusions from Birmingham schools presented to us by the Commission for Racial Equality (CRE) seems to show a similar pattern there. The CRE study also suggests that, in suburban schools where there were fewer Afro-Caribbean pupils as a proportion of the total, they were even more likely to be excluded than in inner-city schools with more Afro-Caribbean pupils. It also suggests that Asian pupils were less likely to be excluded than whites.

61 We recognise that issues relating to gender and ethnicity can provoke strong feelings. In chapter four we suggest that dogmatic or inflexible approaches to racial prejudice are likely to be counter-productive. Questions of gender also need to be handled sensitively, not ignored. We believe that if heads and teachers are to create harmonious school communities they must take action in these areas.

62 In chapter five we recommend that parents should encourage their sons not to behave aggressively. Our evidence suggests that some teachers also have an important role to play in reducing boys' aggression. Our evidence suggest that some teachers, often unwittingly, reinforce such behaviour by automatically responding to it, or by reacting in a way which provides a model of the behaviour that they are trying to discourage. **We therefore recommend that teachers should take account of the gender differences involved in pupils' behaviour, for example by not reinforcing attention-seeking and aggressive behaviour.**

R
89

63 In chapter four we stress the value of multi-cultural education in promoting a sense of community in schools. We emphasise that the school curriculum should recognise and value the cultures of all its pupils, whether they come from majority or minority backgrounds. We believe that this kind of mutual respect should permeate every aspect of school life, including the affective curriculum. **We therefore recommend that headteachers and staff should work to create a school climate which values all cultures, in particular those represented in it, through its academic and affective curricula.**

R
90

64 We have already highlighted the dangers of stereotyping pupils. For teachers to assume that academically less able boys or Afro-Caribbean boys are going to be disruptive is not helpful to them or their pupils. **We therefore recommend that teachers should recognise the potential for injustice and the practical dangers of stereotyping certain kinds of pupils as troublemakers.**

65 It has been suggested to us that non-verbal communciation, or body language, can produce misunderstandings between teachers and pupils

programmes, including those broadcast after 9.00 pm, and that the Broadcasting Standards Council should encourage them to do so.

75   We have emphasised the need for teachers to understand the culture of their pupils. Popular television programmes are an important part of that culture. All of us tend to feel hurt if our tastes and enthusiasms are rejected by others. If teachers ignore or even ridicule pupils' interests in such programmes this is likely to be interpreted as rejection.

76   Media education aims to develop a critical understanding of the modern mass media including television. Our evidence suggests that more schools are now making use of popular television as an educational resource either in special media studies courses or for topic work in other subjects such as English. The National Curriculum English Working Group was specifically asked by the Secretary of State to look at the place of media studies within the English curriculum. The Group's first report emphasises the importance of understanding how words and pictures are used on television. Its second report is likely to amplify this in the context of the secondary curriculum. While we welcome this development, we recognise that it is not for the English curriculum alone to deal with television. We believe that there is also considerable scope for using the issues raised by popular programmes as starting points for discussion in personal, social and moral education. There are also opportunities for involving the parents of younger children in home-school viewing schemes. These entail parents and children watching and discussing particular programmes together as an extension of topic work in school. Teachers and parents can also introduce children to ways of looking at the form as well as the content of television programmes. They can, for example, discuss how they are made or why people want to make them. In this way children can become critical viewers in the same way that they are encouraged to become critical readers by studying literature. **We therefore recommend that teachers and parents should make active use of television as an educational resource, reinforcing the positive messages presented by programmes and encouraging children to become more discriminating and critical viewers.**

77   We have highlighted the anxieties expressed to us about the possible effects of violent 'video nasties' on children's attitudes and behaviour. We have also registered concerns about the future possibility of children with a taste for violent images moving towards 'all-violence' viewing as cable and satellite channels come on stream. We believe that parents have the primary responsibility for ensuring that this does not happen. New technologies themselves may offer parents better means of

regulating their children's viewing through devices such as pre-programmable controls. **We therefore recommend that parents should monitor and, where necesssary, restrict their children's access to network, cable, satellite or video material transmitting violent or other anti-social messages.**

78 In response to public concern over issues like violence in television the Government has recently set up a Broadcasting Standards Council (BSC). One of its functions will be to draw up a code on the portrayal of sex and violence in all forms of broadcasting in order to define standards in these areas more clearly. The BSC will have an important role to play in promoting the responsible use of television.

79 Other steps have been taken to control access to unsuitable programmes. The Video Recordings Act 1984 established a system of classification for videos with penalties for those who supply unclassified videos or make videos classified '18' or '15' available to younger people. The Act requires the British Board of Film Classification to pay special attention to the fact that videos are likely to be viewed at home. The result is that videos are often more heavily cut than their film equivalents. The Criminal Justice Act 1988 has given trading standards officers new powers to enforce the 1984 Act.

80 The Government has also recognised the danger of unacceptable programmes being transmitted into this country from unregulated satellites. It is working towards an agreement, which it hopes will be reached early in 1989 on a Council of Europe convention covering the international regulation of television services. This will include minimum standards on taste and decency, and will specifically prohibit programmes containing gratuitous violence.

81 We welcome these measures and urge the Government to monitor their effectiveness in regulating the content of network, cable, satelite or video material and children's access to programmes containing violent or other anti-social messages.

DIET

82 What children eat has changed in recent years. A few of our correspondents identify aspects of diet, in particular 'fast' or 'junk' food, as causes of bad behaviour in schools. There are two main variations to this argument. The first is that additives in junk foods affect children's behaviour. The second is that 'junk' food diets lack important vitamins and trace elements which may influence behaviour.

83   We have been advised by the Department of Health that there is no firm scientific evidence of links between 'junk food' diets and children's behaviour. This does not, of course, mean that scientists will stop looking. If such links were to be identified, action to improve children's diets could become an important contribution to improving behaviour in schools. **We therefore recommend that the Government should continue to monitor research findings on links between children's diets and behaviour and should take appropriate action if any causal connections are identified.**

7 Attendance

1 The Secretary of State set up this Enquiry in response to strong concerns about pupils' behaviour in school. Many of those submitting evidence to us suggest that standards of behaviour have deteriorated in recent years. Our evidence does not show similar perceptions of an attendance crisis. Although national attendance statistics are not kept, evidence from individual LEAs and from HMI indicates that attendance levels have remained fairly stable for at least the last five years, and probably for much longer, though there has been some deterioration as a result of the teachers' industrial dispute.

2 We are aware of very few LEAs which carry out regular authority-wide surveys of attendance. We looked in some detail at the analysis provided by the ILEA. The results of its annual one day surveys from 1978 to 1987 show a very consistent overall attendance rate for primary schools of about 92%. The pattern for secondary schools shows a marginal decline from about 85% in the late 1970s to just over 83% in 1987. The ILEA figures also illustrate two aspects of attendance which are confirmed by HMI as being consistent features of the national picture. They are:

2.1 significant variations in attendance rates between different schools. The highest secondary school attendance rate in the 1987 survey was 94.3% and the lowest was 63.6%. The recent HMI survey report covering 185 secondary schools identified differences of a similar order. HMI comment that 'poorer attendance was by no means confined to schools serving disadvantaged areas; and

2.2 lower attendance rates among older secondary pupils. In 1987 the rate for 11 year olds was 90.3% and the rate for 15 year olds was 70.9%. A variety of explanations can be suggested. In chapter four we point out the difficulties of motivating lower achieving fourth and fifth year pupils. Some may therefore be 'voting with their feet' against the curriculum. Others may be working illegally, or have domestic responsibilities such as caring for younger brothers and sisters, which they or their parents regard as more important than attending school.

3 The majority of absences are for legitimate reasons such as illness. There is however a persistent level of unjustified absence which may take place with parents' knowledge (condoned absence) or without it (truancy). We are also concerned about the problem of 'internal truancy' which exists in some schools. This consists of pupils coming to school and registering, but missing some of their lessons.

4 Unjustified absence and internal truancy are forms of misbehaviour which are damaging to the pupils involved because they hinder their

educational progress. They also fall within our terms of reference because they affect the progress of other pupils and the atmosphere of the school as a whole. It has been suggested to us that the non-attendance of certain pupils may actually help to improve general standards of behaviour in some schools. We believe this view is rare and, in any case, we reject it as a basis of policy. While some persistent absentees behave disruptively when they actually come to school many do not. The occasional re-appearance of regular absentees can however be disruptive in other ways. Teachers have to give absentees special attention to help them catch up with the work they have missed. This may affect the progress and behaviour of other pupils who become frustrated by the repetition of work or by its slow pace. We believe that high levels of unjustified absence and internal truancy also have a damaging effect on the atmosphere of a school. Some persistent absentees may encourage others to follow suit. The presence of unsupervised pupils about the school during lessons is clearly a disturbing influence. The damaging effect on school atmosphere can be amplified if staff are not seen to be making determined efforts to maximise attendance. Lack of effort in this area may suggest to pupils that teachers do not really care whether they attend or not. This is one of the most negative messages that a school can transmit.

5   It has also been suggested to us that there is a link between unjustified absence from school and juvenile crime. A recent Home Office review of research findings on the links between schools, disruptive behaviour and delinquency concludes that no clear connection has been established in this area (Graham 1988). There is however concern about non-attending pupils becoming the victims of street crime.

6   Our evidence indicates that fourth and fifth year pupils from certain kinds of home background are much more likely than others to become persistent absentees. Research indicates that the majority of persistent absentees come from families which are badly housed and have a multitude of economic, social and health problems (eg Galloway 1985). But while the social and economic characteristics of a school's catchment area may be a strong influence on its attendance rate, they do not rigidly determine it. Schools can and do make a difference.

ACTION AT SCHOOL LEVEL

7   We believe that an important first step is to reject the idea that unjustified absence can be treated as in any way helpful to schools. Heads and teachers should therefore recognise the potentially unsettling effects of any absence, and particularly of unjustified absence, on the

atmosphere of schools and on pupils' behaviour. They should also recognise that the quality of a school's atmosphere and curriculum is an important factor in encouraging regular attendance.

8 We suggest that schools should develop positive strategies for receiving back frequent absentees. Such strategies should have two objectives. The first should be to help absentees catch up with the work that they have missed. The second should be to minimise the negative effects of this catching up process on other pupils.

9 Since lower achieving fourth and fifth year pupils in secondary schools have the highest rates of absence, we believe that the kind of 'alternative curriculum' approaches designed for this group which we refer to in chapter four may be particularly important in encouraging their attendance. So may work experience, compacts with employers and records of achievement, which we discuss in chapter six.

10 In cases of absence, schools should ensure that parents provide notes explaining reasons for absence and that these are collected and checked. When truancy is suspected, parents should be notified as quickly as possible. Education welfare officers have an important part to play in working with parents to deal with cases of truancy and condoned absence. The regular dialogue between education welfare officers and headteachers of primary schools or pastoral staff of secondary schools, which we recommend in chapter four, is particularly important in this connection. **We therefore recommend that headteachers and teachers should make full use of education welfare officers to maximise attendance.**

R 99

11 Good information systems are an important aid to securing maximum attendance. These can be developed and used at classroom, school and LEA level. We consider that regular checking is the most effective means of eliminating internal truancy. In secondary schools, particularly in the fourth and fifth years, a pupil may be in several different groups during the course of a day. Secondary teachers should keep group lists and check them regularly. **We recommend that senior school staff should carry out frequent random attendance checks on individual lessons.**

R 100

12 Governors are responsible for ensuring that attendance registers are kept as required by law, for making them available for inspection, and for making returns to the LEA in certain circumstances. We consider that governors should develop their role in monitoring attendance. **We recommend that governors should obtain regular reports on attendance, including internal truancy, with a view to encouraging and supporting action by the school.**

R 101

ACTION AT LEA LEVEL AND NATIONAL LEVEL

13   In chapter 10 we recommend that LEAs should monitor standards of behaviour in their schools. The main purpose of such monitoring would be to ensure that the consultancy and support services provided by the authority are properly targeted. Maintaining detailed attendance statistics enables an LEA to identify schools in difficulty and, for example, to use this information to give priority to the areas of greatest need when deploying its education welfare service. We understand that at present few LEAs monitor attendance at all their schools on a systematic basis. **We recommend that all LEAs should regularly gather data on attendance at their schools and should use this information to plan the deployment of their resources in the most effective ways to improve attendance.**

14   On our visit to the Netherlands we were impressed by the computerised attendance monitoring system being used by schools in Rotterdam. We were told that the computerised system meant that schools could check on absent pupils more quickly and consistently, identify patterns of non-attendance and significantly reduce the number of unjustified absences. Computerised attendance monitoring systems are not uncommon in colleges of further education in this country, but they are as yet rare in schools. We recognise that there may be considerable practical problems involved in introducing such systems. We are aware, however, that many LEAs and schools are now involved in the development of computerised information systems. **We therefore recommend that those designing school-based computerised information systems should take account of the possibilities of including programmes for monitoring attendance in them.**

15   Parents are required by law to ensure that their children are educated. They can be prosecuted for their children's non-attendance at school, unless education is provided by other means. LEAs decide whether or not to prosecute depending on individual circumstances. We are not convinced that there is a case for changing existing practice by recommending more prosecutions. Although no national statistics exist, evidence from expert witnesses suggests that there is no clear relationship between the willingness of individual LEAs to prosecute parents and levels of attendance in their schools.

16   The role of education welfare officers is crucial in following up cases of unjustified absence. It has been suggested to us that, in some areas, education welfare officers may have such large case loads that they cannot perform all the necessary aspects of their job effectively. There are certainly large variations in the number of education welfare officers

employed by different LEAs. Statistics published by the Chartered Institute of Public Finance and Accountancy for 1987/88 show ratios of education welfare officers to pupils aged five to 16 ranging from about 1:500 to about 1:8500. The average is about 1:2000. It seems to us that education welfare officers in LEAs at the bottom of the range are likely to be hopelessly over-stretched. **We therefore recommend that all LEAs should maintain adequate numbers of education welfare officers to ensure that cases of unjustified absence can be followed up systematically and promptly.**

17 We believe that there may be opportunities for collaboration between LEAs and local police forces to reduce unjustified absence. We have seen accounts of 'truancy sweeps' in Birmingham, Bradford and Bedfordshire which involved the police approaching children of school age seen in the street during school hours with the aim of returning them to their schools. The Bedfordshire sweep involved teams of police officers and education welfare officers working together. This seems to us a promising approach, which may serve not only to get the children back into school but also to prevent them from becoming the victims or perpetrators of crime. However we do not have enough information about the results of these exercises for us to recommend them as general practice. **We therefore recommend that LEAs and chief officers of police should jointly consider the use of 'truancy sweeps' as a means of maximising school attendance and reducing juvenile crime in local circumstances.**

18 It has been suggested to us that a number of persistent non-attenders are working illegally when they should be at school. It is possible that, as the number of school leavers falls, it may become more tempting to employ children illegally. The current penalty for this offence under the Children and Young Persons Act 1933 is a fine at level three on the standard scale, which currently stands at £400. We do not consider this to be an adequate deterrent for unscrupulous employers who profit from illegal child labour. Any employment of school age children beyond what is permissible in law is likely to have harmful effects on their education as well as having the disruptive effects on the work of their classmates which we have described above when they are employed during school hours. We consider this to be a more serious offence than illegal employment out of school hours. **We therefore recommend that the Government review the penalties for the illegal employment of school age children with a view to substantially increasing penalties for employers, especially those who make use of illegal child labour during school hours.**

8 Police

1   Our evidence suggests that there is considerable scope for co-operation between the police, LEAs and schools to promote good behaviour and attendance among pupils. In chapter seven we recommend that more LEAs and police forces should consider carrying out joint 'truancy sweeps' in their areas. In chapter 10 we urge the police to take full account of staff morale when considering whether to refer cases involving attacks on school staff to the Crown Prosecution Service. In this chapter we consider the scope for collaboration between the police and schools on a variety of levels.

DEALING WITH INTRUDERS

2   We have been told that the appearance of intruders during the school day is a persistent problem in some schools. During our programme of visits to schools, we were also shown some examples of property vandalised by intruders. Some of these intruders may be ex-pupils or pupils' relatives. Others will have no connection with the school at all. The presence of an intruder during school hours can be a distracting influence on pupils and a cause of concern to staff. It can also be associated with the theft of equipment or personal property. In some cases it can be dangerous. The analysis of non-accidental injuries to school staff provded by the ILEA (see chapter 10) shows that 20% of them took place as a result of encounters with intruders or ex-pupils.

3   Trespass is not, in itself, a criminal offence but section 40 of the Local Government (Miscellaneous Provisions) Act 1982 makes it an offence for a trespasser to cause a nuisance or disturbance on school premises. Both the police and persons authorised by the LEA, or governing body in the case of aided schools, have powers to remove trespassers whom they have reasonable cause to suspect are committing or have committed an offence under this section. The police also have powers under section 25 of the Police and Criminal Evidence Act 1984 to arrest trespassers if there are reasonable grounds for believing that they may become violent, steal or damage property.

4   It seems clear to us therefore that adequate legal powers exist to remove intruders. School staff may understandably be reluctant to remove certain kinds of intruder themselves. The quality of relationships between the school and local police is therefore important. We consider that headteachers should establish a clear understanding with their local police about the circumstances in which the police will be called upon to intervene. In some cases it may be appropriate for chief education officers to make initial contact with chief officers of police to establish a general framework of response for the area as a whole. Once these

understandings are established, we believe that the police should always intervene if asked to do so by the headteacher or other senior members of staff.

5   In its evidence to us, the National Association of Head Teachers suggests that the maximum penalty for trespassers found guilty of causing a disturbance in a school is too low. This penalty consists of a fine at level two on the standard scale, which currently stands at £100. We agree that this would probably not be enough to act as an effective deterrent to intruders on its own. However, more serious disturbances can be dealt with under section 5 of the Public Order Act 1986 which provides for fines at level three on the standard scale, which currently stands at £400. We consider that this provides a sufficient deterrent.

COLLABORATION WITH SCHOOLS

6   The Secondary Heads Association provides us with examples of collaborative projects involving schools with other agencies. Most of these projects included the police. The recent publication by Her Majesty's Inspectorate of Schools on good practice in school-police liaison, **Our Policeman,** contains many more examples of such schemes. Much of this work is not directly related to behaviour in schools, but two types of project seem to be directly relevant to this enquiry.

7   'School watch' schemes aim to raise pupils' and parents' awareness of vandalism to and theft from schools. These schemes encourage pupils and parents living near schools to report suspicious activities to the police. In chapter four we emphasise the importance of promoting a sense of community and 'ownership' of the premises among pupils. School watch schemes may help in this process.

8   **Our Policeman** points out the valuable contribution that the police can make to personal and social education programmes in schools. An example quoted in the report involved a teacher, two police officers and a group of low achieving fourth year pupils in a project based on planning and carrying out work to repair damage done by vandals in a local park. We believe that there is considerable scope for practical projects of this kind, as well as more conventional work in the classroom, and that the police can play a positive role in promoting the principles of social responsibility and good citizenship among pupils.

9   **We recommend that all LEAs and schools should recognise the practical and educational value of good relations with the police and promote the development of school-police liaison projects.**

171

THE ROLE OF GOVERNORS

1 Very few of the submissions we received mention governors. The most notable exception is the evidence provided by the National Association of Governors and Managers (NAGM), an organisation to which many governors belong and which is involved in their training. The NAGM emphasises the contribution that governors can make to developing whole school approaches to pupils' behaviour. We welcome this emphasis.

2 Governors are drawn from a variety of groups including parents, teachers, the local community, the LEA and, in the case of aided and controlled schools, the church or other organsiation which set them up. They have a wide range of responsibilities which has been significantly increased by the 1986 (No. 2) and 1988 Education Acts. Between now and 1993 the governing bodies of all secondary schools and all primary schools with more than 200 pupils, and probably some smaller primary schools, will take over responsibility for managing school budgets. This initiative is called local management of schools (LMS). The governing bodies of aided schools employ staff and have responsibility for most building work. Under LMS the governing bodies of county and controlled schools with delegated budgets will be able to decide how many and which staff should work at the school. They will however have to satisfy the LEA, which remains the employer, that these people are appointable. Governors will also be responsible for the day-to-day maintenance of school buildings (see chapter four).

3 In relation to pupils' behaviour and discipline, section 22(b) of the Education (No. 2) Act 1986 gives heads a duty to act in accordance with any written statement of general principles on disciplinary matters provided by the governing body. Governors also have specific responsibilities relating to attendance and the exclusion of pupils from school for bad behaviour. We discusss attendance in chapter seven and exclusions in chapter 11.

4 Governors are not expected to take detailed decisions about the running of the school, nor would we encourage them to do so. That is the role of the headteacher. They have however a general responsibility for its effective management. In discharging this duty, they should ensure that they know their school well and make arrangements to visit it regularly. We believe that governors can and should make a positive contribution to whole school approaches to pupils' behaviour. Our comments in the rest of this chapter focus on what is likely to become the most typical school – a county or controlled school with a delegated budget. But most of them should apply with equal force to all LEA maintained schools.

5   Most governors are not teachers or professional educationalists. They are lay people such as parents, local businessmen, councillors, and clergymen who are interested in how a particular local school is run. We believe that this is as it should be. Professionals need to take account of the views of lay people. The wide range of training now available to governors can help make them more effective, without losing the important perspective they provide as lay representatives. Governors, for their part, must recognise the value of the professional advice which they are given by headteachers, LEA officers and inspectors. We respect the right of governors and other lay people to hold and express their own views about running schools. Professionals should not assume that they have a monopoly of wisdom on these matters, but neither should governors. Senior professionals such as heads and chief education officers have extensive knowlege and experience of the education service. This often enables them to focus more clearly on the question of what works.

6   We consider that, within the area covered by our terms of reference, two aspects of the governors' role are particularly important – the development of school behaviour policies, and the appointment and dismissal of staff.

BEHAVIOUR POLICIES

7   In chapter four we emphasise the need for heads and their staffs to develop whole school behaviour policies which are clearly understood and supported by governors and parents. Governors have a right to lay down guidelines for such policies, and we consider that they should do so. We stress the importance of each school working out its own behaviour policy. This report does not include a detailed specification for such policies. It does, however, offer guidelines and examples. Working out the policy collectively may ensure commitment to it, but we do not consider commitment to a bad policy to be a useful contribution to improving standards of behaviour. **We therefore recommend that, when governors choose to draw up a written statement of general principles for a school's behaviour policy, they should take account of the principles of good practice identified in this report as well as the professional advice of the headteacher and the chief education officer.**

R
108

8   Behaviour policies need to be monitored and evaluated. In chapter four we recommend that heads and their staffs should do this regularly. Governors need to keep in touch with all significant developments in their school. They have a right, under section 32 of the Education (No.

2) Act 1986, to obtain a report from the headteacher on such matters connected with the discharge of his function as they may require. Governors should, of course, give heads a reasonable amount of time to prepare such reports. **We recommend that governors should obtain regular reports on the standards of behaviour in their schools from headteachers.**

9 Sections 30 and 31 of the Education (No. 2) Act 1986 require governors to provide parents with an annual report on their management of the school and to hold an annual parents' meeting to discuss it. The recent DES publication **School Governors: a guide to the law** (1988) suggests that governors may wish to include information in such reports on pupils' behaviour and attendance. We strongly support this suggestion. We consider it essential for governors' annual reports to deal with standards of behaviour, and that this should be a regular item for discussion at annual parents' meetings. We recognise that this can be an emotive issue. In chapter five we emphasise the need for responsible discussion at annual parents' meetings. The chairman of governors does not have to chair the meeting, but he or she is the person most likely to do so. We consider that all governors, and the chairman in particular, have a responsibility to ensure that behaviour-related issues are discussed constructively. **We recommend that governors' annual reports should contain a section on the standards of behaviour in and attendance at the school.**

THE APPOINTMENT AND DISMISSAL OF STAFF

10 Appointing a new headteacher is a governing body's single most important job. In county or controlled schools, the LEA employs the headteacher but candidates are recommended for appointment by a selection panel. In schools with delegated budgets, the chief education officer or his representative will be entitled to attend meetings of the selection panel, but only governors on the selection panel will be able to vote. Governors are required to consider, but not necessarily to take, the advice offered by the LEA.

11 The headteacher plays a central role in promoting good behaviour. The quality of leadership provided by heads is crucial to the development of a school community in which high standards of attainment can be achieved. Governors should therefore approach the process of appointment with the utmost care. They may be choosing the person who will be their school's chief executive for more than a decade.

12 We recognise that governors will be looking for wide and differing ranges of skills and experience when making these appointments. It is

not for us to advise them on what that range should be in any particular case. We are sure, however, that it will never be adequate if it does not include the skills and experience necessary to establish a whole school behaviour policy; nor would we expect a candidate who does not place importance on establishing or maintaining good standards of behaviour throughout the school to meet the requirements of a conscientious governing body.

13 The whole school, team-based approaches recommended in this report require particular styles of school management. In our view, governors should look for candidates able to combine purposeful leadership with a consultative management style. They should look for evidence of this both in applications and at interview.

14 Governors are also responsible for appointing other teaching and non-teaching staff. The ability to form relationships with pupils based on mutual respect is an essential qualification for effective teaching. Governors should not appoint candidates who appear to lack this ability. Team work and mutual support are also important in promoting good behaviour throughout the school. Governors should look for candidates who are temperamentally suited to this style of working.

15 Governors will, of course, be aware that discrimination in appointments on grounds of race or gender is illegal. They will need to guard against any unconscious assumptions that the qualities we have identified can only be found in particular sections of the population.

16 Interviewing and selecting candidates require skill and tact. Experience of this sort of work, particularly in the educational field, is invaluable. So is first hand experience of teaching. Chief education officers and headteachers have legal rights to offer advice on appointments. Governors should take full account of this professional advice when making appointments.

17 **We recommend that, in selecting applicants for interview and appointing headteachers, or recommending them for appointment, governors should take care to select only those candidates who have the leadership and management qualities necessary for establishing whole school behaviour policies on the lines set out in this report.**

18 **We recommend that, in selecting applicants for interview and appointing other teaching staff, or recommending them for appointment, governors should take care to select candidates temperamentally suited to staff team work and mutual support and able to form relationships with pupils based on mutual respect.**

R
113

19 **We recommend that, in making or recommending appointments, governors should give full weight to the professional advice offered by chief education officers and headteachers.**

20 There are circumstances in which governors are not directly in control of adults servicing the school for which they are responsible. This can arise both under present arrangements where, for example, school meals are delivered and served under arrangements made by the LEA; or it may arise in the future where a school chooses to contract out certain services to the private sector. In both cases, headteachers and governors will need to bear in mind the effects which these adults will have on the school's behaviour policy. All adults working at the school should be required to comply with the school's behaviour policy, including members of the LEA's direct labour organisation and employees of private sector companies to whom LEAs or governors, in the case of schools with delegated budgets, have contracted a service. **We recommend that LEAs and governing bodies which employ contractors should make adherence to the relevant parts of the school's behaviour policy a condition for the letting or renewing of contracts.**

R
114

21 The dismissal of a teacher is a rare event, but it is sometimes necessary. Teachers can be dismissed for breach of contract, professional misconduct or incompetence. Both misconduct and incompetence can relate to the management of pupils' behaviour. Questions of misconduct may, for example, arise if a teacher or headteacher is found to be administering illegal physical punishment. Our impression is that cases involving incompetence tend to be less straightforward. The introduction of systematic appraisal should help to ensure that teachers receive help and support in dealing with discipline problems, but problems may still persist. In chapter three we comment on the tradition of 'classroom isolation' which still exists in many schools. We have heard of situations where heads and colleagues have turned a blind eye to a teacher's apparent inability to control classes. We do not doubt that such situations are rare, but where they exist they can continue for years. When a crisis is reached in such cases, governors who decide to recommend dismissal on the grounds of incompetence will find their action difficult to justify to an industrial tribunal if the teacher has been sacked after several years of service during which there is no record of any systematic attempts to provide professional support or supplementary training. In chapter three we discuss the kind of action that heads and LEAs can take to support teachers in difficulty. If all reasonable action has been taken, including consideration of transfer to another school, and it is clear that there is no prospect of the teacher involved achieving an acceptable standard of competence in classroom

management, we believe that governors should not hesitate to recommend dismissal.

22   **We recommend that:**

22.1   **governors and LEAs should recognise that teachers who are unable, with the training and support recommended in this report, to control their classes in a school should cease to be employed in that school; and**

22.2   **in such cases, as in all personnel matters, that governors should follow professional advice on good employment practice. This can be provided by LEAs.**

23   Governors will need training to carry out their responsibilities effectively. In 1989/90 the Government is supporting expenditure of £5.3 million on training for school governors in England and Wales through the Education Support Grant scheme. Further funding will be available in 1990/91 and 1991/92. We welcome this initiative. **We recommend:**

23.1   **that LEAs should ensure that governors' training includes their role in developing school behaviour policies and in the appointment and dismissal of staff; and**

23.2   **that governors should take full advantage of the training opportunities which are becoming available to them.**

VOLUNTARY BODIES

24   Our terms of reference mention voluntary bodies. The best known of these are the Church of England and Roman Catholic Diocesan Boards of Education. Although these bodies offer valuable support and advice to voluntary schools, particularly in relation to building matters, they do not have statutory powers and responsibilities for the running of schools analogous to those of LEAs. Their influence is exercised mainly through the 'foundation' governors whom they appoint. All the recommendations in this report relating to the running of schools apply with equal force to the voluntary sector. Voluntary bodies will wish to note in particular the recommendations addressed to governors.

10 Local Education Authorities

THE ROLE OF LEAs

1 There are 105 LEAs in England and Wales. The abolition of the ILEA and the transfer of its functions to the inner London councils in 1990 will increase their number to 117. LEAs vary greatly in size, but they all have similar functions. The 1988 Education Reform Act will mean significant changes in these functions. Some of the changes made by the Act, like local management of schools (LMS see chapter four), will be phased in over several years. This report has been written with the implications of the Act in mind. We start this chapter by outlining the role of LEAs in this new context.

2 With the exception of the ILEA, all LEAs are part of councils which are responsible for running a range of public services of which education is only one. Local education services, which include schools and colleges, are controlled by education committees consisting mainly of elected councillors. Education committees have general responsibilities for the management of education services in their areas. Chief education officers are responsible for giving professional advice to education committees and for managing education departments which provide a wide range of services for schools, colleges and individual clients.

3 LEAs will provide four general kinds of service relevant to schools in the new environment created by the 1988 Act. All of these can relate to the question of pupil's behaviour. They can be summarised as follows:

3.1 LEAs will be responsible for co-ordinating the introduction into their schools of national initiatives such as LMS and the National Curriculum (see chapter four), and for monitoring and providing advice and support for the development of those initiatives. They will also be responsible for monitoring the performance of their schools, advising schools on how to improve their performance and providing support for such action. This chapter deals with their responsibilities for monitoring performance and providing consultancy services.

3.2 LEAs will provide a range of personnel services including professional advice to governors on appointments and dismissals (see chapter nine), in-service training (see chapter three and four) and staff appraisal (see chapters three and four). As the employers of most school staff, LEAs will continue to be responsible for their welfare. We consider an important aspect of this responsibility in this chapter.

3.3 LEAs will continue to provide a range of services for individual pupils, parents and teachers. These are sometimes called 'client based' services to distinguish them from those provided through schools, although they can support whole schools as well as individuals. Client based services include school meals (see chapter four), the education welfare and psychology services (see chapters four, six and seven), alternative provision for disturbed or difficult pupils (see chapter six) and the youth and careers services. This chapter deals with the co-ordination of client based services and with the youth and careers services.

3.4 LEAs will continue to be responsible for the long term planning of educational provision in their areas. This includes making sure that there are enough school places of the right kind in the right locations and that surplus places are taken out of use, which may involve reorganisation of existing schools. LEAs will also retain their responsibilities for school building programmes and for structural repairs to school premises (see chapter four). We do not discuss the reorganisation of schools in detail in this report. The 'settling in' period for a new school made up of staff and pupils from others which have been closed can be difficult, but problems involving pupils' behaviour in these circumstances tend to be short term. We are not suggesting that reorganisation schemes which may have major benefits in terms of improving the quality of pupils' education and making it more cost-effective should be abandoned because of such difficulties. When merging schools, LEAs should assess the effects of the merger on the behaviour of the pupils in the new school and take account of these effects in their provision of support services to it during the 'settling in' period.

CONSULTANCY SERVICES

4 All LEAs have senior officers responsible for the management of services for schools. They also have advisors or inspectors responsible for monitoring and improving the quality of the curriculum which schools provide. Both officers and inspectors visit schools. Many LEAs give their inspectors 'pastoral' responsibility for a group of schools. Our impression is that this may amount to an effective consultancy service for heads and teachers in some LEAs, but in many it does not. We consider that the quality of consultancy services available to schools can be an important factor in promoting good behaviour. The clear message emerging from the 'effective schools' research to which we refer throughout this report is that one of the best ways of improving standards of behaviour in a school is to change the way in which the institution works. We know that this can be a very difficult process. It may be particularly difficult for 'insiders' like heads and their management teams to recognise that some of the features built into the

organisations that they run are actually increasing the likelihood of bad behaviour among pupils. Heads and their senior colleagues may also find it difficult to accept advice from 'outsiders', particularly if it is seen as a criticism of their management styles. But it is common practice both in commercial and public sector organisations to use management consultants to identify organisational weaknesses and suggest remedies for them. LEAs themselves sometimes make use of external consultants to help them improve the quality and cost-effectiveness of their education departments. If consultants can show themselves to be well qualified, well informed and sensitive to the practical constraints faced by managers, their advice will be seen as constructive by their clients.

5 We are, however, aware of two problems which restrict the value of the consultancy services that LEAs currently provide for their schools. The first relates to the traditional roles and capabilities of LEA officers and inspectors. The second is the quality of management information currently available to them.

6 LEA officers and inspectors are equipped to provide heads with advice on technical, legal, financial and curriculum matters. Systematic management advice is not readily provided by many LEAs to their schools. Our impression from talking to heads is that it is often not clear who is responsible for giving management, as distinct from technical or curriculum, advice to headteachers and that consequently that advice is not given. We believe that many heads would welcome and make good use of effective management consultancy services if they were provided by LEAs, and that such services could make a significant contribution towards improving standards of behaviour in schools. **We therefore recommend that all LEAs should provide effective management consultancy services for headteachers.**

7 We recognise that this recommendation is likely to present LEAs with practical difficulties. Smaller LEAs in particular would have difficulty in adding a 'school management consultant' to their officer or advisory teams. Some LEAs would argue that 'advisory heads' have sometimes been employed with very limited success. They might also point out that heads can be encouraged to seek each other's advice on management problems through 'peer consultancy' arrangements. We are not suggesting a single solution to the consultancy problem which will work for all LEAs. Solutions need to be tailored to local circumstances. Smaller LEAs could, for example, group themselves into consortia made up of several authorities to provide a consultancy service more economically. LEAs may be able to combine services provided by officers and inspectors with a peer consultancy network for headteachers.

8 Effective consultancy is based on good management information. LEAs already have a wealth of statistical information on numbers, costs, examination results and so on. The picture of an organisation painted by statistics alone can however be misleading. 'Hard' information has an important part to play in improving the quality of school management, and of the consultancy services available to headteachers, but it needs to be interpreted in the light of other knowledge. There is among officers and inspectors in every authority a pool of information about schools in the area, covering such matters as differences in the nature of school catchment areas, the history of schools, the composition of their staff and the personal styles of different headteachers. Such so-called 'soft' information, based on professional judgements rather than statistics, can be of immense value to those seeking to advise headteachers. LEAs should make arrangements to ensure that it is accessible.

9 Our evidence from LEAs indicates that, in most of them, the 'hard' information available about pupils' behaviour in their schools is very limited. Some collect and analyse school attendance statistics. In chapter seven we recommend that all LEAs should do so. Some maintain detailed records of the exclusion of pupils from their schools. Only one LEA appears to maintain records of violent incidents involving school staff. Later in this chapter we recommend that all LEAs should maintain detailed records of serious incidents in and exclusions from their schools. Such records should help them target consultancy and support on the schools that need them most.

10 The development of performance indicators for schools is a complex process which is in its early stages. We consider that, when they are more fully developed, such indicators could be useful to officers and inspectors for targeting LEA consultancy and support services more precisely. But they will have to be used with care. Even sophisticated indicators cannot be used as performance measures. Their purpose is not to provide answers but to enable managers and consultants to ask pertinent questions.

11 **We recommend that LEAs should develop information systems covering pupils' behaviour in their schools which will enable them to make timely and effective use of their consultancy and support services.**

12 Section 28 of the Education (No. 2) Act 1986 gives LEAs a reserve power to intervene directly in the running of a county or controlled school maintained by them in the event of a breakdown of discipline, or the likelihood of such a breakdown occurring. An LEA can use this

power if it judges that the behaviour of pupils is such that their education is severely prejudiced or is likely to become so in the immediate future. It is clear that this power is intended for use as a last resort and that it will be used rarely, but this does not diminish its importance.

13 **We recommend that if an LEA is convinced that a breakdown of discipline has occurred or is likely to occur in a school, it should not hesitate to use its powers of intervention under section 28 of the Education (No. 2) Act 1986.**

SUPPORT SYSTEMS

14 LEAs must also provide routine practical support for schools and pupils in difficulty. In many LEAs this does not at present appear to be done as part of a coherent system. We asked all LEAs about the guidelines they provide for their schools on disciplinary matters. A considerable number of LEAs sent us examples of the written advice they provide. These examples vary considerably in their approaches. Some simply provide legal guidance covering the procedures involved in excluding pupils from school laid down in the Education (No. 2) Act 1986. Others provide much more detailed guidance on, for example, the steps that can be taken before a pupil is formally excluded, sometimes including ways of involving parents, education welfare officers and educational psychologists. We received a number of examples of documents outlining such guidance which seemed well thought out. Circumstances of different LEAs will vary. We do not therefore put forward a model for others to copy. We set out below the main features which we think good LEA guidelines should have. They are:

14.1 advice on the law as it applies to headteachers, governing bodies and the LEA;

14.2 clear guidelines for headteachers covering what they should do themselves and what they can expect LEA officers and others to do;

14.3 suggestions for a 'staged' approach to exclusions, with clear objectives and procedures at each stage of the process. Under such an approach the parents might for instance be formally notified as soon as a pupil's behaviour was causing concern, and warned of the risk of exclusion. If the pupil's behaviour did not improve the parents might receive a further warning that the LEA and governing body had been notified, and the education welfare service would be brought in;

14.4   formal procedures for ensuring that the LEA considers the possibility that a pupil who is at risk of exclusion may have special educational needs;

14.5   procedures for bringing in the full range of LEA and local authority services where a pupil is excluded;

14.6   the use of a re-entry agreement (see chapter four) when a pupil is excluded for an indefinite period;

14.7   if possible, the opportunity for a pupil to be transferred to another school if he or she is excluded permanently; and

14.8   a clear end to the exclusion process, such as the transfer of a pupil to an off-site unit.

15   Under the Education (No. 2) Act 1986, decisions on exclusions are the responsibility of the headteacher. Nevertheless we consider that LEA guidelines have a valuable part to play in providing a coherent support system which co-ordinates the efforts of other LEA and local authority services and includes adequate alternative provision for the most difficult pupils (see chapter six). **We therefore recommend:**

15.1   **that LEAs should develop effective strategies for supporting the behaviour policies of their schools based on clear aims and procedures and backed up by the necessary communication systems and resources; and**

15.2   **that they should regularly evaluate these strategies in relation to their aims and the perceptions of schools, parents and pupils of the quality of service being provided.**

16   In chapter four we recommend that pastoral staff in schools should maintain regular contacts with education welfare officers. We consider that LEAs should do all that they can to encourage such contacts. In chapter seven we recommend that all LEAs should employ adequate numbers of education welfare officers to ensure that excessive case loads do not prevent them carrying out their full range of functions effectively. **We recommend that LEAs should ensure that schools and education welfare officers establish regular pastoral contacts and early warning systems to identify pupils 'at risk' at the earliest possible stage, so that preventive action can be taken.**

17   We visited a large secondary school in Sunderland which had an education welfare officer based on site. He served that school and its 'feeder' primary schools. This arrangement meant that he could work closely with the school's pastoral team and maintain continuous contact with families throughout the school careers of their children. Such an

arrangement would not be suitable in all circumstances. In some authorities with a large number of relatively small and widely distributed secondary schools it would not be a practical arrangement. Some city secondary schools take small numbers of children from so many different primary schools that the idea of 'feeder' school hardly applies. We are also aware that in some instances relations between teachers and education welfare officers are not as good as they might be. It is very important that efforts should be made to maintain good relations and mutual confidence between these two professions. We are convinced of the value of continuity of contact between education welfare officers, schools, and families. **We therefore recommend that LEAs should, wherever possible, ensure continuity of family and school contacts by using education welfare officers to service clusters of secondary and related primary schools.**

18 In chapter six we recommend that all LEAs should employ adequate numbers of educational psychologists to enable them to achieve the six month target for assessing and providing statements of special educational needs for pupils. We consider that educational psychologists should play a much wider role in promoting good behaviour in schools. We know that, in a number of LEAs, educational psychologists are involved in in-service training in classroom management. We consider that LEAs may also get better value in terms of improving pupils' behaviour out of their educational psychology services if they use them for more general consultancy and in-service training work in schools. Traditionally educational psychologists have concentrated on the difficulties and needs of individual pupils. We consider that it is necessary for them to look at the situations in which pupils are behaving badly rather than simply to concentrate on the behaviour of individuals. A number of LEAs are now also using their educational psychologists to provide a more general consultancy service for schools dealing with difficult behaviour. This is easier if educational psychologists are linked to particular schools and have regular contact with them. **We recommend that LEAs should encourage closer working relationships between schools and educational psychologists to develop consultancy services providing advice on the management of behaviour in groups and in the school as a whole.**

19 We know that some pupils and their families are sometimes in contact with a variety of welfare and other agencies. Education welfare officers, educational psychologists, support teachers, social workers, housing departments, health service agencies and the police can all be involved. In its submission to us, the Secondary Heads Association highlights the potential for closer collaboration between these agencies and schools. It points out the problems that can be caused by lack of co-ordination

between various agencies and by misunderstandings between teachers and other professionals working with young people and their families. It emphasises the need for closer inter-agency co-operation at local level and for more mutual understanding. We support this view. We consider that the links between school pastoral systems and external agencies dealing with the same clients can usefully be developed. The local authority, as 'owner' of many of the services involved, is in a good position to develop inter-agency links and promote mutual understanding. This can be done at authority level through inter-agency committees or liaison groups and at operational level through case conferences. **We therefore recommend that local authorities should promote better co-ordination between the various local agencies dealing with pupils with behaviour or attendance problems and their families.**

YOUTH AND CAREERS SERVICES

20   LEA youth services, which cater mainly for young people of secondary school age, are usually based on youth centres run by youth workers. A common pattern is for services to be provided by a combination of LEA-run centres and others run by voluntary organisations which may receive grant-aid from the LEA. In some areas there are also 'detached' youth workers running projects for young people which are not based on centres. There can also be links between youth workers, centres and projects and individual secondary schools. Some youth centres operate on school premises in the evenings. We believe that each of these arrangements can contribute to developing constructive and responsible social attitudes among young people which can have a beneficial influence on their behaviour in schools.

21   Youth workers generally have a good understanding of young people's interests and are able to relate to them well in an informal way. Traditionally, youth centres have been associated with providing social and leisure facilities. But most youth workers emphasise the educational aims of their service. One of these is to provide personal and social education by informal means. Many youth service activities take the form of projects which rely on co-operative effort. Young people are often encouraged to take active responsibility for the management of youth centres. It seems clear to us that, if an LEA has an active youth service which has a positive educational purpose, its curriculum can reinforce school personal and social education programmes in a number of areas. In chapter three we ask LEAs to create opportunities for joint training involving youth workers and teachers. We believe that there is much that they can learn from each other about managing groups of

R
126

young people. **We also recommend that LEAs should encourage schools and youth services to explore the possibilities for developing closer links within particular catchment areas and, where appropriate, for basing youth workers in schools.**

22   A number of the submissions we received link bad behaviour in schools to youth unemployment. Our evidence does not suggest that there is any simple relationship between regional variations in employment levels and the seriousness of behaviour problems perceived by teachers. It seems likely to us, however, that the prospect of unemployment will have a demotivating effect on some pupils which will affect their will to learn and their behaviour or attendance. We consider that LEA careers services have a role to play in improving the motivation of older secondary pupils. Careers officers usually have responsibility for one or more secondary schools. They aim to give guidance to all fourth or fifth year pupils before they leave school. We consider that the quality of the guidance and job placement services provided by careers officers is important for the self-esteem of lower achieving pupils. It must be clear to them that their career prospects are being taken seriously, and that their behaviour in school is a relevant factor. **We recommend that LEAs should make the improvement of the motivation and self-esteem of lower achieving pupils one of the objectives of their careers services.**

R
127

SUPPLY TEACHERS

23   When full time teachers are away from school, substitute or supply teachers are provided by LEAs to take their classes. Under LMS, the budget used by LEAs to pay for supply cover will be delegated to schools. It will be for each school to decide what arrangements it wishes to make for supply cover. The systems which are adopted will not, however, alter the force of the following paragraphs.

24   Heads and teachers in almost all the schools we visited raised the problem of supply teachers with us. We were told that supply teachers often have particular classroom management problems. These may reflect the extra difficulty of the task they have to perform. They may not know the school or any of its pupils or staff. They may be asked to teach an unfamiliar age group or subject. In many respects, therefore, supply teachers have to face repeatedly the difficulties with which other teachers only have to cope when they are first appointed to a school. One result is that pupils will continually test them out. In the case of a planned absence work will usually have been set for classes. In other cases it often will not. A supply teacher may then have neither the

opportunity to plan a lesson properly nor the information to make it relevant to pupils' needs.

25 All this means that supply teachers have a greater need of skill and experience than other teachers if the behaviour of the pupils for whom they are responsible is not to deteriorate. This, in turn, means that high standards are needed both in their selection and in their training for this particular role. **We therefore recommend:**

R 128.1

    25.1   **that LEAs and schools should select supply teachers with as much care as full-time staff; and**

R 128.2

    25.2   **that LEAs should provide them with in-service training in classroom management.**

26 It is clear that in certain parts of the country, such as the London area, LEAs are experiencing considerable difficulties in recruiting supply teachers. We recognise this difficulty but, nevertheless, if their response is to reduce the standard of entry for recruits to the supply pool, increased discipline problems are bound to follow.

27 Nationally supply teachers provide about 5% of total teaching time in schools. This proportion may vary considerably between individual schools and LEAs. Supply teachers are used to replace teachers who are absent or unavailable to teach for a variety of reasons including sickness and in-service training. No systematic national analysis of the facts about teachers' absence and supply cover is available. The results of a survey by one LEA, summarised in the report of the Interim Advisory Committee (IAC) on **School Teachers' Pay and Conditions** (1988), showed that 41% of the teachers for whom supply cover was provided on one day in 1983 were absent because of sickness or family reasons. A further 24% were taking part in school journeys and 15% in in-service training.

28 The IAC report identifies a variety of ways to reduce the unsettling effect on pupils and schools of the frequent use of supply teachers. These include avoiding known peak periods for absence due to sickness when planning school journeys and in-service training, using groups of supply teachers on permanent or longer-term contracts to service clusters of schools or increasing the full-time staff of schools by one or more teachers whose main task is to provide cover for absent colleagues. We commend all these suggestions for consideration by schools and LEAs. The IAC report also recommends that LEAs should carry out a careful analysis of patterns of supply cover as a first step towards improving its management. We support this recommendation.

29   It has been suggested to us that another way of reducing the need for supply cover would be for more in-service training to take place when pupils are on holiday. The recent provision of five non-teaching days in the teacher's working year represents a move in this direction. It seems clear that the teachers' professional associations would oppose any extension of the teacher's working year to provide training days without some form of compensation. At present Local Education Authority Training Grants Scheme funds cannot be used to pay teachers to undertake training. Where such training took the place of training in term time, however, the cost of that compensation could be met from savings in expenditure on supply teachers, whose hourly rates of pay are generally higher than those of full-time teachers. We consider that the consequent reduction in the use of supply teachers would reduce behaviour problems in the schools affected. We recognise that the savings would have to be clearly identified and the risk of reducing the amount of training currently taking place avoided. Any scheme would have to be devised in the light of a full knowledge of its resource and administrative consequences. **We therefore recommend that, in order to increase the amount of in-service training undertaken out of school hours, the Secretaries of State should consider the extent to which it would be possible to finance such training from savings achieved by a consequential reduction in the use of supply teachers to replace full-time teachers absent on in-service training courses.**

30   While it may be possible to reduce the number of supply teachers used by schools, it will not be possible, nor would it be desirable, to eliminate their use altogether. Unavoidable absences, for reasons other than training, will continue to require supply cover. It will be very important therefore to see that supply teachers are chosen, trained and deployed as effectively as possible, and that schools support them properly.

31   Much of the particular difficulty of supply teachers' work results, as we have suggested, from their constant redeployment to new tasks in unfamiliar schools. This difficulty can be reduced to a minimum by administrative means. **We therefore recommend that LEAs should make it their normal practice to attach individual supply teachers to specific schools or groups of schools.**

32   We have received a clear impression that supply teachers are not well treated in some schools. We do not think this is intentional, but the results are no less damaging for that. In some schools supply teachers are not welcomed by the head or senior member of staff on their first day. They are given inadequate information and may be more or less ignored by other teachers. This is not likely to improve their morale, which is an important factor in effective classroom management. We consider

that the problems which seem to be associated with supply teachers could be significantly reduced if schools adopted a code of good practice for their use. As an example they could consider the following, which is based on suggestions made in a recent article by Dr Jean Lawrence (1988). Schools should:

32.1   provide a welcoming environment for supply teachers;

32.2   make a senior member of staff responsible for briefing and managing them;

32.3   provide supply teachers with an information pack containing a school map, staff and form lists, and a summary of the school's behaviour policy and its practical application;

32.4   provide work and instructions for the classes they are to take and a system for reporting their work and behaviour to regular teachers;

32.5   pair supply teachers with experienced colleagues in adjacent classrooms if behaviour problems are expected;

32.6   obtain full information about the qualifications and experience of supply teachers systematically; and

32.7   review supply cover arrangements regularly. This should involve not only the head and senior management team but the whole staff.

33   We recommend that headteachers and teachers should ensure that schools provide a welcoming and supportive environment for supply teachers and adopt a code of practice for the use of supply teachers based on the model provided in this report.

R
131

SERIOUS INCIDENTS REPORTING SYSTEMS

34   In chapter two we conclude that the question of whether there is now more bad behaviour in schools cannot be answered satisfactorily because of a lack of hard information. It is not even possible to say whether there has been a national increase in the number of attacks on school staff or in the number of pupils permanently excluded from schools. Most LEAs do not appear to keep any systematic record of serious incidents in schools. We are aware of only one, the ILEA, which keeps detailed records of violent incidents involving its staff. More LEAs maintain a central record of exclusions from their schools, but variations in the form and level of detail of these records make comparisons between authorities very difficult.

35 We consider this state of affairs to be very unsatisfactory. It represents a serious gap in the management and policy information available to LEAs and to the Government. The report on **Preventing Violence to Staff** recently published by the Health and Safety Executive points out that setting up a proper recording system for incidents is a vital step towards developing effective strategies to deal with the problem of violence to staff.

36 The details provided by the ILEA system of recording injuries resulting from incidents involving two or more people illustrate the potential value of such records. The breakdown of incidents involving staff in ordinary schools in the 1987/88 academic year was as follows:

| Injured person | Stopping fights or re-straining pupils a | Incidents as % of relevant FTE work-force b | Non-accidental injury involving: | | | | | Total non-accidental injury incidents | Incidents as % of relevant FTE work-force b |
			Pupil	In-truder	Ex-pupil	Parent	Other adult		
Teacher	114	0.54	48	10	3	9	3	73	0.35
School meals supervisor or primary helper	95	2.81	22	3	–	–	1	26	0.77
Caretaker	1	0.05	1	7	1	1	1	11	0.66
Other staff	7	0.03 c	9	2	–	2	3	16	0.07 c

a Less than 20% requiring medical attention.
b Full time equivalents (FTE) used to indicate staff time on the premises.
c Estimate.

37 The figures show that the majority of injuries to staff occurred as a result of stopping fights or physically restraining pupils in some way. This has clear practical and training implications particularly for school meals supervisors who are on duty when fights between pupils are most likely to occur and who, according to these figures, are much more at risk of injury in such circumstances than teachers. They also show that the risk from intruders on school premises is not insignificant, particularly for caretakers.

38 Systematic exclusion records would also be useful for targeting consultancy and remedial action. Researchers have noted quite large variations in the rates at which different schools exclude pupils which cannot be explained by the nature of their catchment areas. A recent study of exclusions from secondary schools in Leeds found that the

schools with the highest exclusion rates were those in which pupils who misbehaved were most rapidly referred up to senior staff rather than being dealt with by class teachers or form tutors (McManus 1987). This finding suggests that exclusion rates could be reduced in some schools by reorganising their internal referral systems.

39 **We recommend:**

39.1 **that an LEA/DES/Welsh Office working group should be set up as soon as possible to develop serious incidents reporting systems with the aim of having a pilot system in place by September 1989; and**

39.2 **that, as soon as possible thereafter, all LEAs should establish serious incidents reporting systems and should monitor and act upon the information that these systems provide.**

40 Both the national and local components of serious incidents reporting systems would need to be very carefully designed to maximise clarity and minimise bureaucracy. Different information needs exist at local and national levels. We envisage a system with a standardised 'core' of information needed by the DES or Welsh Office. Each LEA could then add its own more detailed information requirements. The national core might consist only of information about violence to staff, violence to pupils resulting in injury, serious vandalism and the permanent exclusion of pupils from schools. **Preventing Violence to Staff** includes some useful guidance on classifying violent incidents and setting up recording systems, including a model incident report form. We consider that exclusion records should include details of the age, sex and ethnic origin of each of the pupils involved, full details of the reasons for the exclusion and how it was resolved, whether by transfer to another school or unit or home tuition or some other means.

ATTACKS ON STAFF

41 This enquiry was set up by the Secretary of State partly in response to reports of physical attacks on teachers and other school staff by pupils and parents. This issue is a matter of the gravest concern to us.

42 The breakdown of violent incidents resulting in injuries to school staff shown above provides a reasonably precise indication of the number of violent incidents resulting in injury which took place in one inner-city LEA in a year. The problem of attacks does not appear to be large in terms of the number of staff affected. We do not, however, underestimate its seriousness for the individuals and schools involved.

One of the main thrusts of this report is towards minimising the opportunities for bad behaviour of all kinds by improving the group management skills of teachers and other staff, and the organisation and atmosphere of schools. We believe that action in these areas can make an important contribution to reducing the risk of violence for school staff, particularly that which may result from the escalation of minor incidents, but it will not eliminate it. Violent incidents can occur in the best run schools. Teachers and school meals supervisors will occasionally have to break up fights between pupils, putting themselves at risk in the process. School staff will occasionally be attacked by intruders. We consider that the employers of school staff have a duty to support any employee who is attacked, and to facilitate appropriate action against their attacker. **We recommend that LEAs and governing bodies which employ school staff should establish clear procedures for dealing with attacks on staff by pupils, members of pupils' families or intruders.**

43   We consider that such procedures should include the following features.

43.1   Effective reporting systems. Recording attacks on staff would be an important part of the serious incidents reporting systems which we recommend earlier in this chapter. Employers should ensure that prompt action is taken as soon as a report is received.

43.2   Support for victims. School staff must be confident that all violence against them will be taken seriously and that they will be supported by their employers. This support may need to be personal, for example through legal advice or counselling. Serious cases can attract media attention. Victims and other members of the school community may need help in dealing with reporters. Some violent incidents seriously affect the morale of a whole school. Headteachers and LEAs or governors will need to provide support for other staff and pupils during such a crisis.

43.3   Action against attackers. Some violent incidents involving school staff are clear cut cases of attack on them by pupils, parents or intruders. Others are not. The Education (No. 2) Act 1986 makes it clear that staff can legitimately use physical means to prevent a pupil injuring anybody or damaging property. We have, however, been told of incidents not covered by these circumstances which were sparked off by teachers administering illegal corporal punishment of some kind. We do not doubt that such incidents are very rare, and we do not suggest that this justifies the pupil's action. But we must recognise the complexity of such cases. We cannot, therefore, recommend a single course of action for employers covering all violent incidents. We would expect employers to report an alleged criminal act to the police in cases where it has not already been reported by the employee, unless the employee objects. When such an allegation is reported the police will decide whether to refer it to the Crown Prosecution Service (CPS). The CPS will then decide whether or not to prosecute. We consider that the employer should try to find out what action the police and CPS propose to take and pass on this information to the employee. The police may decide not to refer the case to the CPS, or the CPS may decide not to prosecute. In these circumstances we consider that the employer should be prepared to provide legal advice on the other courses of action which remain open to the employee. One is to institute a private prosecution for common assault. The other is to take action for civil damages against the alleged attacker.

44 In chapter five we recommend that the Government should investigate the possibility of imposing on parents civil liability for their children's acts in school. It would be inconsistent for this investigation not to cover the question of civil liability for injuries to school staff, which would also be relevant to cases involving children below the age of criminal responsibility.

45 Attacks on individual members of staff can affect the morale of their colleagues. We believe that damage to morale may be increased if the police decide not to refer the case to the CPS or the CPS decides not to prosecute. **We recommend:**

45.1 **that, in considering whether to refer cases of physical attack on school staff to the Crown Prosecution Service, chief officers of police should take into account the effects of their decisions on staff morale as an aspect of public interest; and**

R
134.1

45.2 **that the Crown Prosecution Service should also take staff morale into account as an aspect of public interest when deciding whether to prosecute such cases.**

R
134.2

46 We consider that compensation should be available to teachers and other staff for personal injury or damage to their property suffered at school. We accept that LEAs and governing bodies cannot be expected to insure their employees against the theft of personal property such as handbags or wallets. This would not be normal practice for any employer. We are, however, concerned by accounts of damage to teachers' motor vehicles parked on school premises. It is not reasonable to expect teachers to supervise these in the same way that they can look

10

R
135

after small items of personal property while they are working. We therefore recommend that LEAs and governing bodies which employ school staff should, either through insurance cover or ex-gratia payments, ensure that adequate compensation is available to school staff for non-accidental injury or for damage to their motor vehicles or other belongings which they bring into school but cannot be expected to supervise properly while they are working.

THE GOVERNMENT'S ROLE

1   Throughout this report we argue that there is no single or simple solution to the problem of disruptive behaviour in schools. We emphasise the need for concerted action to promote good behaviour at classroom, school, community and national levels. There is no single, dramatic step that the Government can take to transform the situation in schools. Our report identifies a variety of specific actions which, taken together, will do much to improve the standards of behaviour in our schools. Some of them should be taken by the Government.

2   In chapters three and four we recommend ways in which the Secretaries of State can help to improve the quality of training for heads and other teachers and reinforce their authority and status. In chapter four we suggest ways in which the National Curriculum could be designed to promote better behaviour. In chapter five we recommend that the Government should consider ways of making parents more accountable for their children's behaviour and promoting the principles of responsible parenthood. In chapter 10 we recommend that the Secretaries of State should help to set up a national reporting system for serious incidents in schools. We also welcome a number of Government initiatives such as the appraisal of heads and teachers (see chapter four) and the development of records of achievement, work experience schemes and compacts with employers (see chapter six), all of which we believe should help to improve the management of schools and classrooms and the motivation of pupils. This chapter deals with two further issues – the funding of the education service and the arrangements for excluding from schools those pupils involved in the most serious misbehaviour.

FUNDING LEAs

3   There is a link between the amount of money which central Government makes available to local authorities and the amount that LEAs spend on schools and support services but it is not always direct and simple. About half the expenditure of a typical LEA is supported by Government grant. Almost all this money comes in the form of Rate Support Grant which does not have to be spent on any particular service. The rest is specific grant such as Education Support Grant or money for in-service training. The other half of a typical LEA's expenditure is supported by the rates and other sources of income.

4   Levels of expenditure on teachers, schools and support services vary considerably between LEAs. For example, figures produced by the Chartered Institute of Public Finance and Accountancy for 1987/88

show a range of expenditure estimates for secondary schools from about £1500 to about £2500 per pupil. The range shown for primary schools is about £800 to £1700 per pupil. These variations reflect policy differences between LEAs as well as different social and economic circumstances in the areas they serve. The amount of Rate Support Grant received can also vary greatly. LEAs serving poorer and more disadvantaged communities tend to get more. A few in the most prosperous or high spending areas get none at all.

5 In chapters four, six and seven we recommend reviews of expenditure levels in five areas. They are the education welfare and psychology services, pre-school education, building maintenance and arrangements for lunchtime supervision. In the first three areas we note the large variations in levels of provision between different LEAs and recommend that those at the bottom of the range ensure that what they provide constitutes an adequate service in terms of this report. We draw attention to more general concerns relating to building maintenance and lunchtime supervision and recommend that the Government should give explicit encouragement to LEAs and governors to provide adequate funding for these activities in its expenditure plans.

CLASS SIZE

6 It is clear that most teachers see smaller classes as an important part of the answer to the problem of disruptive behaviour. This point is made in most of the submissions from the teachers' professional associations and in many letters from individual teachers. The majority of the teachers in our survey identify smaller classes as one of the things that would help them most. We therefore expected to find evidence that smaller classes meant better behaviour and looked very carefully for it.

7 The ratio between the number of pupils and the number of teachers in an LEA (the pupil : teacher ratio or PTR) is often used as a crude indicator of school staffing levels. There are considerable variations in this ratio between LEAs. In January 1987 average primary PTRs in English LEAs ranged from about 17 : 1 to about 24 : 1 and average secondary PTRs from about 12 : 1 to about 17 : 1. The national average PTR fell from just over 18 : 1 in 1983 to just over 17 : 1 in 1987. This must, however interpreted, reflect some improvement in provision. But average PTRs tell us very little about actual class sizes in individual schools, some of which will have ratios outside these ranges. They also tell us nothing about the nature of different schools' catchment areas. Aware of these limitations, we concluded that it would be misguided to look for any general relationship between an LEA's overall PTR and standards of behaviour in its schools.

8   We next decided to look for information about relationships between staffing levels and behaviour at individual school level. We asked our survey team to look at the responses made by teachers in 40 primary and secondary schools serving disadvantaged inner city catchment areas. They could find no significant relationship between the seriousness of the behaviour problems perceived by teachers in these schools and differences between their individual PTRs.

9   We knew that even individual school PTRs are not a very good guide to class sizes. They include heads and other senior staff who may do little or no teaching. In a primary school, the size of different age groups can affect class sizes and the age range within them considerably. Secondary schools with small sixth forms may have larger classes lower down the school than those with larger sixth forms or with none. There may also be marked differences in size between fourth or fifth year groups doing different subject options. We therefore decided that we needed information about the relationship between the size of individual classes and behaviour.

10   Research into the effects of class size seems to have concentrated more on academic achievement than on behaviour, and there does not seem to be any clear consensus among researches on whether smaller classes produce better results in either area. Studies by Glass and his colleagues in the USA in the early 1980s appeared to show that class size was a key factor in raising pupil achievement, but this work has come under some criticism in recent years. In this country Rutter looked for the relationship between class size and behaviour of the third year classes of secondary schools in his sample. Class sizes ranged from 22 to 30. He found no significant association between the size of these classes and the standard of behaviour observed. In his study of junior schools, Mortimore found some association between smaller classes and better behaviour. He found that teachers of smaller classes made more use of praise and neutral comments rather than critical comments about pupils' behaviour. The difference between these findings suggests that there may be a case for smaller classes for younger pupils.

11   The weight of professional opinion which considers that a general reduction in class sizes would be an effective means of improving standards of classroom behaviour is impressive and ought not be ignored. It is clearly the view of the majority of teachers that teaching smaller groups of pupils would reduce stress and make it easier for them to keep order in their classrooms. We could, however, find no consensus on what constitutes the optimum class size for this purpose.

11

12   This is not surprising. The range of other critical factors involved, such as the age and sex of the pupils, the experience and skill of the teacher and the teaching methods used, is very wide.

13   We have already emphasised that, for most of the time, most classes are well behaved and well taught. We do not accept, therefore, that a reduction in the number of pupils in all classes across the board would be an appropriate response, even if it were affordable. Much of the very considerable cost would be applied where it was not needed.

14   We consider that, in schools where discipline problems are acute, there is a case for deploying extra teachers as one medium term measure. This can at present be done by LEAs on a pragmatic basis and we recognise it as an effective strategy in appropriate cases. We regard this as particularly important in primary schools because large classes are more common there, and because it is important to establish habits of good behaviour as early as possible in a pupil's school career. We recognise that there are different ways of deploying extra staff. Behaviour may be improved by reducing class sizes, by introducing skills which are in short supply among the regular staff of the school in question, by reducing teachers' class contact time or by a combination of all these and other measures.

15   It has been pointed out to us that most primary teachers have no non-teaching periods. Demands on teachers have been increased by recent developments like the General Certificate of Secondary Education, and will be further increased by the changes which will be brought about by the Education Reform Act 1988, such as the national assessment system. If implemented, some of our recommendations would have the same effect in some schools. We have no way of assessing the effect of teachers' workloads on their performance as class managers.

16   Throughout this enquiry we have sought only to make recommendations that can be supported either by evidence that was already available or by the results of our own survey. Conclusive evidence of the sort needed to establish a firm relationship between pupil behaviour and class size is not available. The response to our own survey reveals a general belief in the virtue of reducing class sizes but no indication of what the actual size should be in any circumstances. We suspect that there are circumstances where that relationship is important and relevant to the effective deployment of staff resources; but information does not even exist to define accurately what those circumstances are. In this one area only we consider that further research would be justified.

17   Such research would have to be very carefully designed and take full account of existing work in this field. It would not be appropriate for us to suggest a detailed specification. We consider it particularly important for the relationships between pupils' behaviour and the following factors to be investigated:

  17.1   the size and composition of classes,

  17.2   teaching styles,

  17.3   teacher stress, and

  17.4   class contact time and teachers' workloads.

18   **We therefore recommend that the Secretaries of State should commission research to investigate the relationships between school staffing levels, class size and pupils' behaviour.**

EXCLUSIONS

19   Pupils involved in serious or persistent misbehaviour may be excluded from school. They may be excluded for a fixed or an indefinite period. In the past this was called suspension. In the most serious cases they may be permanently excluded. In the past this was called expulsion.

20   Before 1986 there was no clear legal basis for dealing with exclusions. Different LEAs had different procedures. The intention of sections 23 to 27 of the Education (No. 2) Act 1986 was to make exclusion procedures clear and consistent. This part of the Act came into force for most schools from September 1988, but for voluntary aided schools will not do so until September 1989.

21   Four of the seven submissions we received from the heads' and teachers' professional associations commented on exclusion. Three recommended that the 1986 Act should be amended. All four referred to the question of reinstating excluded pupils. Under the 1986 Act only the head has the right to exclude a pupil. If a pupil is excluded for a fixed term or indefinitely, both the school's governing body and the LEA can order that the pupil should be reinstated. If a pupil is excluded permanently from a county or controlled school, the school's governing body and the LEA can direct that the pupil should be reinstated. The governing body alone has the power to direct that a pupil who has been permanently excluded from an aided or special agreement school should be reinstated. Provision is made for appeals against decisions not to reinstate a pupil following a permanent exclusion which has been confirmed by the LEA or governing body. This gives parents the right to

put their child's case to an appeal committee. For county and controlled schools, that committee consists of members nominated by the LEA. They are members of the LEA itself, or its education committee, and other people who are not members of the LEA but have experience of education. Those who are members of the LEA or its education committee may not outnumber the other members by more than one, and a person who is a member of the education committee may be the chairman. Governors can appeal to the same committee against an LEA decision to reinstate a pupil. For aided schools the appeal committee is set up by the governing body.

22   The comments made about these procedures by the heads' and teachers' professional associations were as follows:

22.1   the Professional Association of Teachers and the National Association of Head Teachers recommended that the LEA should have no power to overrule decisions made by the head and governors;

22.2   the National Association of Schoolmasters/Union of Women Teachers (NAS/UWT) recommended that staff in county and controlled schools should be given the right to appeal independently of the head and governing body against LEA decisions to reinstate pupils; and

22.3   the Secondary Heads Association did not recommend any change in the law but advised LEAs to be wary about overruling the decision of heads and governing bodies in cases of permanent exclusion.

23   In chapters four and nine we emphasise the importance of unity of purpose between the heads, teachers and governing bodies of schools. It would therefore be wholly inconsistent for us to support the suggestion made be the NAS/UWT. The right of collective appeal would be unnecessary for the staffs of schools where good relations with the head and governing body exist. In the few schools in which relations have broken down to a point at which a collective appeal might be contemplated, we believe that this would simply make a bad situation worse.

24   The arguments for and against the LEAs powers to order the reinstatement of pupils seem to be more finely balanced. The issue was highlighted by the controversy surrounding the reinstatement of pupils to Poundswick School by Manchester LEA in 1985 which resulted in industrial action by some of the school's staff.

25 The strongest argument for removing the power of LEAs to direct the reinstatement of pupils lies in the damage which may be done to the authority and morale of the head and staff if pupils whom they wish to see permanently excluded are reinstated. We also recognise that reinstatement under these circumstances is unlikely to be successful in most cases, as the events leading to exclusion and the exclusion process itself may have done irreparable damage to relationships between staff and the pupil involved. This breakdown may also have an effect on the behaviour of other pupils. We therefore find it difficult to imagine that reinstatement of a permanently excluded pupil, against the wishes of the headteacher, in the school from which he or she had been excluded could be either justified or successful except under quite exceptional circumstances.

26 The case for leaving the present legal position unchanged can be supported by at least two arguments.

26.1 LEAs need to have reserve powers to enable them to discharge their statutory responsibility for providing education. LEAs have to provide enough school school places to meet the needs of their areas. Governors do not have an equivalent responsibility. The governors of aided schools already have the last word on permanent exclusions, but only about 17% of schools fall into this category.

26.2 There is also real concern arising from our lack of knowledge about the reasons for existing patterns of exclusion. Evidence that we received from a number of LEAs suggests that there are striking variations between the exclusion rates of different schools which cannot be explained by differences in catchment area. This is confirmed by research findings. In their study of exclusions in Sheffield, Galloway and his colleagues (1982) found that six of the 37 secondary schools in the sample accounted for about half of all the exclusions. There is no evidence to suggest that schools with high exclusion rates achieve better standards of behaviour than those with lower rates. In chapter four we argue that the way in which schools are run has a strong influence on pupils' behaviour and that institutional change is the best way of improving standards in less effective schools. Heads can usually persuade governors to back their decisions to exclude pupils. It can be argued that the absence of an external check from the LEA would encourage some schools to export more of their problems, and reduce the head's incentive to review and change the features of the school's organisation which make bad behaviour more likely.

27   In chapter two we comment on the general lack of information about exclusions. One of our difficulties is that we simply do not know how frequently LEAs order the reinstatement of pupils against the wishes of headteachers and governing bodies. Our impression is that it happens rarely, but that could only be confirmed by the serious incidents reporting systems which we recommend in chapter 10. In the absence of any systematic national information, the arguments for and against the present legal position are difficult to evaluate. What is clear, however, is that the procedures established by the 1986 Act have not been tested properly. At the time of writing they have been in force for the great majority of schools for less than six months. Poundswick, and the few similar though less well publicised cases which have been mentioned to us, took place before this legislation came into force. We consider that the most sensible course of action would be to monitor and evaluate the workings of the exclusion procedures established by the 1986 Act for a reasonable period of time before considering any change in the law.

28   The effect of schools opting out of LEA control from September 1989 is another unknown factor in this area. The governing bodies of grant-maintained schools will have the power to exclude pupils without reference to LEAs. If significant numbers of schools opt out in particular areas, the role of LEAs as providers of alternative places for excluded pupils may need to be more systematically reviewed. The future number and distribution of grant-maintained schools is as yet unknown. The pattern will take some years to emerge. We believe that it would be prudent to monitor developments for five years before reviewing their impact on the role of LEAs.

29   The proposed national reporting system for serious incidents and permanent exclusions could be used to monitor the operation on the exclusion procedures established by the 1986 Act. We therefore **recommend:**

29.1   **that the DES and the Welsh Office should systematically monitor for five years the operation of the procedures for the exclusion of pupils from schools established by the Education (No. 2) Act 1986; and**

29.2   **that at the end of this period the Secretaries of State should decide, in the light of all the evidence then available, what amendments, if any, should be made to these provisions. They should act sooner if the accumulating evidence warrants it.**

30   Although we do not recommend any immediate changes to the law, we remain deeply concerned at the possible damage that could be done to a school by the ill-advised insistence on readmission of a permanently

excluded pupil against the wishes of the headteacher and governors. We believe lasting damage would also be done to the relationship between that school and its LEA. We believe that the incidence and nature of such cases will be of the first importance when the Secretaries of State come to review the workings of the 1986 Act in the light of the statistics accumulated in its early years. Section 92 of the Education Act 1944 enables the Secretary of State to require LEAs to furnish him with such reports, returns and information as he may require to exercise his functions under the Education Acts. **We recommend:**

30.1 that the appropriate Secretary of State should **require any LEA which directs the reinstatement of a permanently excluded pupil to a school against the wishes of the headteacher and governing body to supply him with a written report of the circumstances contributing to this decision within 14 days;**

30.2 that the headteacher should **be asked to supply his own account to him within the same period; and**

30.3 that similar procedures should apply in cases where the **governing body directs the reinstatement of a permanently excluded pupil against the wishes of the headteacher.**

The following organisations and individuals submitted written evidence to the Enquiry.

Local education authorities (68)

Avon
Barking and Dagenham
Barnet
Berkshire
Bexley
Birmingham
Bradford
Bromley
Calderdale
Cambridgeshire
Cheshire
Cleveland
Clwyd
Cornwall
Croydon
Cumbria
Derbyshire
Devon
Dudley
Dyfed
East Sussex
Enfield
Essex
Gateshead
Gloucestershire
Gwent
Gwynedd
Hampshire
Havering
Hereford and Worcester
Humberside
Inner London Education Authority
Isle of Wight
Kent
Kingston upon Thames
Kirklees
Lancashire
Leeds
Leicestershire

Lincolnshire
Liverpool
Newcastle upon Tyne
Norfolk
Northamptonshire
Northumberland
North Tyneside
North Yorkshire
Nottinghamshire
Oldham
Oxfordshire
Powys
Redbridge
Richmond upon Thames
Rotherham
Salford
Sandwell
Sefton
Sheffield
Solihull
Somerset
South Tyneside
St Helens
Surrey
Trafford
Wakefield
Warwickshire
West Glamorgan
Wiltshire

Initial teacher training establishments (59)

Bangor Normal College
Bath University
Bedford College of Higher Education
Birmingham Polytechnic
Birmingham University*
Bradford and Ilkley Community College*
Brighton Polytechnic
Bristol Polytechnic
Bristol University*
Brunel University
Bulmershe College of Higher Education, Reading

Cambridge University, Department of Education
Central School of Speech and Drama, London
Charlotte Mason College of Education, Ambleside, Cumbria
Chester College
College of Ripon and York St John, York
College of St Mark and St John Foundation, Plymouth
College of St Paul and St Mary, Cheltenham
Crewe and Alsager College of Higher Education
Durham University
East Anglia University
Edge Hill College of Higher Education, Liverpool
Exeter University
Hatfield Polytechnic
Homerton College, Cambridge
Hull University
King Alfred's College, Winchester
Kingston Polytechnic
Lancaster University
La Sainte Union College of Higher Education, Southampton
Leicester University
Liverpool Institute of Higher Education
London University, Institute of Education
Loughborough University of Technology
Manchester Polytechnic
Middlesex Polytechnic
Nene College, Northampton
Newcastle upon Tyne Polytechnic
Oxford Polytechnic
Oxford University, Department of Educational Studies
Reading University
Roehampton Institute, Whitelands College, London
S. Martin's College, Lancaster
Sheffield City Polytechnic
Sheffield University*
South Glamorgan Institute of Higher Education, Cardiff*
Thames Polytechnic
Trent Polytechnic, Nottingham
Trinity College, Carmarthen
University College, Cardiff*
University College of North Wales
University College of Wales, Aberystwyth
University College of Swansea
Warwick University

West London Institute of Higher Edcuation*
West Midlands College of Higher Education, Walsall
Westminster College, Oxford
West Sussex Institute of Higher Education, Bognor Regis
Worcester College of Higher Education

* submissions from individual members of staff which do not necessarily represent the views of the establishment as a whole.

Other national and regional organisations (88)

Advisory Centre for Education
Arts Education Forum
Assistant Masters and Mistresses Association
Association for Behavioural Approaches with Children
Association of Chief Education Social Workers
Association of Chief Officers of Probation
Association of County Councils
Association of Educational Psychologists
Association of Metropolitan Authorities
Association of Workers for Maladjusted Children
Barnardo's
British Association for Ideal Education
British Association of Counselling
British Association of Social Workers
British Housewives' League
British Psychological Society
Campaign for the Advancement of State Education (Camden
    Branch)
Caribbean Teachers Association
'Catch 'Em Young' Project Trust
Catholic Education Council
Centre for the Study of Comprehensive Schools
Central Council of Probation Committees
Children's Legal Centre
Children's Society
Church of England Board of Education
Commission for Racial Equality
Community Education Development Centre
Conservative Western Area Local Government Committee
Department of Education and Science
Department of Education for Northern Ireland
Department of Health
Department of Employment
Educational Institute of Scotland

Education Management Information Exchange
Education Policy Information Centre
Focus in Education
Forum for the Advancement of Educational Therapy
General Synod of the Church of England, Board of Education
Girls' Schools Association
Grubb Institute
Headmasters' Conference
Health and Safety Executive (Education Service Advisory
    Committee)
Hereford Diocesan Council of Education
Her Majesty's Inspectorate of Schools
Home Office
Incorporated Association of Preparatory Schools
Initiative to Promote a General Teaching Council
Inter-Diocesan Schools Commission
Llandaff Diocesan Council for Education
Lord Chancellor's Department
Manpower Services Commission (now Department of
    Employment – Training Agency)
Methodist Church, Division of Education and Youth
Monday Club Law and Order Committee
'Muppet Club' Project
Muslim Educational Trust
National Association for Gifted Children
National Association for Pastoral Care in Education
National Association for the Care and Resettlement of
    Offenders
National Association of Governors and Managers
National Association of Head Teachers
National Association of Social Workers in Education
National Association of School Masters/Union of Women
    Teachers
National Children's Bureau
National Confederation of Parent-Teacher Associations
National Council for One Parent Families
National Foundation for Educational Research in England
    and Wales
National Union of Teachers
National Viewers' and Listeners' Association
National Youth Bureau
Professional Association of Teachers
Professional Development Foundation
Programme for Reform in Secondary Education
Project Fullemploy

Scottish Education Department
Secondary Heads Association
Sikh Education Council, UK (Leicestershire)
Socialist Educational Association
Society of Education Officers
Society of Teachers Opposed to Physical Punishment
Special Educational Needs – National Advisory Council
Sports Council
Tavistock Institute of Human Relations
Training, Consultancy, Resources, in Health, Personal and
    Social, and Drug Education
Undeb Cenedlaethol Athrawon Cymru
Welsh Counties Committee
Welsh Joint Education Committee
Welsh Office
Youthscan

Other organisations and individuals

A further 394 submissions were received from other organisations and individuals. These included a number of schools and parent-teacher associations; medical and academic bodies and researchers.

The following individuals met the Committee and, in their role as witnesses, gave oral evidence and answered members' questions:

Representatives of headteachers' and teachers' professional associations

Miss J Baird Mr D Clout Mrs M Gotheridge Mr R Rainey	Assistant Masters and Mistresses Association
Mr J C Wootton Mr D Burbidge Mr D Baldwin Mr D Best	National Association of Head Teachers
Mr N de Gruchy Mr D Battye Mr J Rowland Mrs O Gunn	National Association of School Masters/ Union of Women Teachers
Mr A Evans Mrs J Fisher Dr A Leach Mr J Williams	National Union of Teachers
Mr P Dawson Miss J Miller Mr N Henderson Mrs C Hicks	Professional Association of Teachers
Mr J Sutton Mr B Stevens Mr C Lowe	Secondary Heads Association
Mr G Wyn-Jones Mr W Williams Mr I Morgan Mr G Hughes Mr H Thomas	Undeb Cenedlaethol Athrawon Cymru

Representatives of other organisations

Mr S McMahon Mr D Bowes Mr A Hazell Mr R Grant	Association of Chief Education Social Workers

Mr G German Mr P Oteng	Commission for Racial Equality
Mr K Ashken Mr G Martin	Crown Prosecution Service
Mr J Coleman Mr C Saville Mr J Gardner Mr R Jain	Department of Education and Science
Mr A Marshall Mr D Jones Mr J Singh Mr J Learmonth	Her Majesty's Inspectorate of Schools
Mr J Graham Mr G Sutton	Home Office
Ms S Finn	Lord Chancellor's Department
Mrs M Bennathan Dr R Davey Dr T Charlton	National Children's Bureau

Other expert witnesses

Dr K Wheldall Dr F Merrett	Birmingham University
Mr W Rogers	Department of Education, Melbourne, Victoria, Australia
Mr J McGuiness	Durham University
Professor P Mortimore Dr D Galloway	Lancaster University
Mrs H Russell	Liverpool University
Mr D Hutchinson	National Foundation for Educational Research in England and Wales
Mr Y Yasuhara	National Institute for Education Research, Tokyo, Japan
Professor J Rudduck Professor J Gray Dr D Gillborn Dr J Nixon Mr N Sime	Sheffield University
Mr D Kearney	Somerset LEA (co-author of **Preventive Approaches to Disruption**)

During the course of the Enquiry, groups of Committee members visited the following 25 institutions:

Birmingham University, Department of Education
Brentfield Primary School, Brent
Bristol Polytechnic, Department of Education
Dillwyn Llewelyn Comprehensive Community School, Swansea
Edgar Stammers Junior School, Walsall
Filwood Park Junior School, Bristol
Glyncorrwg Primary School, West Glamorgan
Hainault High School, Redbridge
Hartridge School, Newport
Holyhead School, Birmingham
Loxford High School, Redbridge
Lowton High School, Wigan
Oxclose School, Sunderland
Philips High School, Bury
Spurley Hey High School, Manchester
St George School, Bristol
Sedgemoor Centre, Bridgewater
Seaton Burn High School, North Tyneside
Stephenson Memorial Middle School, North Tyneside
Speke Community Comprehensive School, Liverpool
Trelai County Primary School, Cardiff
The Mead (Stage 5) Centre, Bristol
Tirmorfa County Primary School, Port Talbot
Urban Studies Centre, Poplar, London
Wideopen Middle School, North Tyneside

The following 10 institutions also contributed to the Enquiry:

Chaucer Comprehensive School, Sheffield
Fairfax Community School, Bradford
Homelands School, Derby
John Ellis Community College, Leicester
Kersal High School, Salford
Park View School, Birmingham
Play Comprehensive School, Nottingham
Primrose Hill School, Leeds
Sidney Stringer School and Community College, Coventry
Thrybergh Comprehensive School, Rotherham

Committee members also visited the following 20 institutions abroad:

The Netherlands

Ministry of Education and Science, Zoetermeer
Project Bureau OVB, Rotterdam
Education Priority Field 9, Hoogvliet (centre for co-ordinating the
    region's education priority policy)
Anne Frank MAVO School, The Hague
De Starrenburg School SG, Rotterdam
J W Willemsen/Prinses Irene School, Amsterdam

Norway

Ministry of Church and Education, Oslo
Oslo City Education Authority
Fjell Primary School, Drammen
Hersleb Junior Secondary School, Oslo
Sagene Primary School, Oslo

USA

Carnegie Foundation for the Advancement of Teaching, Princeton
US Department of Education – Centre for International Education,
    Office of Elementary and Secondary Education and Office of
    Educational Research and Improvement, Washington
Council of Chief State School Officers, Washington
United States Information Agency, Washington
National Association of Secondary School Principals, Washington
Capitol Hill Cluster Schools – Peabody Elementary School, Watkins
    Elementary School and Stuart/Hobson Middle School, Washington
City-As-School, New York
Middle College High School, New York
The Door – A Center of Alternatives for Youth, New York

Committee members also met teachers involved in the US/UK
exchange visit programme, at a conference at the Central Bureau for
Educational Visits and Exchanges in London.

TEACHERS AND DISCIPLINE

*A Report
for the Committee of Enquiry
into Discipline in Schools*

*Members of the
Educational Research Centre
at Sheffield University*

November 1988

*Gillian Squirrell was also involved in the planning and interviewing for this part of the research.

The research brief we were given by the Committee of Enquiry into Discipline in Schools was 'to examine teachers' perceptions and concerns about discipline'. We chose to pursue this in two related ways.

One was to undertake a national survey of primary and secondary teachers in England and Wales in order to obtain a general picture of their experiences and views. What kinds of behaviour did they have to deal with during the course of a week in the classroom? What sorts of problems did they encounter during the course of their duties round the school? How serious did they think discipline problems were in their school? Were any particular classes, pupils or pupil behaviours particularly difficult to deal with? What strategies and sanctions were they currently employing to tackle discipline problems? And, finally, what action would teachers themselves suggest should be taken?

At the same time we wanted to go beyond the kinds of information we could obtain in a national survey. We decided to interview one hundred teachers about their experiences and perceptions in order to establish a better understanding of what having to deal routinely with discipline problems was like. Given limited time and resources, we could only visit a small number of schools. We therefore concentrated our interviews in ten inner-city comprehensive schools. We chose inner-city comprehensives because we believed they would give us important insights into experiences and practices in schools where, traditionally at least, both teachers and the public might expect there to be greater problems. If we had had more time we would have liked to extend this part of the research to other types of school and, crucially, to the primary sector as well.

Research is a cumulative process and we have learnt much from previous studies; most of them are summarised in a review of the literature undertaken recently by Mr John Graham. There are two other major contributions which we should also like to acknowledge. First, the various studies conducted over the past year into these issues by the professional associations. And second, the work of Dr Kevin Wheldall, Dr Frank Merrett and their colleagues at the Centre for Child Study, Birmingham University, whose earlier research in this field contributed in several ways to the practical tasks of constructing questionnaires for the national survey.

The heads and teachers in the schools we contacted for the national survey deserve especial mention. We knew, when we agreed to contact them on the Committee's behalf, that many teachers would be interested in co-operating but also that we were approaching them during a particularly busy period. In the event over three and a half thousand primary and secondary teachers responded producing, in the process, one of the highest response rates for a national survey of this kind ever achieved.

Finally, we are in debt to the one hundred teachers and their heads who agreed to be interviewed. Our promise to maintain confidentiality prevents us from naming them. They gave generously of their time, welcomed us into their schools and talked openly about their experiences and concerns. They clearly recognised the importance of the Enquiry and we are grateful to them for their ready co-operation.

John Gray and **Jean Rudduck**

Sheffield, December 1988

PART I

**Findings from the
National Survey of Teachers
in England and Wales**
(John Gray and Nicholas Sime)

The national survey of discipline in schools was designed to answer five questions:

(1)   What were primary and secondary teachers' routine experiences of discipline, both in the classroom setting and around the school?

(2)   How serious did they think the problems of discipline were in their school?

(3)   What particular pupil behaviours did they find difficult to deal with?

(4)   How were they trying to deal with difficult pupils and difficult classes?

(5)   What action did they think might best be taken to help with the problems of discipline in their schools?

A.   THE SURVEY

A questionnaire was sent to teachers in primary, middle and secondary schools during the first week of October 1988. It covered a wide range of topics and took between 20-30 minutes to complete.

The sample was drawn up with the aid of DES statisticians. A stratified random sample of schools was selected to be statistically representative of the regions and different types of school in England and Wales (for fuller details see Technical Appendix A). Headteachers were then approached for permission to contact members of their staff. Teachers' names were selected at random from staff lists provided by the schools. The teachers were then approached individually by means of a postal questionnaire.

A total of just under 4400 teachers in main grade and promoted posts were sent questionnaires; no fewer than 82% returned them. Just under 3200 questionnaires were sent to teachers in secondary schools (or middle schools deemed secondary) whilst just over 1200 questionnaires were sent to teachers in primary schools (or middle schools deemed primary). 79% of the secondary teachers who were believed to have received questionnaires returned them as did 89% of the primary teachers. About seven per cent of all the replies were returned by teachers who had exercised their option to reply anonymously. With one or two exceptions response rates by region and school type were high. These high response rates contribute to our belief that the survey's findings are likely to be generally representative of the overall sample of teachers originally contacted and, more generally, of the population of teachers in England and Wales (for fuller details see Technical Appendix A).

For the purposes of explication we have decided to report on the primary and secondary school samples separately. We shall commence with the secondary school sample and then turn, at a later point, to the question of whether the experiences of the primary teachers' sample were similar or different.

B. SECONDARY TEACHERS' ROUTINE EXPERIENCES OF DISCIPLINE

Most of our secondary sample spent most of their time teaching in the classroom. It seems appropriate, therefore, to begin our analysis with a brief account of what discipline problems teachers reported having to deal with on a regular basis. To make their reports more specific, however, we asked teachers to confine themselves to those classroom experiences which had occurred during the previous week; for a period as recent as this there was little chance of memories being faulty. Given the timing of the questionnaire, these would mostly have covered a period in the first half of October 1988. We also asked them, after they had reported their particular experiences, to reflect on 'how typical . . . the pattern of occurrences they had (just) described was of their general classroom experiences'. 94% thought it was 'typical' or 'fairly typical'. We can be fairly confident, therefore, that the types of pupil behaviour reported were seen by teachers as being generally representative of their routine classroom experiences.

B.1 Discipline inside the classroom

The fourteen types of pupil behaviour listed in Table 1 are not intended to be exhaustive of all the possible categories of pupil behaviour teachers in secondary schools might have encountered during the course of the survey week. What they offer are some general indications of the reported incidence of behaviours, ranging from the fairly mundane to the more serious, against which subsequently to assess their concerns.

A note of caution must, we believe, be sounded here in interpreting the data emerging from Table 1. Whilst any examples of pupil misbehaviour or indiscipline are to be deprecated and are potentially undesirable, it would be inappropriate to interpret each and every one of these as offering cause for concern. Indeed, there are strong indications later in this analysis that most teachers are quite accustomed to dealing with certain kinds of pupil misbehaviour and treat them as routine. In interpreting the evidence in Table 1, therefore, we use it in two ways: first, to establish the common patterns and experiences teachers shared; and second, to establish those specific areas of experience which departed from this general picture.

Table 1: Percentages of secondary teachers reporting that they had to deal with different types of pupil behaviour during the course of their classroom teaching the previous week

Type of pupil behaviour (listed by frequency of occurrence)	Reported frequency with which dealt with during lessons:	
	At least once during week (%)	At least daily (%)
Talking out of turn (eg by making remarks, calling out, distracting others by chattering)	97	53
Calculated idleness or work avoidance (eg delaying start to work set, not having essential books or equipment)	87	25
Hindering other pupils (eg by distracting them from work, interfering with equipment or materials)	86	26
Not being punctual (eg being late to school or lessons)	82	17
Making unnecessary (non-verbal) noise (eg by scraping chairs, banging objects, moving clumsily)	77	25
Persistently infringing class (or school) rules (eg on dress, pupil behaviour)	68	17
Getting out of seat without permission	62	14
Verbal abuse towards other pupils (eg offensive or insulting remarks)	62	10
General rowdiness, horseplay or mucking about	61	10
Cheeky or impertinent remarks or responses	58	10
Physical aggression towards other pupils (eg by pushing, punching, striking)	42	6
Verbal abuse towards you (eg offensive, insulting, insolent or threatening remarks)	15	1
Physical destructiveness (eg breaking objects, damaging furniture and fabric)	14	1
Physical aggression towards you (the teacher)	1.7	0

Note: 16% of teachers wrote in about some 'other pupil behaviour'. Of these 23% reported that it occurred at least daily and 57% reported that it had occurred at least once during the week. The percentages are based on total numbers of responses of around 2500. Respondents who missed out particular questions averaged around 1% in every case.

Four pupil behaviours would appear to have been common experiences for the vast majority of secondary teachers. In each case they were reported as occurring by 80% or more of those in the sample. At some point during the week, then, most teachers said they had had to deal with instances of pupils 'talking out of turn', 'hindering other pupils', engaging in 'calculated idleness or work avoidance' and 'not being punctual'.

A majority of teachers (around 60% or more in each case) also reported that they had had to deal with pupils 'making unnecessary noise', 'persistently infringing class rules', 'getting out of (their) seats without permission', directing 'verbal abuse towards other pupils', 'general rowdiness, horseplay or mucking about' and 'cheeky or impertinent remarks or responses'. 'Physical aggression towards other pupils' was also mentioned quite frequently (by 42%).

In brief, at some point during the course of their week's classroom teaching, the vast majority of teachers reported having to deal with examples of pupil behaviours that had impeded the flow of their lessons. Furthermore, at some point during the week a majority had had to deal with behaviours which had actually disrupted their lessons or produced an atmosphere which was not conducive to learning. These seem to have been common shared experiences amongst secondary school teachers and they provide the backdrop against which we now assess some teachers' daily experiences.

'Talking out of turn' was the only pupil behaviour a majority of teachers reported having to deal with on a daily basis (see Table 1). About one in four teachers mentioned 'calculated idleness or work avoidance', 'hindering other pupils' and 'making unnecessary (non-verbal) noise' whilst somewhat lower percentages than this mentioned 'not being punctual', 'persistently infringing class rules' and 'getting out of seat without permission'. Around one in ten mentioned 'verbal abuse towards other pupils', 'general rowdiness, horseplay or mucking about' and 'cheeky or impertinent remarks or responses'. About one in twenty reported dealing with 'physical aggression towards other pupils' on at least a daily basis.

Clearly, all these behaviours, to a greater or lesser extent, disrupted classroom teaching and were likely to have been experienced as, at best, irritating and, at worst, wearing by the teachers concerned. Depending on which specific items were included, between one out of ten and two out of ten secondary teachers, therefore, reported experiencing disruptive behaviours on a daily basis.

To this point we have not considered teachers' responses to three items that were designed to pick up considerably more serious examples of pupil indiscipline. It is clear from the drop in the overall percentages reporting these three items that, compared with the remainder, they were experienced differently. During the course of the week about one in seven (15%) teachers reported being the target of 'verbal abuse' from a pupil(s); and about one in eight (14%) dealt with instances of 'physical destructiveness'. However, fewer than two per cent (1.7%) of teachers reported that they themselves had actually been the target of some 'physical aggression' that week (for a fuller discussion see Section B.4 below).

The overall picture of classroom life suggested by Table 1 is one in which 'talking out of turn' is the only area of pupil misbehaviour that was reported as a common daily occurrence for the majority of teachers. However, there were a variety of 'minor' disruptive behaviours which up to two out of ten teachers found themselves dealing with on a daily basis whilst four out of ten teachers had had to deal with 'physical aggression' between pupils at some point during the week. One in seven teachers had been 'verbally abused' during this period but only one in fifty reported having been the target of some form of 'physical aggression' (see Footnote 1).

B.2   Discipline around the school

Teachers' experiences of pupil indiscipline were not, of course, confined to the classroom. We asked a series of questions designed to establish their common experiences during the course of their duties around their schools (see Table 2). Almost all (98%) thought the experiences they reported during the week of the survey were 'typical' or 'fairly typical'.

A number of pupil behaviours emerged as ones that were encountered by the vast majority (80% or more) of secondary teachers at least once during the week (see Table 2). These included: showing a 'lack of concern for others', 'unruliness while waiting', 'running in the corridors', 'general rowdiness, horseplay or mucking about' and 'persistently infringing school rules'. Between two out of ten and three out of ten teachers reported encountering these behaviours on a daily basis (see Table 2).

Common encounters (reported by 60% or more) included experiencing at least once during the week: 'verbal abuse towards other pupils', 'loitering in 'prohibited' areas', 'cheeky or impertinent remarks or responses' and 'physical aggression towards other pupils'. Between one out of ten and two out of ten teachers encountered these behaviours on a daily basis.

Of the three more serious behaviours, one in four (26%) teachers reported examples of 'physical destructiveness' and one in eight (12%) reported being the target of 'verbal abuse' at some point during the week. However, only about one per cent (1.1%) reported some form of 'physical aggression towards themselves' (for a fuller discussion see Section B.4 below).

226

Table 2: **Percentages of secondary teachers reporting different types of pupil behaviours they encountered during the course of their duties round the school**

Type of pupil behaviour (listed by frequency of occurrence)	Reported frequency with which encountered round the school:	
	At least once during week (%)	At least daily (%)
Lack of concern for others	93	31
Unruliness while waiting (eg to enter classrooms, for lunch)	90	29
Running in the corridors	89	34
General rowdiness, horseplay or mucking about	85	21
Persistently infringing school rules (eg on dress, pupil behaviour)	85	28
Verbal abuse towards other pupils (eg offensive or insulting remarks)	76	19
Loitering in 'prohibited' areas	71	17
Cheeky or impertinent remarks or responses	67	12
Physical aggression towards other pupils (eg by pushing, punching, striking)	66	11
Leaving school premises without permission	44	7
Physical destructiveness (eg breaking objects, damaging furniture and fabric)	26	2
Verbal abuse towards you (eg offensive, insulting, insolent or threatening remarks)	12	0.5
Physical aggression towards you (the teacher)	1.1	0

Note: 14% of teachers wrote in about some 'other pupil behaviour'. Of these 25% reported that it had occurred at least daily and 45% at least once during the week. The percentages are based on total numbers of responses of around 2500. Respondents who missed out particular questions averaged around 1% in every case.

In some respects the picture of life around the school parallels that within the classroom. There were a large number of relatively 'minor' problems which formed part of the experiences of the vast majority of teachers at some point during the week. Depending on the particular behaviour concerned around two out of ten teachers experienced these at least daily. The incidence of direct 'physical aggression' towards teachers was extremely rare but about one in eight teachers received 'verbal abuse' at some point during the week. Again, as with the classroom data, extrapolating these figures over longer time periods would be inappropriate (see Footnote 1).

B.3 The relationships between different pupil behaviours

We were interested in whether teachers who reported dealing with or encountering one type of pupil behaviour more frequently reported experiencing others more frequently as well. As a general rule we found that they did. For example, in relation to the behaviours listed in Table 1, teachers who reported more 'talking out of turn' also reported more of the other behaviours such as 'hindering other pupils', 'calculated idleness or work avoidance' and 'general rowdiness'. They were also somewhat more likely to report higher levels of 'verbal abuse' towards themselves.

There was one exception to this general clustering of behaviours occurring in the classroom. Teachers who reported being the target of 'physical aggression' were, on the whole, no more likely to report experiencing higher levels of most of the other pupil behaviours with two exceptions: they were somewhat more likely to report 'physical destructiveness' and 'verbal abuse towards themselves'.

Similar patterns prevailed with respect to the behaviours listed in Table 2. On the whole, teachers who reported, for example, more 'general rowdiness, horesplay or mucking about' in the course of their duties around the school also reported encountering more of the other behaviours.

When we compared teachers' reports of pupil behaviours in the classroom (listed in Table 1) with their reports of behaviours around the school (listed in Table 2) we found similar patterns prevailing (tables not shown). Teachers who reported higher incidences of undesirable pupil behaviours in one setting were more likely to report higher incidences of pupil behaviours in the other. This was especially true of the examples of pupil behaviours that were common to the two lists (in Tables 1 and 2). For example, teachers who reported more 'cheeky or impertinent responses' in the classroom were considerably more likely to report higher levels of this same behaviour around the school; and teachers who reported more 'physical aggression towards other pupils' in their classroom were likely to encounter more 'physical aggression' amongst pupils around the school.

Eight pupil behaviours were common to the lists in Tables 1 and 2. For six of these, teachers were likely to report considerably higher levels outside the classroom compared with inside it (table not shown but for details see Tables 1 and 2). These were: 'persistently infringing class (or school) rules', 'general rowdiness', 'verbal abuse towards other pupils', 'cheeky or impertinent remarks', 'physical aggression towards other

228

pupils' and 'physical destructiveness'. Only in relation to 'verbal abuse' and 'physical aggression' towards themselves were there no substantial differences.

The evidence suggests that teachers' experiences of disruptive pupil behaviours inside the classroom and around the school went hand in hand. Teachers who reported more disruptions in their classrooms were also likely to report more disruptions around their schools.

B.4   The incidence of physical aggression by pupils towards teachers

That any teachers in the survey should have reported being in receipt of some form of 'physical aggression', either in the classroom or around the school, is clearly a matter of concern. We therefore looked in greater detail at the questionnaires of all those teachers reporting any experience of 'physical aggression'.

Just under two per cent (1.7%) of teachers reported experience of 'physical aggression' directed towards them in the course of their lessons at some point during the survey week. Almost all reported that their experiences during the previous week had been 'typical' or 'fairly typical'. Most chose not to elaborate further on these experiences elsewhere in their questionnaires. We interpreted their responses as implying that they were in receipt of some form of physical contact that was 'aggressive' in intent; they did not necessarily mean by this that the experience was a 'violent' one as the fuller discussion that was possible during the interview-based part of the research makes clear (see Part II, Section B.2).

A handful of teachers (making up about one in ten of all those teachers who reported any 'physical aggression' and less than 0.2% of the total secondary school sample) reported that their experiences during the week had 'not been typical'. Of these, two referred directly to being struck.

Just over one per cent (1.1%) of teachers reported some form of 'physical aggression' towards them in the course of their duties around the school. All of these teachers reported that their experiences were 'typical' or 'fairly typical'. Again, we inferred, from the general patterns of their responses, that they were referring to physical contact with pupils rather than violence; and, again, there is further support for this view in the interview-based part of the research (see Part II, Section B.2).

Overall, just over two per cent (2.1%) of teachers reported some form of 'physical aggression' towards themselves, either in the classroom and/or around the school.

A small number of teachers (again making up less than 0.2% of the total) used the open-ended part of the questionnaire to describe incidents in the fairly recent past during which they had been subjected to very serious threats or violence. One of the incidents so described had originated inside the classroom, the others outside it. These teachers' descriptions left no room for doubt about the seriousness of the particular incidents being described.

Neither the evidence on the 'atypicality' of teachers' experiences nor the open-ended reports are conclusive as regards the full extent of physical violence directed towards teachers in the classroom or around the school. Teachers who reported no examples of 'physical aggression' being directed towards them during the week of the survey could, of course, have experienced it during other weeks of the school year. Furthermore, although very large numbers of teachers took the opportunity to comment on their experiences in an open-ended way, by no means all will have chosen (or seen fit) to use the space provided to recount their previous experiences of 'violent' incidents. However, the data we have collected do offer some estimates of the probable limits.

Somewhere in the region of two per cent of teachers reported experiencing some form of 'physical aggression' towards them during the week of the survey (see Footnote 2). However, it should be recognised that this is an estimate based on a particular time-period of one week and that extrapolation to longer time-periods would be inappropriate because the vast majority of teachers reported that their experiences during the week were 'typical' or 'fairly typical'.

Our detailed analysis of all those questionnaires reporting 'physical aggression' of some form suggested that the proportion of teachers referring to incidents of a clearly violent nature was considerably lower than the above figures. Our best estimate is that about one in two hundred (0.5%) teachers had had experiences of this kind. Again extrapolation to longer time-periods would be inappropriate (see Footnote 3).

C. SECONDARY TEACHERS' VIEWS ON THE 'SERIOUSNESS' OF DISCIPLINE PROBLEMS

We have confined ourselves up to this point to teachers' factual reports of the discipline problems they were encountering. But how 'serious' did secondary teachers believe the problems of discipline were in their schools?

About one in six (16%) teachers thought they were 'serious' (see Table 3). A majority (53%) thought they were 'not very serious'. One in four (26%) thought they were 'not at all serious' but only one in twenty (4%) was prepared to say they were 'no problem at all'.

Table 3: **Secondary teachers' perceptions of the 'seriousness' of discipline problems in their school**

Reported 'seriousness' of problem of discipline	% of teachers
'Very serious'	1
'Serious'	15
'Not very serious'	53
'Not at all serious'	26
'No problem at all'	4
Total	99

Note: The question asked was as follows: 'Discipline problems vary from school to school in their seriousness. Looking at your own school as a whole, how serious is the problem of discipline in your opinion?'

In general, teachers' perceptions of the 'seriousness' of the problems in their schools were associated with the patterns discussed earlier in Tables 1 and 2. Teachers who reported that the problems were 'serious' in their school were somewhat more likely to report higher incidences of 'talking out of turn', 'cheeky or impertinent remarks' 'verbal abuse towards other pupils', 'unruliness while waiting' and so on (tables not shown).

C.1   Differences between schools

We were particularly interested in the question of how much teachers in one school differed from teachers in others in terms of their perceptions of the 'seriousness' of the position. We therefore aggregated the responses of the individual teachers in each school to create an overall 'seriousness' score for each of the schools in our study, where a score of 1 meant that the individual teachers thought the problem was 'very serious' and a score of 5 meant they thought it was 'no problem at all' (see Table 4). A score of around 2.0 meant that, on average, the teachers from a particular school thought the problems in their school were 'serious' whilst a score of around 4.0 meant that, on the whole, they thought they were 'not at all serious'.

231

From Table 4 it can be seen that only in a very small number of schools were matters as extreme as this. Teachers in fewer than one in ten (8%) schools thought the problem was verging on the 'serious' (average scores of 2.5 or lower) whilst teachers in about two out of ten (21%) schools thought that matters were 'not at all serious' or, indeed, 'no problem at all' (average scores of 3.5 or higher). The average scores of the staff in more than half the schools clustered round the view that the problems were 'not very serious'.

Table 4: **Secondary teachers' perceptions of the 'seriousness' of discipline problems in their school aggregated to the school level to show variations between schools**

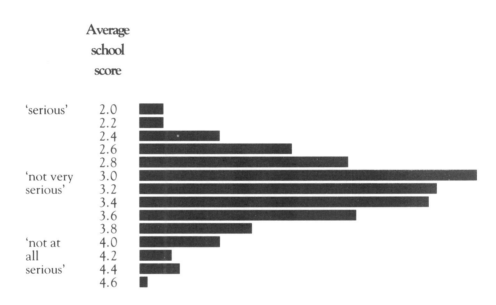

Total number of responses = teachers in 255 secondary schools

What Table 4, by itself, does not tell us is the extent to which teachers in any particular school agreed amongst themselves about the 'seriousness' of the problem. To answer this question we used a statistical technique (known as analysis of variance) which allows one to make an estimate of how much of the overall differences in responses is made up: (a) of differences in the replies of teachers in one school as opposed to another (the 'between-schools' variance); and (b) of differences in the replies of teachers within any one school (the 'within-schools' variance).

This analysis indicated that just under 40% of the variance lay between schools whilst the remaining 60% lay within schools (see Footnote 4). In short, although there were some differences of perception between teachers in any one school, there was quite a strong tendency for teachers in some schools to maintain that they had discipline problems and for teachers in others to maintain that they did not.

We explored a number of factors relating to the circumstances of teachers in different types of school with a view to seeing whether any of them systematically related to teachers' perceptions of the 'seriousness' of their own school's discipline problems.

Some relationships between the circumstances of particular schools and teachers' perceptions did emerge. For example, teachers were more likely to report that discipline problems were 'serious' in their school when they had also reported that they had higher proportions of pupils of 'below average ability' 'compared with the national picture' or higher proportions coming from 'economically disadvantaged areas' (table not shown). They were a little more likely to report problems if they had more pupils from the 'inner areas of large towns or cities', more pupils from 'ethnic minority' groups or more boys. And they were also a little more likely to report problems if their school had made greater use of corporal punishment around the time when it was formally abolished (table not shown). Since all these relationships were based on teachers' reports of the situation in their school, rather than independently-collected evidence, they need to be treated with some caution. Teachers may not always be in the best position to know the particular circumstances of their own school or pupils relative to others. It would also be unwise to single out any one of these factors as being necessarily more important than the others. All point to the view, however, that schools serving areas of social disadvantage (however measured) were more likely to be seen by their staffs as having 'serious' problems. The size of the school (as measured by the numbers of pupils on roll or the numbers of teaching staff) did not appear to matter (table not shown).

We considered, in addition, a limited number of aspects of the career backgrounds and circumstances of individual teachers in relation to their perceptions of the 'seriousness' of discipline problems in their schools. The teachers' sex, age, years of teaching experience and years of experience in their present school, as well as the number of schools they had taught in, did not appear to make any difference to their views, except that those with little or no experience of teaching were slightly more likely to report that the problems were 'serious' (table not shown). There was some small indication that teachers who had gained most of their experience with the 11-14 age-range felt the problems were slightly worse than other teachers whilst those who had gained most of their experience in 11-18 schools felt they were slightly better (table not shown). Teachers who spent more of their 'contracted time' on classroom teaching were also slightly more likely to report 'serious' problems as were those on the 'main professional' grades as opposed to the higher ones (table not shown). However, none of the factors we have discussed regarding teachers' background characteristics were sufficiently strongly related to their perceptions of the 'seriousness' of discipline problems in their school to merit much further comment.

About one in six secondary teachers thought there was a 'serious' problem of discipline in their schools. Statistical analysis of the distribution of responses indicated that there were likely to be a few members of the teaching staff in a majority of secondary schools who believed the problems were 'serious'. The more notable finding, however, was the extent to which there were differences between schools. Teachers in some schools differed in their perceptions of the 'seriousness' of the problems from teachers in others. Teachers in about one in ten secondary schools thought (collectively) that the problems in their school verged towards the 'serious'.

Most of the information collected on the backgrounds and circumstances of schools and teachers did not appear to be systematically related to their perceptions about the 'seriousness' of the problems. However, teachers who reported that they taught in schools with higher proportions of children from 'economically disadvantaged areas' or with 'below average' attainment levels tended to perceive the problems as more 'serious' than those teaching in other sorts of schools.

D. THE CLASSES AND PUPIL BEHAVIOURS SECONDARY TEACHERS FOUND DIFFICULT

In this section we consider the particular pupil behaviours teachers found difficult to deal with, either in the classroom, around the school or with respect to the teaching of difficult classes or pupils. But first we offer some perspective on the proportions of teachers who reported that some aspect (or aspects) of their work was 'difficult'.

D.1 The incidence of difficult classes and pupils

Just over one in three (37%) teachers reported that they found one or more pupil behaviours they had experienced in their classroom 'difficult to deal with' whilst three out of ten (30%) reported finding something difficult to deal with during the course of their duties around the school (see Table 5a). One in five (20%) teachers reported finding something 'difficult' in both settings whilst rather lower proportions than these found something 'difficult to deal with' in one setting but not in the other.

Table 5: Percentages of secondary teachers who reported finding certain pupil behaviours difficult to deal with

(a) | Teachers finding one or more pupil behaviours difficult to deal with: | Yes (%) | No (%) | Total (%) |
|---|---|---|---|
| in the classroom | 37 | 63 | 100 |
| around the school | 30 | 70 | 100 |
| in the classroom **and** around the school | 20 | 80 | 100 |
| in the classroom but **not** around the school | 16 | 84 | 100 |
| around the school but **not** in the classroom | 9 | 91 | 100 |

(b) | Number of their classes teachers reported finding difficult to deal with: | % of all teachers |
|---|---|
| more than one or two classes | 7 |
| one or two | 52 |
| none | 40 |
| Total | 99 |

(c) | Number of individual pupils teachers found difficult to deal with: | in the classroom (%) | around the school (%) |
|---|---|---|
| quite a lot | 1 | 3 |
| several | 17 | 20 |
| one or two | 60 | 48 |
| none | 22 | 30 |
| Total | 100 | 101 |

Six out of ten (59%) teachers reported finding one or more of the classes they taught difficult to deal with (see Table 5b). Not altogether surprisingly, the classes teachers described as 'difficult' tended to contain pupils from the older age-bands (23% were 14+ and 40% were 15+ or over) and they were likely to have more boys in them than girls. More than half of these classes (56%) were grouped by ability in some way (by sets, streams or bands) and three out of four (74%) of these ability groups were of 'below average attainment level compared with other pupils in the school' (tables not shown).

Eight out of ten (78%) teachers reported finding one or more individual pupils 'difficult to deal with' in the classroom. Again, these pupils tended to be from the older age-bands (23% were aged 14+, 45% were aged 15+ or over) and three out of four were boys (tables not shown). Over half were 'below average' in ability 'compared with other pupils in the school' and only one in ten was of 'above average' ability. Contrary to some prevalent stereotypes, teachers reported that difficult pupils were no more or less likely to come from 'ethnic minority' backgrounds than others. Just under one in four were receiving 'special provision or support' whilst, in addition, just over one in twenty were 'being considered' for it (table not shown).

In short, whether they were reporting on difficult classes or difficult pupils, teachers found male pupils of lower ability more difficult to deal with than others. Most teachers had at least one or two pupils they were prepared to say they found difficult to deal with whilst a majority had at least one class which they found difficult.

D.2   The nature of the pupil behaviours teachers found difficult

After we had requested teachers to report on the frequency with which they had had to deal with various pupil behaviours during the course of their week's classroom teaching (see Table 1), we asked them which of the pupil behaviours they had actually experienced they found 'most difficult' to deal with. They were offered the opportunity to list one or two specific behaviours. It should be remembered, as we have already reported, that just over one in three (37%) mentioned something whilst about two out of three (63%) did not (see Table 5a).

In terms of the sheer frequency with which they were reported, three items stood out from the rest. These were: 'talking out of turn'; 'calculated idleness or work avoidance'; and 'hindering other pupils'. But this was not altogether surprising since these were also overwhelmingly the three items which the vast majority of teachers reported having some experience of (see Table 1). In Table 6, therefore, we confined the analyses to those teachers who had reported actually experiencing particular pupil behaviours at some point during the course of the week and then used these as the bases for deciding what percentages of teachers found them really difficult to deal with.

When we looked at the results in this way we still found that 'talking out of turn' was commonly reported as the 'most' or 'next most difficult' behaviour (see columns 1 and 2 of Table 6). No fewer than 15% (11% plus 4%) of the 2440 teachers who had experienced dealing with it described it in this way. 'Calculated idleness or work avoidance' was as frequently mentioned (by 15%) whilst dealing with 'verbal abuse towards other pupils' (11%) and 'hindering other pupils' (11%) were also prominent. 'Physical aggression towards other pupils' was also reported by one in twenty (6%) of the sizeable number of teachers (over 1000) who had had some experience of dealing with it during the week. Interestingly, only just over one in six (17%) of the small number of teachers (42) who had experienced 'physical aggression (directed) towards themselves' thought this was the 'most difficult' or the 'next

Table 6: Pupil behaviours secondary teachers reported finding difficult to deal with: (a) in all classes taught and (b) in particularly difficult classes

Type of pupil behaviour	In all classes taught:		In particularly difficult classes*:		
	Most difficult behaviour	Next most difficult behaviour	Most difficult behaviour	Next most difficult behaviour	
	(of those experienced)		(of those experienced)		
	(%)	(%)	(%)	(%)	
Talking out of turn	11**	4	18	8	(of 2440)
Physical aggression towards you (the teacher)	10	7	5	2	(of 42)
Calculated idleness or work avoidance	8	7	14	10	(of 2187)
Verbal abuse towards you (the teacher)	7	4	4	2	(of 380)
Verbal abuse towards other pupils	6	5	8	1	(of 1542)
Hindering other pupils	4	7	7	14	(of 2134)
Cheeky or impertinent remarks or responses	3	2	6	5	(of 1454)
General rowdiness, horseplay or mucking about	3	3	6	5	(of 1527)
Physical aggression towards other pupils	3	3	3	3	(of 1055)
Making unnecessary (non-verbal) noise	2	3	2	5	(of 1917)
Persistently infringing class (or school) rules	2	2	2	2	(of 1671)
Physical destructiveness	2	1	2	3	(of 345)
Not being punctual	1	2	2	3	(of 2045)
Getting out of seat without permission	0	1	1	1	(of 1518)

Note: * The question was not tied to a particular week but referred to recent experiences with the class concerned.

** The percentages should be interpreted as follows. Of those teachers (2440 in all) who reported that they had at least some experience of this pupil behaviour (talking out of turn) 11% reported that this was the most difficult problem they had to deal with whilst a further 4% thought it was the next most difficult. Some sense of the numbers of teachers reporting experiences of particular problems can be gained by referring to Table 1 or the figures in brackets which indicate the numbers of teachers actually experiencing each type of behaviour.

237

most difficult' pupil behaviour to deal with, which tends to confirm our earlier conclusion that most of the incidents so described were not deemed to have been particularly serious by the teachers concerned.

When teachers were asked to frame their replies within the context of a 'particularly difficult' class (see Table 6, columns 3 and 4) rather more chose to list some behaviour(s). However, the general patterns were not much changed: 'talking out of turn', 'calculated idleness' and 'hindering other pupils' were the most frequently mentioned.

Three out of ten teachers reported that they had found one or more pupil behaviours that they had encountered during the course of their duties round the school 'difficult to deal with' (see Table 5a earlier). 'Showing lack of concern for others' was a common encounter amongst virtually all teachers (see Table 2 earlier) and just over one in ten (11%) of those teachers (2315 in all) who reported that they had experienced it nominated this behaviour as the 'most' or 'next most difficult' they had had to deal with (see Table 7). 'Verbal abuse towards other pupils' and 'verbal abuse towards themselves' were other behaviours which were nominated as 'difficult' ones (by just over one in ten of those with experience of them in each case). Just under one in five of the very small group of teachers (28 in all) who had experienced some 'physical aggression towards themselves' around the school put this top of their list of difficult behaviours.

Table 7: Pupil behaviours secondary teachers reported finding most difficult to deal with around the school

	Teachers reporting this as:		
	Most difficult behaviour	Next most difficult behaviour	
	(of those experienced)		
Type of pupil behaviour	(%)	(%)	
Physical aggression towards you	14*	4	(of 28)
Verbal abuse towards you (the teacher)	9	4	(of 310)
Showing lack of concern for others	7	4	(of 2315)
Verbal abuse towards other pupils	5	6	(of 1902)
Cheeky or impertinent remarks or responses	4	3	(of 1671)
Persistently infringing school rules	3	2	(of 2120)
Unruliness while waiting	3	2	(of 2254)
General rowdiness, horseplay or mucking about	3	3	(of 2131)
Physical aggression towards other pupils	3	4	(of 1641)
Leaving school premises without permission	1	1	(of 1101)
Loitering in 'prohibited' areas	1	1	(of 1756)
Physical destructiveness	1	2	(of 639)
Running in the corridors	1	1	(of 2228)

Note: * The percentages should be interpreted as follows. Of those teachers (28 in all) who reported that they had had at least some experience of this pupil behaviour (physical aggression) 14% reported that this was the most difficult problem they had to deal with whilst a further 4% thought it was the next most difficult.

238

In brief, around two out of three teachers reported that they had found none of the pupil behaviours they encountered during the course of their classroom teaching difficult to deal with. Roughly the same proportion reported in similar terms on their encounters round the school. 'Talking out of turn', 'calculated idleness or work avoidance', 'hindering other pupils' and 'verbal abuse towards other pupils' were reported as being the 'most difficult' behaviours to deal with in the classroom. Outside the classroom, 'showing lack of concern for others', 'verbal abuse towards other pupils', 'verbal abuse' towards themselves and 'physical aggression towards other pupils' were the most frequently mentioned.

E. THE STRATEGIES AND SANCTIONS SECONDARY TEACHERS USED WITH DIFFICULT CLASSES AND PUPILS

Teachers reported a variety of strategies and sanctions which they had 'recently used in dealing with difficult classes or pupils'. Before we consider them in greater detail, however, it is important to remember something of the past. Until fairly recently another sanction or deterrent had been available, namely corporal punishment.

We asked our sample whether corporal punishment had been used in their schools about three years ago. About two out of three teachers told us it was still in use at that time. However, they varied in their reports on the frequency with which it was employed: only 3% said it was used 'quite frequently'; 23% 'occasionally'; and 36% 'hardly at all' whilst just over one third (37%) said it was 'not used at all' (table not shown). For a majority of secondary teachers, therefore, the complete removal of corporal punishment as a sanction or deterrent was a fairly recent experience.

Table 8 shows the strategies or sanctions teachers had been employing to deal with difficult classes or pupils. Efforts to 'reason with pupils', either in the classroom setting or outside it, were strategies that most had had some recent experience of (reported by 80% or more). 'Requiring pupils to do extra work', 'discussing with the whole class why things were going wrong', 'keeping pupils in' for detentions and 'asking pupils to withdraw temporarily from the room' were also common strategies (reported by 60% or more). Substantial minorities also indicated that they had taken further steps such as 'referring pupils to another teacher' and 'removing privileges' (40% or more). About one in ten (27%) teachers had found it necessary to 'send pupils direct to the head, deputy or another senior teacher' and about one in ten (9%) had, in the recent past, 'requested (that a pupil) be suspended from school'.

239

Table 8: The strategies and sanctions secondary teachers were employing to deal with difficult classes or pupils and their perceived effectiveness

| | Teachers reporting recent use: | | Perceived effectiveness (of strategies used) | | |
| | | Often or | | | |
Type of strategy or sanction	At least once (%)	quite often (%)	Most effective (%)	Most ineffective (%)	
Reasoning with a pupil or pupils in the classroom setting	92	55	21*	12	(of 2281)
Reasoning with a pupil or pupils outside the classroom setting	89	46	32	2	(of 2194)
Requiring a pupil or pupils to do 'extra work' of some sort	76	23	8	10	(of 1871)
Deliberately ignoring minor disruptions or infringements	71	19	3	10	(of 1755)
Keeping a pupil or pupils in (ie detention)	67	17	15	7	(of 1645)
Discussing with the whole class why things are going wrong	66	21	9	10	(of 1626)
Asking a pupil to withdraw temporarily from the room or class	61	11	13	5	(of 1500)
Referring a pupil or pupils to another teacher	50	7	7	4	(of 1237)
Removing privileges	44	9	5	7	(of 1064)
Sending a pupil or pupils direct to the head, deputy or another senior teacher	27	2	14	6	(of 653)
Requesting suspension from school	9	0	9	5	(of 224)

Note: 20% of teachers mentioned some 'other strategy' they had used.

*The figures should be interpreted as follows. Of those teachers (2281 in all) who reported that they had used this particular strategy recently, 21% said it was the 'most effective' strategy they had used whilst 12% said it was the 'most ineffective'.

Over three out of ten (32%) of those teachers who had recently 'reasoned with pupils outside the classroom setting' thought it the 'most effective' strategy they had used whilst only 2% actually considered it the 'most ineffective' (see Table 8). Opinions were more divided, however, on the 'effectiveness' of many of the other strategies and sanctions that had been employed. No one approach stood out as being uniformly identified by teachers as highly 'effective' or 'ineffective', suggesting strongly that the 'effectiveness' or otherwise of a particular approach depends both on the individual teacher and on the circumstances of the particular school.

F. THE EXPERIENCES OF PRIMARY SCHOOL TEACHERS

In many respects the experiences of primary school teachers paralleled those of secondary teachers. They had had many of the same experiences in the classroom or around the school as secondary teachers reported. However, the frequency with which these occurred was lower and, in general, they felt less needed to be done. Nonetheless, there were some distinct ways in which their experiences differed from those of secondary teachers and it is to these that we pay particular attention in the following sections.

F.1 Discipline in the classroom and around the school

Like their secondary counterparts, the vast majority of primary teachers (80% or more) reported having to deal with pupils 'talking out of turn', 'hindering other pupils' and 'making unnecessary (non-verbal) noise' at least once during the week (see Table 9). A majority of primary teachers (60% or more) also reported that they had had to deal with 'getting out of seat without permission', 'calculated idleness' and 'general rowdiness' at least once. Whilst the general patterns of the other pupil behaviours that were dealt with paralleled the experiences of secondary teachers, their incidence was usually somewhat lower.

There was one major respect in which the experiences of primary teachers differed. Whereas about four out of ten (42%) secondary teachers reported having to deal with 'physical aggression towards other pupils' at least once during the week, over seven out of ten (74%) primary teachers had had this experience (see Table 9). And one in six (17%) of them had had to deal with this behaviour on a daily basis compared with only 6% of secondary teachers.

In the course of their duties around the school, the vast majority (over 80%) of primary teachers reported encountering pupils showing a 'lack of concern for others', 'running in the corridors' and 'unruliness while waiting' (see Table 10). 'General rowdiness' and 'verbal abuse towards other pupils' were also common experiences (reported by over 70%). Primary teachers reported less experience of having encountered

Table 9: Percentages of primary teachers reporting that they had to deal with different types of pupil behaviour during the course of their classroom teaching the previous week

Type of pupil behaviour (listed by frequency of occurrence)	Reported frequency with which dealt with during lessons:			
	At least once during week (%) (%)		At least daily (%) (%)	
Talking out of turn (eg by making remarks, calling out, distracting others by chattering)	97	(97)*	69	(53)
Hindering other pupils (eg by distracting them from work, interfering with equipment or materials)	90	(86)	42	(26)
Making unnecessary (non-verbal) noise (eg by scraping chairs, banging objects, moving clumsily)	85	(77)	42	(25)
Physical aggression towards other pupils (eg by pushing, punching, striking)	74	(42)	17	(6)
Getting out of seat without permission	73	(62)	34	(14)
Calculated idleness or work avoidance (eg delaying start to work set, not having essential books or equipment)	67	(87)	21	(25)
General rowdiness, horseplay or mucking about	60	(61)	14	(10)
Verbal abuse towards other pupils (eg offensive or insulting remarks)	55	(62)	10	(10)
Not being punctual (eg being late to school or lessons)	53	(82)	11	(17)
Persistently infringing class (or school) rules (eg on dress, pupil behaviour)	50	(68)	13	(17)
Cheeky or impertinent remarks or responses	41	(58)	6	(10)
Physical destructiveness (eg breaking objects, damaging furniture & fabric)	16	(14)	1	(1)
Verbal abuse towards you (eg offensive, insulting, insolent or threatening remarks)	7	(15)	1	(1)
Physical aggression towards you (the teacher)	2.1	(1.7)	0	(0)

Note: 15% of teachers wrote in about some 'other pupil behaviour'. Of these 30% reported that it occurred at least daily and 58% reported that it had occurred at least once during the week. The percentages are based on responses of around 1050. Respondents who missed out particular questions averaged around 1% in every case.

* The figures in brackets are the comparable percentages for secondary teachers (taken from Table 1).

'persistent infringe(ment) of school rules', 'cheeky or impertinent remarks' or 'loitering in 'prohibited areas'' (reported by about half) whilst 'physical destructiveness' and 'verbal abuse' towards themselves were rather rare (reported by around one in twenty).

Table 10:   **Percentages of primary teachers reporting different types of pupil behaviours they encountered during the course of their duties round the school**

| Type of pupil behaviour (listed by frequency of occurrence) | Reported frequency with which encountered round the school: | | | |
| | At least once during week | | At least daily | |
	(%)	(%)	(%)	(%)
Lack of concern for others	90	(93)*	25	(31)
Running in the corridors	89	(89)	40	(34)
Unruliness while waiting (eg to enter classrooms, for lunch)	86	(90)	31	(29)
Physical aggression towards other pupils (eg by pushing, punching, striking)	86	(66)	21	(11)
General rowdiness, horseplay or mucking about	74	(85)	16	(21)
Verbal abuse towards other pupils (eg offensive, or insulting remarks)	71	(76)	15	(19)
Persistently infringing school rules (eg on dress, pupil behaviour)	59	(85)	13	(28)
Loitering in 'prohibited' areas	57	(71)	9	(17)
Cheeky or impertinent remarks or responses	49	(67)	7	(12)
Physical destructiveness (eg breaking objects, damaging furniture & fabric)	7	(26)	1	(2)
Verbal abuse towards you (eg offensive, insulting, insolent or threatening remarks)	6	(12)	0.5	(0.5)
Leaving school premises without permission	5	(44)	0	(7)
Physical aggression towards you (the teacher)	1.6	(1.1)	0	(0)

Note: 13% of teachers wrote in about some 'other pupil behaviour'. Of these 17% reported that it had occurred at least daily and 40% at least once during the week.

* The figures in brackets are the comparable percentages for secondary teachers (taken from Table 2).

'Physical aggression towards other pupils' was again the one major area of pupil behaviour where primary teachers' experiences differed significantly from those of secondary teachers. Just under nine out of ten (86%) primary teachers had encountered this at some point during the course of their week's duties round the school and two out of ten (21%) on a daily basis (see Table 10). The figures for secondary teachers were under seven out of ten (66%) and about one out of ten (11%) respectively.

As in the secondary survey, very small percentages of primary teachers reported 'physical aggression' by pupils directed towards themselves. Only 2.1% reported this experience occurring once during the week in the classroom (see Table 9 and Footnote 5). The figure for encounters around the school was only 1.6% (see Table 10). As in the secondary survey, extrapolation of these figures to provide estimates over longer time-periods would be inappropriate. The overwhelming majority of primary teachers reported that their general experiences were 'typical' or 'fairly typical'. We inferred that by 'physical aggression' they meant physical contact initiated by a pupil and this interpretation was borne out by the fuller comments some teachers made in the open-ended section of their questionnaires. 'Aggression' was most frequently described as occurring whilst primary teachers were trying to restrain individual children. Unlike a few of their secondary counterparts, none of the primary teachers in the whole sample used the opportunity to comment on 'any matters they wished' in order to describe 'violent' incidents which had happened to them personally, although a few wrote about incidents which they knew of. We conclude, on the basis of our primary sample's reports, that the incidence of 'violence' directed towards primary teachers, either in the classroom or outside the school, was very low indeed, certainly no higher than the figures reported for the secondary sample and almost certainly considerably lower.

F.2 Primary teachers' perceptions of the 'seriousness' of discipline problems, their particular difficulties and concerns

The generally lower incidence of potentially problematic pupil behaviours was reflected in primary teachers' assessments of the 'seriousness' of the situation in their schools. Fewer felt it was 'serious' (11% compared with 16% of secondary teachers) and more were prepared to say it was either 'not at all serious' or 'no problem at all' (51% compared with 31%) (table not shown).

We have already suggested that there were quite considerable differences between teachers in different secondary schools regarding their perceptions of the 'seriousness' of discipline problems. In only about one in twenty (6%) of primary schools did primary teachers think the problem was verging on the 'serious' (average scores of 2.5 or lower) whilst teachers in two out of three (66%) thought the problems were either 'not at all serious' or, indeed, 'no problem at all' (average scores of 3.5 or higher) (see Section C.1 and Table 11).

Table 11: **Primary teachers' perceptions of the 'seriousness' of discipline problems in their school aggregated to the school level to show variations between schools**

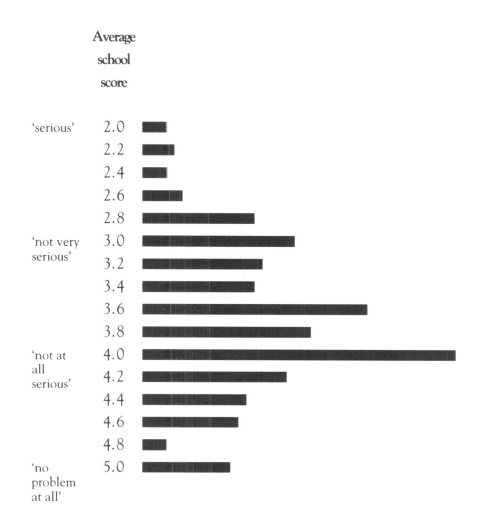

Total number of responses = teachers in 222 primary schools

In the case of primary schools the differences between schools were still larger than in secondary schools. Over half of the variation lay 'between schools' and under half 'within' them (see Footnote 6). This analysis served to emphasise the extent to which primary teachers in some schools believed that the problems were 'serious' and to which those in other schools did not. As with their secondary counterparts, primary

245

teachers working in schools with greater proportions of pupils from 'economically disadvantaged areas' or of 'below average ability' were more likely to report that the position in their schools was 'serious' (tables not shown.)

Primary teachers were considerably less likely than secondary teachers to report that they found individual pupils 'difficult to deal with'. Four out of ten (40%) said, for example, that they had no difficult pupils in the classroom setting compared with two out of ten (22%) secondary teachers. And only about two out of ten reported finding particular pupil behaviours difficult to deal with, either in the classroom or around the school, compared with well over three out of ten secondary teachers (table not shown).

The particular pupil behaviours that this relatively small group of two out of ten primary teachers said were 'most difficult' to deal with corresponded in most respects to the concerns of secondary teachers. 'Talking out of turn', 'hindering other pupils', 'calculated idleness or work avoidance' and 'physical aggression towards other pupils' were the behaviours the vast majority of primary teachers reported having to deal with in the classroom situation (see Table 10). They were also the behaviours that they found 'most' or 'next most difficult' to deal with although, in each case, fewer than one in ten of the 900 or more teachers with actual experience of them nominated them as 'most/next most difficult'.

'Physical aggression towards other pupils' was nominated as the 'most (or next most) difficult' problem to deal with outside the classroom (mentioned by about one in eight primary teachers). 'Showing lack of concern for others' and 'verbal abuse towards other pupils' were also mentioned, but less frequently, by around one in twenty (tables not shown). Hardly any of the 17 primary teachers who reported 'physical aggression' directed towards themselves thought this was the most difficult behaviour they had to deal with. The pupils primary teachers found most difficult to deal with were overwhelmingly male.

F.3 The strategies and sanctions primary teachers used with difficult classes and pupils

Half (50%) the primary teachers reported that corporal punishment had not been in use in their school three years ago compared with about one third (37%) of secondary teachers; only just over one in ten (12%) reported that it had been used 'occasionally' compared with one in four (26%) secondary teachers (table not shown).

246

Given that their pupils were younger, most of the strategies and sanctions primary teachers reported using recently differed from those employed by secondary teachers, but only insofar as they were more appropriate for the age of their pupils. There was widespread use of 'reasoning' with pupils, both in the classroom and outside it, as well as 'class discussion about why things were going wrong' (mentioned by over 80% of primary teachers as being used at least once recently). There was less imposition of 'extra work' (reported by 61%) or 'keeping pupils in' (reported by 33%) compared with secondary teachers whilst 'removing privileges' was more commonly used (by 71%).

This latter sanction featured highly on teachers' list of 'more effective' strategies along with 'reasoning with a pupil in the classroom setting' (both mentioned by over one out of four who had used them). 'Requiring pupils to do extra work', asking a pupil to 'withdraw temporarily from the room' and 'deliberately ignoring minor disruptions' were all seen as 'ineffective' strategies by those who had used them (tables not shown).

G. PRIMARY AND SECONDARY TEACHERS' PRIORITIES FOR ACTION

Given the very different circumstances facing schools, as well as teachers' widely differing perceptions of the 'seriousness' of the problems in their schools, it is scarcely surprising that a wide variety of priorities for action were put forward. We listed fourteen forms of action that could be taken and asked teachers to say, with respect to each, whether it was 'needed', 'possibly needed' or 'not needed' in their own school. The particular structure of the question allowed teachers to recommend several priorities if they wished. Their choices reveal, to some extent, their analyses of the prevailing situation in their own schools.

Over six out of ten secondary teachers (63%) recommended 'establishing smaller classes' (see Table 12). The other strategies they mentioned can be considered as proposals for action in relation to five particular areas.

About half the secondary teachers recommended two strategies that were designed to tackle directly the problems posed by individual pupils or groups of pupils. These were: 'tougher sanctions for certain forms of indiscipline' and 'more opportunities for counselling for pupils whose behaviour is often difficult' (see Table 12).

247

Table 12: **Primary and secondary teachers' perceptions of the priorities for dealing with pupils' behaviour problems in their own schools**

Strategy or priority for action	'Needed' Secondary (%)	'Needed' Primary (%)	'Needed/possibly needed' Secondary (%)	'Needed/possibly needed' Primary (%)
Establishing smaller classes	63	57	88	81
Tougher sanctions for certain forms of indiscipline	52	30	82	64
More opportunities for counselling for pupils whose behaviour is often difficult	49	34	88	73
Building more parental involvement	45	31	84	68
More opportunities for personal guidance or support from colleagues for teachers facing problems with discipline	41	21	86	57
Firmer communications to pupils about what they can and cannot do	40	28	77	65
More in-service training focusing on discipline problems and strategies	40	27	84	68
Building more respect for the school within the local community	39	29	73	58
More discussions of discipline amongst staff as a whole	39	29	81	71
More opportunities for personal guidance or support from LEA staff for teachers facing problems with discipline	30	19	70	49
Changing the content of the curriculum	20	5	62	26
Changing teaching styles	19	8	78	44
Changing the climate or atmosphere of the school	18	8	51	30
Creating more opportunities for team teaching	17	8	62	35

Note: 14% of secondary teachers and 12% of primary teachers mentioned some other strategy or priority which they believed was needed.

About four out of ten teachers diagnosed the problems as stemming from the community and wanted to 'build more parental involvement' and 'more respect for the school in the local community'.

Similar proportions thought that more support for the individual teacher 'facing problems with discipline' would be valuable. The 'personal guidance or support' could come either from 'colleagues' or from 'LEA staff', although more favoured the former than the latter. 'More in-service training' was also recommended, either for individual teachers or for groups.

Around four out of ten teachers again favoured collective action on the part of the staff, recommending 'more discussions of discipline amongst staff as a whole' and 'firmer communications to pupils about what they can and cannot do'.

Changing 'the content of the curriculum', 'teaching styles', 'the climate of the school' and 'creating more opportunities for team teaching' attracted the support of around two out of ten teachers.

We also asked which strategies teachers felt were 'most/next most important'. 'Smaller classes', 'tougher sanctions', 'counselling for pupils' and 'building parental involvement' all received strong support (table not shown). However, it was very clear from the very high percentages of secondary teachers in Table 12 reporting that certain strategies were 'needed/possibly needed', that action across a broad front would be likely to command support from a considerable majority of secondary teachers and that they felt there were several starting points for tackling the problems. No fewer than eleven of the fourteen items listed in Table 12 received support from seven out of ten (or more) secondary teachers.

In general terms, primary teachers' priorities for action matched those of secondary teachers. However, given the lower incidence of behaviour problems and the extent to which the situation was perceived by a considerable majority of primary teachers as less serious, correspondingly fewer reported that particular approaches were 'needed', apart from 'establishing' smaller classes (mentioned by 57%).

As with the secondary teachers, views on which approaches were required varied quite considerably (see Table 12). There was much less support for 'tougher sanctions' than amongst secondary teachers and lower proportions recommended 'firmer communications to pupils about what they could and could not do' (recommended as 'needed' by about three out of ten teachers in each case).

Around three out of ten primary teachers were in favour of 'building more parental involvement' and 'respect for the school in the community' whilst similar proportions favoured 'counselling for pupils', 'counselling and support for teachers with discipline problems' (both from colleagues and from LEA staff), more 'in-service training' and more 'staff discussions'. Less than one in ten recommended changing the 'content of the curriculum', 'teaching styles' or the 'climate of the school' (see Table 12). And whereas only a small minority of secondary teachers (between two and three out of ten) were prepared to state that particular approaches were 'not needed' between three and five out of ten primary teachers reported that many of the items we had listed as possible priorities were definitely 'not needed' in their school (table not shown). We took this, in part, as reflecting their view that there was no major problem that demanded immediate action.

Footnotes to Part 1

(1) In order to obtain estimates of the relative frequency with which teachers had experienced particular forms of pupil behaviour it was decided to confine the survey to a period (one week) during which their memories of what had happened were likely to be reliable. It is not possible to extrapolate the teachers' replies to provide reliable estimates of the percentages of teachers who would be likely to encounter particular types of behaviour over longer periods. In order to produce such figures it would be necessary to make assumptions about the extent to which particular teachers would or would not be more likely than others to experience such behaviour. Such assumptions would clearly be unsafe.

(2) Allowing for simple sampling errors, the 95% confidence intervals surrounding this estimate are plus or minus 0.5%.

(3) The 95% confidence intervals surrounding this estimate are plus or minus 0.3%.

(4) The exact estimates were: 'between-groups' 38.3%; 'within-groups' 61.7%.

(5) The 95% confidence intervals surrounding this estimate are plus or minus 0.7%.

(6) The exact estimates were: 'between-groups' 54.2%; 'within-groups' 45.8%.

PART II

Teachers' Experiences and Perceptions of Discipline in Ten Inner-City Comprehensive Schools
(David A. Gillborn, Jon Nixon and Jean Rudduck)

A. INTRODUCTION

This paper reports the findings of an interview-based research project. After a brief methodological introduction and a consideration of the problems of generalisation across ten sites, teachers' experiences and perceptions of discipline are discussed in relation to four main areas: the nature of discipline problems; responses to discipline problems; issues relating to curriculum and pedagogy; and links with parents, family and the community.

A.1 The conduct of the study

This project was specifically designed to complement the national postal survey of teachers (also carried out by members of Sheffield University's Educational Research Centre) and sought to explore in detail the perceptions and experiences of teachers who spend the majority of their working day in the classrooms of inner-city comprehensive schools.

Because of time constraints, we decided to approach schools in ten LEAs which were within a couple of hours travelling distance of Sheffield. This offered a good range, taking in several Northern and Midland authorities.

Census data were used to identify schools whose location might reasonably be described as 'inner-city'; these reflected the characteristics of the school's electoral ward in relation to indices of multiple disadvantage such as the level of unemployment, proportion of one-parent families and percentage of households lacking basic amenities. We made telephone contact with the headteachers and where the school was confirmed as an inner-city comprehensive we sought their co-operation in organising a series of interviews over a two day visit to each school. In addition to the headteachers themselves, we asked to see ten classroom teachers who would offer a cross-section of the views, concerns and experiences in each school (a total of 100 classroom teachers in all).

We specifically requested that interviewees should represent different subject areas, years of teaching experience and both sexes. Throughout our analysis we have been sensitive to the complexity of factors which may influence teachers' experiences. Although our interviewees must remain anonymous, in presenting our findings we have chosen to indicate the following characteristics of those whom we quote: gender (M/F); years experience in teaching (in total/in present school); salary scale (main professional grade/allowance for special responsibility/ deputy/headteacher): main subject specialism (see Footnote).

251

So as to maximise comparability across the ten research sites the interviewers were guided by a semi-structured schedule. The main areas explored during the interviews were:

- the behaviours that are of most concern to the school staff **as a whole**

- the behaviours that **individual classroom teachers** have to deal with on a regular basis

- the kinds of thing that individual teachers and the staff as a whole are doing **in response** to discipline problems.

The interviews were tape-recorded and the transcripts read by each member of the team.

A.2   The problems of generalisation across the schools

At one time or another each member of the research team encountered an interviewee who queried what we meant by the term 'discipline'. We had deliberately avoided being prescriptive about such matters, wanting to explore each teacher's own perceptions. The teachers' questions served to highlight the dynamic and complex character of discipline in schools: across the ten research sites we were told of many different problems and of the varied responses to these problems.

The themes explored in this paper are those which consistently emerged in interviews as important areas of concern across all ten schools. In many cases there was striking similarity between the schools despite their very different histories and location within specific LEA and local community contexts. However, each school had its own identity and it was therefore not possible to generalise across all ten schools on some issues. We asked, for example, whether interviewees thought that, during their time in the school, discipline had got worse, better or remained about the same. Within each individual school the interviewees were consistent in their replies, yet **between** schools there was often significant variation. This reflected very different factors in the location and history of each school.

We chose to concentrate the interview-based study on inner-city schools; it may be that teachers in schools in less 'disadvantaged' areas experience and perceive discipline problems differently. For example, when we asked teachers to describe the general level of discipline in their school they usually qualified their answers by adding, '...for an inner-city school'. This reflected an assumption that teachers in other schools might view certain issues differently:

'I think all organisations, particularly schools, have a tolerance level, which is built up by the culture of the school, about what they will say is the 'bottom line' and members of staff are not prepared to work beyond that. I think the staff here, whether they know it or not, have a particularly high tolerance level, so that a problem does not become a serious problem until much later than it would in some other situations in other schools, in other contexts...most staff have developed a capacity for dealing with the situation.'
(M 18/2 headteacher)

As our report shows, developing such 'a capacity for dealing with the situation' requires a major investment of time, energy and commitment.

B.   THE NATURE OF DISCIPLINE PROBLEMS

Teachers often revealed complex feelings which were sometimes ambivalent about their working lives. On the one hand they tended to display a strong personal and professional concern for their pupils, yet the job of teaching was made both physically and emotionally wearing through seemingly incessant problems related to discipline:

'I've got two very strong feelings about school; one is I enjoy my job and I enjoy teaching my subject to the children. I mean, 95% of individual cases – I've got no children that I actually dread coming into the classroom... I get quite a bit done and I can measure my success, and that's very nice. That's positive. But on the social side of the school I have a horrible feeling of gloom, constant nagging: 'so and so's said this' and 'so and so's pushed me.' This kind of thing, bubbling under the surface...'
(F 1/1 MPG modern languages)

Occasionally, violent incidents had occurred and these could have important consequences, both for the individuals concerned and for the general morale and atmosphere of the school (see section B.2). Although significant, incidents of pupils' physical aggression against staff were isolated and exceptional; they did not emerge as the teachers' most pressing concern. In terms of their day-to-day experience of working in an inner-city comprehensive school, teachers' main worry was the wearing effect of a continuous stream of relatively 'minor' disruptions.

B.1   Teachers' experience of frequent and wearing indiscipline

For many of the teachers we spoke to, teaching had become a struggle: a sense of frustration and the slow erosion of their energies frequently emerged when teachers explained their concerns regarding discipline:

'I think one of the reasons people outside teaching think it's such an easy job is that they think that 100% of your energy goes into merely teaching pupils, whereas in some schools a large proportion of your energy – probably **most** *of your energy – goes into disciplining them in the first place.'*
(F 20/5 MPG+incentive allowance chemistry)

'Just can't get them to settle down to work to the best of their abilities. And this seems to be the constant hassle that teachers are having in the classroom these days... It becomes more of a battle, more of a hassle. All the time, you know, the teacher is having to say, 'Come on.' 'Get on with your work.' 'Stop turning around and talking to the person behind you'.'
(M 18/18 MPG+incentive allowance special needs)

It was the **cumulative** nature of such problems which was most significant. In isolation many of the examples which teachers gave could appear to be relatively trivial. However, it would be foolish to underestimate the cumulative force of pupil-pupil bickering, shouting, jostling and lack of concentration. Teachers regularly reported problems getting pupils settled and working at the start of each lesson. Once this had been achieved lessons were characteristically punctuated by a succession of interruptions as things had to be repeatedly explained or pupils reminded of the rules of the group concerning, for example, gossiping with friends, name-calling and safety procedures in laboratories and workshops:

'. . .they cannot concentrate. . .general chatter and you fight against that the whole time. . .You are continually having to stop, make sure everybody is quiet, carrying on for five or so minutes until the noise level is unbearable again and you make them stop, put their pens down, and give them **another** *speech on keeping quiet. . .'*
(M 1/1 MPG+incentive allowance technology)

'. . .they will yell out even when they see I am talking to someone else at the other side of the room, and they won't wait their turn. That infuriates me. It might seem a very trivial point but I find it infuriating. And then if I am spending time with one child they tend to be impatient because they want my attention immediately.'
(F 10/10 MPG history)

Such problems led to a sense of being slowly worn down by the sheer number of teacher-pupil interactions which involved some element of control or response to acts of indiscipline. This was a particular problem for staff who held a position of special responsibility, such as head of subject or pastoral head of year, for it meant that they were often the first port of call for teachers who wished to remove a child from their class or report an incident to their senior colleagues. In fact, the frequency of problems was such that even staff with no special responsibilities often found that disciplinary issues came to dominate their experience of school:

A head of subject
*'As head of [subject] I have to deal with discipline, so I would imagine that at least once, on average, in **every lesson** I have to deal with discipline problems. I find that the most irritating part of my school day, because rarely can I go through a lesson without having to deal with somebody else's discipline problem, and often it could be two or three in one lesson.'*
(M 22/5 MPG + incentive allowance design)

A pastoral head of year
'. . .as head of the 5th year you don't get to see the good kids, you don't get to see the middle kids, all you get to see are the flaming troublemakers. You spend all your time chasing these kids round and round the school. You think, 'God, this is crazy.' It's not fair on the rest of the school – when I say 'discipline', that is the big problem.'
(M 15/9 MPG + incentive allowance social education)

A form teacher
'If you need a break you've got to leave the school premises, because otherwise you are totally involved with problems…because there is so much going on in school, every minute you get you're seeing a child, you're dealing with problems…'
(F 18/10 MPG + incentive allowance religious studies)

In addition to their exasperation at the succession of disruptive moments during lessons, teachers often reported a change in the overall nature of their interactions with pupils. Such comments were frequently worded in terms of pupils' poor motivation, 'quarrelsome' attitude and a 'lack of respect for authority'. In such cases, teachers often had difficulty pin-pointing what had led them to their belief in a deterioration in pupil 'attitude'. Examples which were common to several different schools concerned the levels of noise (both inside and outside the classroom), jostling in corridors and a failure to show recognition of the adult's status within the institution. As a woman in her second year of teaching put it, *'A lot of the children don't seem able to discern a difference between addressing a mate on the playground and a member of staff in a classroom'* (F 1/1 MPG modern languages):

'I think within the last two or three years, it's become fairly obvious that the pupils tend to ignore authority in some ways. You know, if you lay down certain rules they tend to disobey more than they used to, let's put it that way. I think they tend to resent being told. . .If you give out an instruction and say, 'This is what we need to do', then there are individuals who might turn around and say blatantly, 'We're not really interested' – period.'
(M 14/14 MPG + incentive allowance physics)

255

A further dimension to the loss of respect which teachers reported concerned the level of insulting language which they encountered in the classroom. Mostly this involved pupils swearing at each other and making a show of aggression to their classmates. However, occasionally pupils did not restrict bad language to interactions with their peers:

> 'A boy that I taught told me to 'fuck off' which has never happened to me before.'
> (F 9/9 MPG mathematics)

> '. . .a fifth year boy had gone to the general office and asked to borrow 50p. When he was told he couldn't – he didn't actually swear **at** the member of staff, he swore **in front** of her, saying 'shit. fuck'. Right, this is one example of disrespect, you know, using that sort of language in front of a member of staff. . .'
> (M 18/18 MPG + incentive allowance special needs)

Overall **we found no significant difference between the levels of disruption reported by male and female teachers.** However, gender could influence the **kind** of problem which they encountered. Female staff, for example, sometimes complained of pupils' use of sexual innuendo in class and again stressed the importance of the continual, wearing nature of these disturbances.

It should be noted that, although the pupils who caused the disruptions were almost always described as a small minority of the whole pupil population, the cumulative demands upon teachers' energies were very great. Similarly, the very few pupils who had been physically aggressive towards staff could have an effect upon morale (and the general 'atmosphere' of a school) which was much more significant than might at first be suspected.

B.2   Teachers' experience of physical aggression in school

We asked every interviewee whether, in the last five years, they had been the recipient of 'physical aggression from a pupil'. Interviewees usually qualified their answers by emphasising the need to understand pupils' actions within their **situational context:** teachers highlighted the importance of several factors which made this a surprisingly difficult question to answer in simple 'yes'/'no' terms.

Some teachers stated that pupils' actions could be 'physically aggressive' without actually involving contact. The following quotation, for example, concerns a pupil who had smashed the windscreen of a teacher's car:

'I walked up to him. He said, Don't touch me or I will hit you with this' [a pick axe handle]. So I said, 'Okay, fine. You are into criminal damage at the moment. If you hit me with that it's grievous bodily harm as well as criminal damage.' He was holding it high and threatening me and all sorts of things. I just very slowly talked to him and walked up towards him and asked him several times to put it down. And in the end he just put it on the ground and said 'Let's go inside'.'
(M 24/5 headteacher)

This incident was presented as an example of physical aggression, even though no physical contact was made ('He was holding it high and threatening me. .'). Therefore 'physical aggression' did not always involve contact: however, interviewees also noted that physical contact did not always signal that the pupil had intended any aggression towards the teacher:

*'I've had confrontation situations in the past where there's been **verbal aggression,** but no **physical aggression.** The only physical aggression has been really just the heat of the moment, due to a fight between two pupils, and it's not really been aimed at me, it's been aimed at the other one. . .but it's just that you've had to get between and separate them.'*
(F 6/6 MPG physics)

'I can't remember any incident where anybody's threatened me with physical violence. . .I've been hit once, when I was separating a fight. I was separating a fight and somebody was swinging a punch at the adversary and I got it on the chin – but that was an accident, there was definitely no way he could have meant it.'
(M 11/11 MPG modern languages)

*'[A pupil] got cross and on his way out [of the classroom] unfortunately he pulled the door very very hard – I think he was basically in a temper – and he got me right down the arm – I got a bruise. . .he did not come towards me to do anything to me, he just didn't control his temper and it was unfortunate that it happened – the door happened to hit **me** – I mean, he wouldn't have taken notice who was there. . .I don't think it was deliberate, he just wasn't in control of what he was doing.'*
(F 11/9 MPG + incentive allowance chemistry)

The three examples above illustrate the interviewees' desire to qualify their answers by reference to their assessment of the situations in which the incidents occurred. Thus, even in those situations where the teacher had felt physically threatened or where contact had been made there was sometimes doubt as to whether the acts were deliberately directed towards themselves as teacher. Moreover, even where there was contact the teacher might not feel that 'assault' was an appropriate description:

'I was actually hit last year, or at least deliberately elbowed out of the way by a very big lad and we managed to sort that out, in that I still teach the child. . .but I don't really class that as being assaulted.'
(F 17/14 MPG + incentive allowance French)

The interviewees' responses, therefore, confirmed the complexity of relationships in school by highlighting the variety of occasions where teachers might have to deal with physical aggression; most importantly, they were quick to point out that **it was very rare for pupils deliberately to direct physical aggression at staff.** Very often teachers noted that with hindsight they would have handled the situation differently and might now be able to avoid escalating the teacher-pupil conflict.

Thus, intended physical aggression by pupils against teachers was not a common experience in the schools which we visited and was not perceived by staff as **the** major disciplinary issue. Cases of physical aggression were isolated and must be viewed within the whole school context. However, the importance of such incidents should not be underplayed. In fact, teachers could have to deal with physical aggression in a variety of forms: for example, by interceding in a pupil fight; or by questioning strangers (often in their late-teens or early twenties) who entered the school site during the day and might respond in a threatening manner if challenged. Schools which acted as community colleges faced a particular problem in this respect; one school we visited had to cope with a public right of way which cut across its site, while another had recently suffered a guerilla-style attack upon one of its pupils:

'[A youth not attending this school] spent most of his time hanging around the fringes of our area and then presumably somebody annoyed him and he was determined, come what may, he was going to get equal. And he literally climbed the drainpipe, in through a window, thumped the lad and was out through the window and was gone again. We had an incident last week where two outsiders walked in and sat in a classroom, two 19-20 year olds. A female member of staff, all she could do was ask a child to go and fetch help. . .There are two lady members of staff who moved classrooms recently because they wanted to be in a kind of suite together, because they both worked in this particular way, and eventually they got two very nice classrooms. Once they were in it, they suddenly realised how exposed they were: they were right out on the far corner of the school at ground floor level, and it was into one of these classrooms that these two yobs [from outside the school] walked in and sat down.'
(M 22/2 MPG + incentive allowance geography)

Although isolated, such incidents dramatically exposed how vulnerable teachers could be and this in turn could lead to a general sense of unease amongst staff in the school.

Very occasionally teachers might have to face physical aggression which seems to have little or no rational basis. However, experienced staff often pointed out that such exceptional cases had always existed and should not be taken as indicative of a disciplinary crisis. The following example of pupil-pupil violence clearly illustrates this:

> '. . .a girl brought a machete to school to sort somebody out. Now we are talking about a machete. We are talking about a real weapon. Now many people might think that is desperate, but in one of my lessons 14 years ago I had a boy chase another boy through the crash doors of a fire exit with a hammer in his hand. Had he caught him, he would have killed him. It's no different to a girl bringing a machete is it? Had she got close to the person she wanted to do in, she would have done him in. So the major incidents haven't changed, they are still as **isolated**. Those are the two that come to my mind after 16 years here. The major incidents haven't changed and I don't think they will. I think you are always going to get a major incident in a place like this once in a while.'
> (M 20/16 MPG + incentive allowance design)

It is clear, therefore, that occasionally teachers had to deal with violent or physically threatening episodes. These incidents were exceptional but could nevertheless have important consequences for the individuals concerned and for the general atmosphere in some schools. However, teachers identified their most pressing problem as the wearing effects of a continual stream of relatively 'minor' disruptions to classroom teaching. Although, viewed separately, the individual disruptions could sometimes appear trivial, their cumulative effect could place staff under enormous physical and emotional strain.

C.   DEALING WITH THE PROBLEMS OF DISCIPLINE

C.1   Reactions to the abandonment of corporal punishment

Among our ten schools were some which had recently abandoned corporal punishment and others which had dropped it six or more years ago. In the latter schools, teachers were, on the whole, markedly less worried about coping **without** corporal punishment: 'We weren't happy at the time of changeover but now we never think about it' (M 9/9 MPG + incentive allowance information technology). Alternative perspectives on discipline have evolved, and new strategies for dealing with discipline problems. These are more in accord with the principles that structure new curricula, new teaching and learning styles, and pastoral work.

There were other schools where corporal punishment had been used, albeit sparingly, until its recent prohibition. It was clear that these schools were in a state of transition. There was, not surprisingly, some disorientation, nervousness and uncertainty as alternative systems were being developed and tried out. An additional factor was that the media had given prominence to pupils' rights following the abandonment of corporal punishment and many pupils had been quick to let teachers know that they were well informed. For example, one teacher, whose habit it was to flick small pieces of chalk at pupils as a way of re-engaging their attention, recalled one boy's recent response: *'Well, you can throw it **to** us but you can't throw it **at** us'*; he added *'– which I thought was a fine distinction for a boy of twelve to make' (M 11/11 MPG + incentive allowance CDT)*. Pupils' remarks were often more aggressively challenging.

A number of teachers in both groups of schools thought they would like firmer sanctions for more serious acts. There were also some who felt that corporal punishment itself still had a place in school. These teachers typically offered the following arguments: pupils 'understand' the cane or the slap because it's the language of the home; parents urge teachers to hit or cane pupils because it's the style of retribution that they are familiar with; it is quick and immediate – you can have a joke with a pupil later the same day – whereas other procedures are protracted and lose their meaning in relation to the act that elicited the punishment; there has to be an ultimate deterrent for the really bad cases; corporal punishment is a deterrent to pupils who wonder how far they can go.

These arguments were counterbalanced by a different set of arguments from other teachers: corporal punishment cannot be an effective deterrent since the same pupils have, in the past, been caned on more than one occasion, and sometimes repeatedly; pupils do not 'learn' from corporal punishment, they merely accept it; pupils become more aware of the seriousness of their misdeeds or irresponsibility when parents and/or other teachers become involved; some pupils need to see that there is, in society, an alternative to the language of violence that they experience outside school; to hit or cane another human being is 'dehumanising' and 'barbaric'. Some teachers recalled the humiliation they had felt at being caned as a child and they mentioned the commitment to retaliation that caning could evoke if pupils felt that the punishment had been unjustified. Some also recorded their own feelings of abhorrence about occasions when they had had to administer corporal punishment themselves.

Overall, the abandonment of corporal punishment seems to have occasioned an important reappraisal among teachers of the coherence of the values and practices of schooling. It has also created a climate in which it is becoming increasingly possible for teachers '*to talk about (discipline) freely*' (F 17/7 MPG + *incentive allowance mathematics*).

C.2   Developing alternative perspectives and strategies

In developing alternative perspectives and strategies, schools have identified a number of important areas:

- the system of incentives, sanctions and support

- shared understanding and mutual support among members of a school staff

- ways of talking things through with pupils

- curriculum content and teaching styles

- home-school relationships.

The issues of curriculum and home-school links will be dealt with more fully in later sections of this report.

C.2.i   **Incentives, sanctions and support.** Schools are tackling the problem of discipline from a number of perspectives. One headteacher said that his school '*is now built on incentives rather than punishment*'. It had been '*a very violent school*'. As the numbers of pupils in the school fell, so the discipline pattern seemed to change. The headteacher commented:

> '*The incidents have gone down in terms of severity but I think the number is still running, for the number of children we've got, at about the level it always has been. In a sense this doesn't concern me because . . . this is the sort of school where you will always have that kind of difficulty*'.
> (M 24/7 headteacher)

'*Disruption in the classroom*', not violence, '*is now the big issue*', confirmed one of the staff (F 17/7 MPG + incentive allowance mathematics). The school serves a '*poor white area*' in the most deprived part of the county. When the headteacher joined the school, 300 pupils were caned in his first year. He changed the regime, and in the following year (now about five years ago) the LEA prohibited corporal punishment. The school already had a support unit, which continued, and staff worked at progressively strengthening the pastoral system, exploring ways of recognising and rewarding regular attendance, commitment to learning and good behaviour, making the school a more comfortable and attractive place to work in (carpeting was mentioned

261

by several headteachers as a desirable development) and raising money to give pupils some residential experience. Staff persisted in trying to build closer links with parents, and tried overall to achieve a sense of 'confidence and consultation' among staff. A similar profile of effort and initiative existed in some other schools.

A clearly articulated and consistently handled set of sanctions is something that classroom teachers strongly urge. Behind sanctions lie expectations about behaviour. It is when these codes of behaviour are challenged – whether the general code of behaviour that the school establishes for all its pupils or the codes embodied in the expectations of individual teachers – that the sanctions and/or support systems come into play.

The most common are the individual report, temporary exclusion, detention, withdrawal and long-term or permanent exclusions. These now form the backbone of the system, and although deemed to be generally effective, each component is seen by some teachers as having drawbacks. It might be helpful briefly to discuss each of these in turn.

The individual report: a pupil who is on individual report carries a proforma from lesson to lesson and each teacher is required to make a written comment on his or her behaviour during the lesson. Although this is a fairly common and conventional form of 'probationary' checking, it is not without problems. The major one is lack of consistency among teachers in interpreting what counts as 'satisfactory behaviour'. Some teachers, it seems, will give a 'satisfactory' comment for attendance, while others also expect evidence of concentration and participation. In addition, there is a limit to the number of days a pupil can be on report before it becomes a tedious device, both for the pupil and for the teacher, and decisions to take the pupil off report may not reflect any substantial commitment to a more constructive outlook or pattern of behaviour. At the same time, the individual report does ensure that a number of teachers are aware of and are communicating about individual pupils whose behaviour has given cause for concern.

Temporary exclusion from the classroom: a teacher who feels that a pupil is disturbing other pupils or who has behaved unacceptably may be excluded from the lesson or, if the behaviour is more serious, from the remaining lessons of the day. This can mean, according to circumstance or policy, that the pupil is isolated in an adjoining room but under the eye of the class teacher, or is required to sit/stand out in the corridor, or is sent to a duty tutor and required to work independently, or is sent to a member of senior staff. The temporary exclusion is generally seen as an immediate and helpful device and one that allows the teacher and the rest of the class to resume their concentration on the task in hand. The problems most often mentioned by teachers were these: on a bad day the duty tutor's room may become crowded and the excluded pupils may themselves become too difficult for the duty tutor to handle; the excluding teacher may be anxious lest pupils see exclusion as a sign of teacher weakness; the teacher may feel that he or she is sacrificing the needs of the individual to the needs of the group; exclusion necessitates a cycle of spoken or written communication among staff; and teachers complain widely about the amount of paper work and time that the bureaucracy of support systems can lead to (this is not to say that they do not find them helpful in principle.

Detention: this is a traditional sanction which schools are reacting to in different ways. One school was about to re-introduce detention as a follow-up to temporary exclusion and as a way of underlining its seriousness. Another school had dropped it. Others continue with it but recognise some of the problems: for example, the time involved in writing to parents to give them warning; the reaction of some parents who are unwilling to allow children to stay on at school; the reaction of some pupils who like staying on at school and may prefer it to going home with the result that the sanction loses its meaning.

Withdrawal: some schools have a withdrawal or support unit where particularly difficult pupils can be given help, usually over a period of time, until they are thought ready to return to the regular work of the classroom. The support unit may be dealing with persistently difficult pupils or with pupils whose need for remedial help is leading, or is likely to lead, to boredom and disruption. Many teachers feel secure in the knowledge that such a unit exists and value its long-term potential for the resocialisation of difficult pupils but the counter-pull in many schools is towards the greater use of support teachers within the normal classroom setting. Teachers mentioned two particular problems: pupils who are not behaving badly can resent the fact that the disrupters, rather than being punished, are getting 'preferential treatment' in being allowed to work in a more comfortable setting where they receive greater individual attention; for pupils who have difficulty, for whatever reason, in keeping up with the progress of their classmates, withdrawal can compound the problem of discontinuity of learning. An additional problem with the withdrawal unit is that schools with such units may be sent difficult pupils by other schools, and while headteachers may pride themselves in being able to cope with pupils that other schools cannot cope with, not all teachers may share the head's enthusiasm for the intake.

Exclusion from school: this may be temporary or permanent. A temporary exclusion will require parental contact and the pupil may not be allowed to return to school until an arrangement has been made between teacher and parents. While this sanction was considered essential for serious misconduct such as fighting or bullying, there was concern about the amount of paperwork and time involved. For extreme cases or for a succession of serious incidents, the school may consider permanent exclusion. Teachers expressed concern at the time taken to achieve a decision, and the damage that may result to the pupil concerned or to others if an 'unmanageable' pupil has to remain in school while a decision is being made. There is some feeling among classroom teachers that governors may oppose the idea of exclusion in order to avoid the school acquiring 'a bad name', ie. a reputation for having pupils whose behaviour is such that they have to be removed.

In addition to these 'school-wide' systems, individual teachers have their own personal systems which include such traditional punishments or privilege withdrawals as: doing extra work, writing out lines, tables or explanations of why what they have done is unacceptable; staying behind (when a break follows the end of a lesson) for as many minutes as the whole class delayed the start of the lesson; and not being allowed to join in favoured communal activities during the course of the lesson.

C.2.ii **Shared understanding and mutual support.** All schools recognise the importance of discussion about discipline. Not all schools, however, have as yet created occasions for open discussion within the staff group as a whole. In schools where this has been achieved, staff value the sharing of experiences and of strategies for responding to problems. The aftermath of the period of teachers' action has worked against the development of corporate planning and in some settings it has left a residue of friction that may be perpetuated in different attitudes to discipline, or even in some distrust. But the sense of community and mutual support that some schools are beginning to achieve is impressive:

> *'The majority of staff are keen to get the place running nice and smoothly for their own sake and they talk about the problems that they've got. We tell each other solutions that we've got, we show how we do that sort of thing and most of them are not afraid to ask for help. Even the better teachers, you know, they say, I've got this problem here. How would you cope?'*
> (M 9/9 MPG + incentive allowance information technology)

Less experienced teachers can, however, feel some ambivalence about disclosing problems before they have 'proved themselves' to colleagues.

The two main concerns teachers have in relation to the quality of mutual support are **consistency** and **reliability of back-up.** Teachers need to feel that they are working to roughly the same standards for interpreting the seriousness of pupil behaviours and working to roughly the same procedures for dealing with them:

'If there was a genuine consistency throughout the school, obviously staff are individuals, but some staff will react to a situation in a totally different way to others. We do have, and operate, school rules – some I don't agree with but I try to enforce each one where some staff will, I'm afraid, say that's a school rule but perhaps it is not an important rule. And perhaps it isn't but … consistency I think would be a help … That would be something I would like to see happen and I think then our users would know better where they stood and would feel happier that they were in a situation where they could sort of live easier perhaps.'
(M 12/12 MPG+incentive allowance English)

While emphasising the need for consistency, teachers still have a strong sense of individuality. This expresses itself in a number of ways: in personal reputation – *'They know that I don't allow them to mess around and they know they're coming to work'* (F 15/7 MPG English); it is also expressed in physical presence and style of command, and in techniques for achieving a disciplined start to the lesson. Teachers talked a lot about the need, against a background of less than perfect consistency in relation to general rules, to develop a habit of orderliness and an atmosphere for learning in lessons that was related to them as individuals and to their subject and setting.

The convention of developing a strong individual style to maintain classroom discipline is in fact quite complex when one examines it closely. Teachers realise that they can no longer take respect for granted:

'You can't go into a classroom and expect their respect. They put more demands on you for that than ever before. Whereas before you went in as a figure of authority, as a figure of respect, because of being a teacher, you now no longer have that automatically. You have to earn it, justify it much more often – perhaps to yourself as well as to the pupils'
(M 11/11 MPG+incentive allowance CDT)

Respect has to be earned and teachers who have a reputation for being 'easy' or 'weak' can be vulnerable: *'once the kids know, they're in there like bull terriers'* (M 13/13 MPG+incentive allowance humanities). The aim of helping pupils to achieve some quality of learning is still high on the agenda: teachers are not content just to *'clown about, keep 'em happy and baby mind'* (M 11/11 MPG+incentive allowance CDT) and they maintain, despite the distractions, a keen commitment to teaching their subject and to helping pupils learn. There is the need to establish a sense of achievement, not just for the pupils but also for the teacher's own sense of professional pride. Teachers often talk about the need to have faith in their own capabilities to manage classroom discipline – partly because pupils might judge them to be weak if they regularly send miscreants to senior staff:

> 'I've had to be seen to be doing something … If I had to go cap in hand to anybody else to sort out any problem in class … If the children see you doing that then they obviously feel that oh that teacher who you sent them to, they are important, they sort out all the problems, and I think that works against us. I personally do not send people to senior members of staff because I don't want to lose face in front of the kids because my own belief is that **I've** got to create an atmosphere in the classroom where learning can take place and I want to have the power to be able to make that happen.'
> (M 9/9 MPG geography)

Where teachers do send pupils out of lessons to senior staff they expect some action to be taken and feel let down if it isn't. Teachers particularly resent it if members of the senior management team exercise their privilege of *ad-hominem* judgements – which may lead to their deciding not to proceed to the usual sanctions. In such circumstances, the teacher can feel that his or her own judgement has been undervalued. On the other hand, senior management staff justify their approach in terms of the need to see both sides of a situation and to take into account background information that a teacher may not have, and this may lead to different interpretations of the episode. Teachers can also feel irritated when information about what difficult pupils have done or how they are being handled is not communicated by colleagues in senior management or pastoral teams. Anxiety about 'not knowing' is also experienced by heads: *'the most disturbing bit'*, said one headteacher, *'is that you never find out. Whenever a staff feels unsupported, you don't actually know'* (M 18/2 headteacher). The complaints tend to be exchanged within the peer group rather than explored directly with members of senior management teams.

C.2.iii **Talking things through with pupils.** One school, which had worked for 16 years without corporal punishment (and which still has 1200 pupils on roll), has reduced its rules to one: *'to respect and show courtesy and kindness to all people at all times'* (M 18/2 headteacher). As one teacher said: *'in this atmosphere, it's hard not to be reasonable'* (M 11/6 MPG+incentive allowance English). The aim, as in other schools, is to create *'a whole net of caring'* (M 12/5 MPG+incentive allowance music). This means being attentive to pupils' concerns, particularly at the point of transition from primary or middle to secondary school, and ensuring that they feel secure, but it can also involve spending time 'teaching pupils how to get out of conflict' (M 18/2 headteacher). It can involve creating good working conditions for pupils and it can also involve taking time to get to know 'a little bit more about the history' of a young person who is disruptive, 'because sometimes it could be the problem is a deep-rooted one' (F 5/5 MPG chemistry).

Teachers recognise the time that it takes to understand and support rather than merely to punish. Problems may be brought in from outside school and many teachers are concerned to undertake a sympathetic diagnosis rather than merely to treat the symptom:

> 'This poor lass has got this trauma so I try and discuss these sorts of things. The others are usually very good and I say, 'Just get on with your work while we have a chat outside or in the other room'. I had one girl the other day who'd snapped at one of the others and I thought well it's not like her and one of the others said, 'Oh, Miss, she has had a lot of worry today. She has had a bit of an upset at home'.'
> (F 13/8 MPG+incentive allowance business studies)

Some teachers may also try to help pupils see discipline from their perspective as a person rather than just as a teacher. For example, one teacher outlined a situation when she herself was feeling upset and her tolerance was lower than usual. This led to an episode with a boy who upset her and her rebuke led to 'a little shouting match in front of the rest'. She handled it by taking him aside and talking to him on a one-to-one basis; her explanation of how she felt had, she thought, a positive effect:

> 'I was on the level with him and said, 'I am human and I have a lot of problems, especially today. So you could have picked another day' and he could see how much he had upset me. I didn't cry or anything, I saved that 'til later. I think that would have been really bad, breaking up in front of a pupil – but he could see that I was upset and he was really sorry for what he'd done and he saw that he was wrong, and he was ever so apologetic'.
> (F 5/5 MPG chemistry)

There was evidence of growing commitment to treating young people in a more adult fashion; in particular a recognition that if teachers require pupils to be courteous then they should show courtesy to pupils:

> 'Come in, sit down and let's sort of discuss this now', and they can see that perhaps someone is taking them a bit seriously for once and wants to know'.
> (F 9/6 MPG+incentive allowance home economics)

Talk is also used to help individual pupils set their learning targets and to help them review and recognise their achievements. Teachers may feel awkward at first in managing such dialogue with pupils but 'a

267

number of staff are already seeing the advantages' (M 26/11 headteacher). Individual discussion may be supplemented by class discussion of responsibilities and problems:

> *'We sort of discuss most things and we have lots of majority decisions on as many things as possible so that they realise they are very important. Lots of children don't realise. They have no worries. They just don't value themselves at all ... I have got to try and get them to realise that what they think is important.'*
> (F 16/16 MPG general subjects)

Here, as in other developments, schools recognise the importance of helping pupils to build more positive images of themselves.

D.   THE INTRODUCTION OF NEW CONTENT AND TEACHING STYLES

Many teachers, in speaking of discipline within their own classrooms, expressed a concern, as one interviewee put it, with ensuring that *'boredom doesn't have a chance to set in'* (M 17/17 MPG+incentive allowance French). Not surprisingly, therefore, 'motivation' and 'relevance' were key terms in teachers' accounts of lessons which they felt had been successful. Classroom discipline, in other words, was seen as having a great deal to do with *'the way you ... turn your teaching towards the children you have got'* (F 9/6 MPG+incentive allowance home economics). The introduction of new curriculum content was considered to be of particular significance in this respect:

> *'If the actual content of the lesson is boring, that's when you start losing them. So that's the struggle. You've got to make it interesting all the time.'*
> (M 9/9 MPG+incentive allowance information technology)

Content, however, was only one aspect of this general concern among the interviewees with ensuring that pupils were well motivated and that lessons engaged their interests. The way in which classrooms are organised, the kinds of activities that are introduced, and the quality of the relationships within the classroom were also seen as important factors governing the kind of discipline that might be achieved. Changes in the content of particular subject specialisms were almost always discussed in relation to corresponding changes in teaching styles. *'It's both,'* insisted one interviewee, *'the content of the curriculum has got to change and teaching styles have got to become more informal'.* (M 23/13 MPG+incentive allowance CDT).

D.1 Approaches to classroom discipline

Perceptions of what constitutes 'a discipline problem' or 'disciplined behaviour' would seem to vary considerably according to the particular teaching style adopted:

> 'If you take what seems by many people to be a traditional kind of lesson – the teacher in front gives some instructions, maybe does some question and answer work, maybe writes one or two points on the board and has a worksheet where the youngsters have a list of the questions they are going to be doing – that means a certain kind of discipline . . . a certain style of discipline which is often teacher-led. If we take some of the more, what some people might call risky activities – you know, the discussion group, small-group work – that depends a lot more on personal discipline.'
> (M 16/16 MPG+incentive allowance geography)

The distinction here – between the style of discipline associated with 'a more traditional kind of lesson' and that associated with 'risky activities' in which pupils have greater responsibility for managing their own learning – was central. Few interviewees, however, saw themselves as operating solely within one mode. Different groups of pupils, it was argued, required different approaches and most teachers, therefore, rejected any typification of their role in terms of such simplistic dichotomies as traditional/progressive, formal/informal, etc. 'You play different roles ... with different groups,' as one teacher put it, 'until you get what you think is the best out of them' (F 18/18 MPG+incentive allowance humanities).

Even those teachers who favour a more 'informal' approach insisted upon the importance of there being certain clearly defined expectations regarding pupil behaviour. One teacher, for example, who acknowledged that 'we have a 'freer' approach now,' stressed that 'you still expect certain things and ultimately you're still the one in charge' (M 20/12 MPG+incentive allowance English as a second language):

> 'There are standards that you set and you make it clear to the kids what your standards are and that you're going to stick to them.'
> (M 9/9 MPG geography)

There is also a clear sense of discipline, not as an achieved state, but as a process which takes time and requires the willing participation of the learner. Discipline, from this perspective, is part and parcel of what it means to learn – which is why, as one interviewee pointed out, 'it's very difficult to isolate discipline from interest and learning methods. It's not something separate' (F 14/14 MPG+incentive allowance art and design). The aim is for pupils 'to take authority for their own minds'
(M 28/1 headteacher).

269

D.2 Discipline with a purpose

Different curriculum areas would seem to vary considerably in the kinds of opportunity they offer for developing self-discipline in pupils. A science teacher, for example, pointed to the way in which *'science lends itself to . . . group work and problem solving, activities'* which, she claimed, *'give the kids something meaningful to do'* (F 21/17 deputy biology). Similarly, an art and design teacher explained how, within her subject, discipline has to be understood in terms of *'the way an artist works or the way a designer approaches the work'*:

> *'You can't have discipline for discipline's sake. Discipline has to have a purpose within the learning situation. There has to be a point to it, not just that you don't want to hear them making any noise or they get on your nerves. There has to be a reason for the discipline to be there. For example, when we are doing printing, you have to understand that if you don't keep your work surface in reasonable condition your work will get into a mess and the sequence will be destroyed and you won't be able to organise your ideas or your methods. It will become chaotic, so that's discipline. It's discipline within the subject area, in what you're doing, and you have to understand that and the children have to understand. They have to see the purpose of it.'*
> (F 14/14 MPG + incentive allowance art and design)

A number of interviewees mentioned the safety aspects of their particular subject as providing a readily understood logic relating to matters of discipline. Teachers of subjects such as science, home economics, art and design and physical education, which necessarily involve some practical work together with the use of specialist equipment, were particularly aware of the strength of that logic, based as it is upon the pupils' own personal safety:

> *'You've got to have discipline, because you have to have regard to personal safety, handling apparatus, movement around the building, moving around the field ... that's got to be laid down on day one and continue right through the school, so it becomes after a while second nature for the majority.'*
> (M 22/16 MPG + incentive allowance physical education)

D.3 The emphasis on learning

Regardless of their subject specialisms, interviewees stressed that for them discipline in the classroom was primarily about creating, *'an atmosphere in which kids can learn'* (M 9/9 MPG geography). Many felt that, in order to create such an atmosphere, teachers needed to stimulate pupils through the use of teaching methods designed to encourage a greater degree of collaboration and active participation.

Several cited CPVE, GCSE and TVEI as examples of initiatives which had helped to promote work of this kind and thereby raise the level of motivation in the classroom. Above all, however, they felt that discipline should be associated, in the minds of both teachers and pupils, with the process of learning itself. Indeed, one of the major benefits to have accrued from the introduction of a broader range of teaching methods was, in the words of one interviewee, *'that there is now more learning than teaching going on generally in classrooms'* (M 20/12 MPG+incentive allowance English as a second language).

The emphasis on learning goes some way to explaining the premium placed by many interviewees on talk and interactive activity as a key element in pupils' classroom experience. *'They are all working'*, said one teacher of his pupils, *'there is a lot of talk going on, but it is all to do with the work'* (M 15/5 MPG history). While acknowledging that a lesson organised in this way may appear from the outside to lack order, they argued that it in fact makes heavy demands on the teacher in terms of developing alternative organisational structures and pupil expectations. Such an approach, in other words, was seen to require a different kind of orderliness which gains its rationale from the nature of the tasks being undertaken and the interests and insights that these generate. It requires, as one interviewee put it, *'discipline from the teacher. It may look very informal, but it is actually very structured'* (F 10/1 MPG+incentive allowance personal and social education).

Off-site activities, such as residential and work experience, were also seen as providing important opportunities for developing in pupils the collaborative skills that are central to group work. Activities of this kind were valued not only as being worthwhile in themselves, but as having a positive impact on the subsequent attitudes and behaviour of pupils in the classroom. One interviewee, for example, spoke of *'the difference in relationships when people have been on a residential … you find a totally different attitude in the classroom'* (F 16/11 MPG+incentive allowance pre-vocational); another spoke of her own experience of *'taking kids out of the classroom'* as having been *'the greatest influence on changing my teaching methods generally'* (F 21/17 deputy biology).

There was broad agreement among the interviewees that unless learning takes place within a context that is genuinely caring, the outcomes of that learning will inevitably suffer in quality. One of the interviewees articulated very clearly the view that, to be effective, teaching necessarily involves the teacher in close and sustained relationships with pupils:

> *'You've got always to be there. You've got to face up to pupils, acknowledge them, talk to them – with your eyes, with your voice. It takes some doing*

271

but you can't give up … It's a persistent thing.'
(M 31/15 deputy English)

One way in which many classroom teachers had attempted to *'acknowledge them'* was by instituting what one interviewee referred to as *'systems of praise, report and encouragement: valuing youngsters' work, seeing that it's marked, seeing that it's appreciated'*. Clearly, the relation here between consistent whole-school strategies and the individual teacher's professional commitment is crucial if *'schools are to be maintained as places where respect and good working relationships can continually improve'* (M 28/1 headteacher).

There was a very strong sense among the teachers interviewed that there are no simple answers to the problem of classroom discipline. Relevant and stimulating materials, careful lesson preparation and classroom organisation, varied teaching methods and learning experiences and a commitment to the personal welfare of pupils were all mentioned as elements in the equation. None of these elements in itself was seen as sufficient. Taken together, however, they were seen as significantly increasing the likelihood of classrooms becoming places in which pupils want – and are able – to learn. The commitment of teachers to that possibility is – arguably – the most significant element in that complex equation.

E. LINKS WITH PARENTS, FAMILY AND COMMUNITY

E.1   The importance of home-school links

All schools considered their links with pupils' parents and communities to be a crucial factor in relation to discipline. Teachers distinguished between occasions when it was easier to bring parents into school (for example, a specific invitation which allows a one-to-one conversation, whether in response to a crisis or to hear about their child's progress) and the occasions when it is less easy to attract parents (for example, information giving sessions in a large group):

'When we had a parents' evening to discuss the Governors' report to parents we only had – as most schools – about a dozen parents turn up [approximately 550 pupils are on the school roll]. But at least it's a start.'
(M 28/20 headteacher)

Clearly, there is an increasing need for contact to help parents understand how the structures of curriculum and assessment are changing, as well as to understand what pattern of sanctions and support the school is operating in relation to discipline. Schools' attempts to improve links with the family and community were often based upon familiar initiatives, such as fairs, sales, performances, outings and parent teacher associations. Evening or day classes may be run at schools and parents were sometimes involved in voluntary work. In addition to the **range** of activities which schools ran, the most significant aspect was the amount of **effort** it takes for schools to win (or maintain) the interest, confidence and support of families in the community, or communities, which they serve.

Although some schools had very good links with the local community, many teachers felt that some of the discipline problems in the school reflected a parental and/or community influence. There were many references to the problems created by protracted unemployment and family tensions and upheavals. In addition, some teachers believed that there had been a loss of discipline and 'respect for adults' in the home which could carry over into school. There was also some feeling that communities which had once been supportive of schooling and teachers were now becoming less so. Teachers suggested that this change in attitudes may have been strongly influenced by public attacks on the quality of teaching and a tendency to seize upon dramatic incidents that often present a poor image of the school:

> '[When public figures] say that the standard of teaching is much inferior than it used to be – even though they qualify it in later interviews – the press pick these things up and it undermines the status, the level of expertise, the quality of the teaching profession ... And that in itself breeds disrespect from parents, and that disrespect is passed on to their children.'
> (M 18/18 MPG + incentive allowance special needs)

E.2 Teachers' knowledge of home and community

A key problem in interpreting what teachers say about the communities which they serve is that of judging how well teachers **really** know and appreciate the values and perspectives of parents. Teachers were often troubled by their lack of time and opportunity to build better understandings of the local communities. In fact, the teachers themselves were sometimes the first to point out that one of the benefits of close home-school contact would be the greater **mutual** understanding that this would create. This was particularly true in the case of ethnic minorities whose attitudes to school and schooling may be very different from those of neighbouring 'poor white areas'. In such cases the situation was further complicated by problems of language and tradition. In some of our schools tentative first steps had been taken towards addressing some of these issues:

> 'English is not the first language for many of our parents. One of the things

we try and do is work via the children to try and give their parents more confidence. A couple of 'for instances'; always on reception we have children who are the first people to greet visitors to the school. The make up of the school suggests that one of the people, if not **both** *the people on reception, will be able to speak community languages – Punjabi or Urdu or Bengali. That immediately means that if Mum comes up – who may have very little English – mum can talk to someone in her own language, in the language where she knows she will be understood and she will get some assistance. On parents' evenings, all our paperwork we send out is sent out in community languages and again we have young people who will assist the adults as soon as they come in … '*
(M 21/16 deputy history)

In schools where Asian pupils made up a substantial part of the roll, language was a vitally important issue: one of the schools' headteachers was instigating moves to increase the number of teachers drawn from the Asian communities, and although the policy was still in its infancy it was viewed as a positive move by staff at all levels within the school.

However, links between the school and home do not necessarily rely upon the parents approaching the school. Visits by staff to meet parents at home was an important feature of the pastoral system in some of the schools. This required a great deal of time and effort on the teachers' part, but where the practice had been established there was a very strong feeling that school-home links had improved as a result. **Home visits were seen as being a very great help regardless of the nature of the school's catchment area:** home visiting was not seen as a resource for multi-ethnic schools alone. However, in areas of substantial ethnic minority settlement this was viewed as a particularly important resource. An interviewee of South Asian origin (speaking as both a teacher and a parent) offered an insightful account of the mutual benefits of home visiting:

'From my own experience you see I know that at my daughters' school – my greatest need was to go and meet the teachers, to see who they were, what they were like and so on and so forth. Until I actually went and met them I somehow felt uneasy about what was happening in the school … Now as a teacher I find whenever I've met parents – as a school-community tutor I've gone and met parents and talked about their children in their homes – I find I come back to school and my concern for the child, for that particular child, assumes a slightly greater depth. And what is more, the child himself or herself looks upon me in a very different light altogether, not just as a teacher who stands over there and delivers his lectures, but somebody who knows Dad … Do you see?'
(M 11/11 MPG + incentive allowance English)

Regardless of the particular characteristics of the catchment area, both teachers and headteachers in several schools saw it as important to have a staffing allowance which would support home visiting.

Some teachers identified tensions between the norms and values which pupils met at home and in the school. There were many accounts, for example, of parents urging teachers to control their children through 'a quick slap' or even a more extended beating'. Indeed, there were instances of parents doing this themselves on the school premises after being called in and informed of their child's behaviour. Sanctions could cause further disagreements between home and school when parents refused to agree to their child staying at school for a detention. Such actions are further evidence of differences in perception between parents and teachers.

Forging good and mutually beneficial links with parents is a difficult, yet crucial, task. Although relationships with parents were generally good in some schools, in all ten schools which we visited there were many teachers who wanted **greater** parental support. The reasons for some parents' reluctance to be involved will tend to vary according to local circumstance. For instance, one of our schools was situated away from its catchment area Most pupils walked up to a mile to school, few families had cars and the neighbourhood had a reputation for violence at night: attendance at evening meetings was poor. Part of the school's response was to reschedule its parents' meetings for 3.30 pm (rather than later in the evening). Where relationships **are** developing well, constant effort is needed to sustain them. For example, in one school the year tutor encouraged parents to telephone before school started (or even during the day) to talk about children who might not be attending school or who were facing problems. Clearly, both schools and parents must work at improving and sustaining home-school relationships.

There were occasions when the lack of parental support and control was seen as so serious that the school might be powerless to help:

> 'Where they are out of control here **and** at home, I do feel that we are spitting in the wind, that really we can do absolutely nothing.'
> (F 22/1 headteacher)

As we have already stated, we visited schools whose location indicated a relatively high degree of social and economic deprivation. However, it would be wrong to assume that the composition of the catchment areas necessarily had negative consequences. Teachers often held positive views concerning some aspects of life in the local community. The following quotation from a headteacher illustrates the 'riches' which

275

may be an untapped resource in some school-community relationships:

'The catchment is made up of a poor working class side of the city. In terms of all the indices that you could want to look at – which would include the number of people unemployed, number of people who receive free school meals, the number of people who are receiving FIS [Family Income Supplement], the smallest number of car ownership – it comes top of the list in the city by every measure that you could look at; so it is the poorest working area of the city … The proportion of single parent families is quite high. Having said all that, it is culturally the most rich and diversified of the whole city, with populations drawn from a variety of Asian cultures, Afro-Caribbean cultures, Anglo-Saxon and European cultures – because it's a diversified city in itself. It has these enormous riches and I think the greatest strength of the catchment area is that very fact.'
(M 18/2 headteacher)

F. A NOTE ON TEACHERS' NEEDS IN RELATION TO DISCIPLINE

Real problems exist in schools. In many cases, these problems are being contained by strategies that require considerable professional commitment. Teachers are trying to achieve a coherence of purpose and practice that goes beyond mere coping.

Teachers are investing considerable amounts of energy, time and effort in maintaining or developing a balanced system of sanctions, incentives and support. Some improvements are within the capacity of the school itself and can be achieved by careful planning. These would include better communication between senior management teams and other teachers, a clearly formulated system of sanctions, reliable back-up in relation to agreed sanctions, and greater consistency in the application of sanctions. There are other sources of support that teachers identify but cannot be provided from within the school. The items most often mentioned were the following:

Support from agencies or services outside the school: teachers would find it helpful to be able to rely on better liaison with, and quicker response from, outside agencies that are called on to give specialist help and advice in relation to pupils who find it difficult to accept the discipline of schooling.

Exclusion procedures: teachers would find it helpful if decision-making procedures could be somewhat faster for those pupils for whom exclusion seems the only possible solution. If procedures are protracted, pupils are held within an environment that has already proved unsuitable or uncongenial, and other pupils may suffer as a result of sustained contact with the disaffected pupil.

Class size: in smaller classes, teachers can give more attention to individual, or small groups of, pupils; a sense of group identity is more easily established; the possibility of disruptions escalating into minor disorders is decreased. Overall, teachers feel that they can help pupils to learn more effectively when class sizes are smaller.

Staffing: teachers would value a staffing complement that would allow regular collaboration with support teachers and that is generous enough to allow more staff to make regular home visits. All staff would gain from the greater recruitment of bilingual and ethnic minority teachers.

Resources: teachers would welcome more resources, not only for curriculum development but also to improve the quality of the environment. Schools and classrooms are sometimes of depressing appearance, acoustically inadequate, and generally dispiriting. While teachers make every effort to brighten the appearance through displays and exhibitions, the fabric of the building and its general demeanour may remain unwelcoming.

Footnote to Part II

(1) For example, a female chemistry teacher on the main professional grade only, who has taught for a total of fourteen years, the last nine in her present school, would be identified as:
(F 14/9 MPG chemistry).

KEY TO THE INTERVIEW TRANSCRIPTS

highlighted text	Denotes emphasised speech or raised voice.
[Square brackets]	Signify background information or where speech has been paraphrased for clarity of understanding.

A. **Sampling procedures and response rates for the national survey**

Sample design

The target population for the national survey was defined as all teachers (of whatever status) in the state-maintained primary and secondary schools in England and Wales. The selection of teachers from this population was performed in two stages.

Stage 1: DES statisticians provided a national stratified random sample of the names and addresses of 300 secondary and 250 primary schools, drawn to ensure the appropriate representation of the various school types and regions.

The headteachers in these schools were contacted for permission to approach members of their staff. Unfortunately, shortly after the process of seeking such permissions was under way, progress was halted by a national postal strike. During this period chief education officers were approached to contact schools in the sample and forward the required staff lists from them by facsimile transmission.

Table A1: **Responses of primary and secondary schools to requests for staff lists**

	Primary*	Secondary**	Total
Schools in sample	250	300	550
Schools responding to requests for staff lists	234	269	503
Schools responding to requests after the deadline	13	14	27
Schools included in the survey	221	255	476

Notes: *Primary schools included the following types of schools: infants only, junior only, junior and infants, infants, first and middle as well as middle deemed primary.

**Secondary schools included: middle deemed secondary, 11-16 comprehensive, 11-18 comprehensive, other comprehensive, grammar and other secondary.

The ten regions represented in the sample design were: North, Yorkshire and Humberside, North West, West Midlands, East Midlands, East Anglia, Greater London, South East, South West, Wales.

In the circumstances, the numbers of headteachers agreeing to allow staff in their schools to co-operate was most encouraging (see Table A1). In all, 91% of those believed to have been approached replied. However, the time being taken to obtain such replies meant that decisions had to be taken about going into the field with the questionnaires shortly before absolutely all the staff lists had been returned. The result was that 476 of the 550 schools originally sampled (that is 87% of the total) were actually included in the survey. Inspection of the relevant tables (not shown) indicated that schools' responses were spread evenly over the various regions and school types.

Stage 2: the sampling of teachers from the staff lists provided by schools was performed on a systematic random basis. For the secondary schools a sampling fraction of 1 in 4 names was used whilst for primary schools it was 5 in 8.

These procedures generated an overall sample of 4444 names. 37 teachers were withdrawn from the sample as they were either on secondment, maternity leave or were not, in fact, members of the school's current teaching staff. A further ten questionnaires were returned as 'undelivered' by the Post Office. This left a total of 4397 teachers who were believed to have been contacted.

Response rates

Each teacher in the sample was initially sent a questionnaire to complete along with a reply-paid envelope. Those who failed to reply were subsequently sent a reminder. After about three weeks from the time of the initial mail-out those who had still not responded were sent a second questionnaire to complete. As a result of these procedures 89% of those primary teachers and 79% of those secondary teachers believed to have been contacted returned their questionnaires (see Table A2). Just under 7% exercised the option to respond anonymously.

Table A2: **Response rates amongst teachers to the postal survey**

	Primary Teachers	Secondary Teachers	All Teachers
Questionnaires mailed out	1229	3215	4444
Returned as 'ineligible'*	10	27	37
Returned by Post Office 'undelivered'	7	3	10
Effective sample size	1212	3185	4397
Questionnaires returned	1083	2525	3608
OVERALL RESPONSE RATES	89%	79%	82%

Note: Of the teachers who responded just under 7% chose to do so anonymously.
  *Includes those who were on secondment, on maternity leave, no longer teaching in the school, etc.

During the period when the questionnaires were being mailed out there were continuing disruptions to postal services in some parts of the country. These circumstances may have contributed, in part, to the slightly lower response rates in the Greater London and Welsh regions amongst the secondary sample; amongst the primary sample response rates were, however, almost uniformly high (table not shown).

Response rates did not vary significantly amongst the different types of primary schools. Amongst secondary schools the response rates for '11-18 comprehensives' and 'middle deemed secondary schools' lagged somewhat behind those for other types of school (tables not shown).

B. The background characteristics of the interview sample

We requested schools participating in this part of the study to provide us with interviewees who represented different subject areas, years of teaching experience and both sexes.

In all, 100 teachers and nine (out of 10) headteachers were interviewed. 55% of them were male. They averaged about 15 years of teaching experience each, nine years of which had been in their present schools. Just over one in 10 had between 0-five years experience; one in five had 20 or more years experience. They had mostly pursued their teaching careers in comprehensive schools, although about one in four had had some experience in secondary modern schools and just under one in 10 in grammar schools.

One in four of those interviewed were on the main professional grade whilst a further one in three were on main professional grades with allowances A or B. Well over half said they spent 'all or most' of their contracted time on classroom teaching whilst, in total, four out of five said they spent 'over half' their time in the classroom.

Allowing for the over-representation of headteachers in the sample, these figures compare favourably with those obtained for similar schools from the postal survey.

CLASSROOM MANAGEMENT

Some recent books and in-service training materials which seemed useful to us are listed below. This list is not intended to be comprehensive:

Chisholm, B, et al (1986) **Preventive Approaches to Disruption (PAD).** Macmillan Education.

Gray, J and Richer, J (1988) **Classroom Responses to Disruptive Behaviour.** Macmillian Education.

Kyriacou, C (1986) **Effective Teaching in Schools.** Basil Blackwell.

Robertson, J (1981) **Effective Classroom Control.** Hodder and Stoughton.

Wheldall, K and Merrett, F (1985) **Manual for the Behavioural Approach to Teaching Package (BATPACK): for use in primary and middle schools.** Postive Products.

Wragg, E C (ed) (1984) **Classroom Teaching Skills.** Croom Helm.

RESEARCH REVIEWS

We found the following reviews particularly useful:

Docking, J W (1987) **Control and Discipline in Schools: perspectives and approaches.** Harper and Row.

Graham, J (1988) **Schools, Disruptive Behaviour and Delinquency.** Home Office Research Study 96, HMSO.

Johnstone, M and Munn, P (1987) **Discipline in School: a review of 'causes' and 'cures'.** Scottish Council for Educational Research.

OTHER REFERENCES

Department of Education and Science (1988) **Secondary Schools: an appraisal by HMI.** HMSO.

Department of Education and Science (1988) **The New Teacher in School: a survey by HMI in England and Wales 1987.** HMSO.

Galloway, D et al (1982) **Schools and Disruptive Pupils.** Longman.

Galloway, D, (1985) **Schools and Persistent Absentees.** Pergamon.

Gray, J, et al (1983) **Reconstructions of Secondary Education: theory, myth and practice since the war.** Routledge and Kegan Paul.

Hargreaves, D H (1984) **Improving Secondary Schools.** Inner London Education Authority.

Houghton, S, et al (1988) Classroom behaviour problems which secondary school teachers say they find most troublesome. **British Educational Research Journal,** 14(3), pp 297-312.

Jowell, R, et al (ed) (1988) **British Social Attitudes.** Gower (for Social and Community Planning Research).

Lawrence, J (1988) On the fringe. **Education,** 172(8), pp 175-176.

Lefkowitz, M M (1977) **Growing up to be Violent.** Pergamon, New York.

McManus, M (1987) Suspension and exclusion from high schools: the association with catchment and school variables. **School Organisation,** 1987, 7(3), pp 261-271.

Milner, M (1938) **The Human Problem in Schools.** Methuen.

Morgan, V and Dunn, S (1988) Chameleons in the classroom: visible and invisible children in nursery and infant classrooms. **Education Review,** 40(1), pp 3-12.

Mortimore, P, et al (1988) **School Matters: the junior years.** Open Books.

Olweus, D (1984) Aggressors and their victims: bullying at school. In *Frude, N and Gault, H (1984)* **Disruptive Behaviour in School.** Wiley.

Ramsay, P D K (1983) Fresh perspectives on the school transformation – reproduction debate: a response to Anyon from The Antipodes. **Curriculum Enquiry,** 13(3), pp 295-320.

Reynolds, D and Sullivan, M (1987) **The Comprehensive Experiment: a comparison of the selective and non selective systems of school organisation.** Falmer Press.

Rutter, M, et al (1979) **Fifteen Thousand Hours: secondary schools and their effects on pupils.** Open Books.

Social Trends 18 (1988). Central Statistical Office, HMSO.

Steed, D and Lawrence, J (1988) **Disruptive Behaviour in the Primary School.** Goldsmiths' College, University of London.

Tattum, D P and Lane, D A (ed) (1989) **Bullying in Schools.** Trentham Books.

Wheldall, K and Merrett, F (1988) Discipline: rewarding work. **Teachers' Weekly,** 16 May, pp 25-27.

West, D J (1982) **Delinquency: its roots, careers and prospects.** Heinemann Educational.

Extract from a booklet for pupils.

CODE OF CONDUCT

The one rule for all of us in school is **Everyone will act with courtesy and consideration to others at all times.**

This means that:

1. **You always try to understand other people's point of view.**

2. **In class you make it as easy as possible for everyone to learn and for the teacher to teach.** (This means arriving on time with everything you need for that lesson, beginning and ending the lesson in a courteous and orderly way, listening carefully, following instructions, helping each other when appropriate and being quiet and sensible at all times.)

3. **You move gently and quietly about school.** (This means never running, barging or shouting, but being ready to help by opening doors, standing back to let people pass and helping to carry things.) In crowded areas **please keep to the left.**

4. **You always speak politely to everyone** (even if you feel bad tempered!) and use a low voice. (Shouting is **always** discourteous.)

5. **You are silent** whenever you are required to be.

6. **You keep the school clean and tidy** so that it is a welcoming place we can all be proud of. (This means putting all litter in bins, keeping walls and furniture clean and unmarked and taking great care of the displays, particularly of other people's work.)

7. **Out of school,** walking locally or with a school group, you always remember that the school's reputation depends on the way you behave.

Guidance for pupils displayed in classroom

CLASSROOM EXPECTATIONS

Classrooms (including labs, workshops and gyms) are your places of work. Just as in any factory or office, there need to be clearly understood rules and expectations to allow everyone to work successfully, safely and enjoyably.

1. **Start of Lessons**

   - Enter rooms sensibly and go straight to your workplace.
   - Take off and put away any outdoor wear (not on desks).
   - Take out books, pens and equipment.
   - Put bags away (not on desks).
   - Remain silent during the register (except when your name is called!)

2. **During Lessons**

   - When your teacher talks to the whole class, remain silent and concentrate.
   - If the class is asked a question, put up your hand to answer: do not call out (unless you are asked for quick ideas).
   - You must have pen, pencil, ruler, diary and any books or folders needed.
   - You are expected to work sensibly with your classmates: do not distract or annoy them.
   - If you arrive late without justifiable cause you must expect to be detained for the amount of time you missed in order to make up the work.
   - Homework must be recorded in your diary.
   - Eating, drinking and chewing are not allowed: if caught you will have to empty your mouth and hand in any other food or drink.
   - Walkmans, radios, magazines or other distractions are not allowed: they will be confiscated.
   - You must not leave a lesson without a note from a teacher.

3. **End of Lessons**

   - The pips and the clock are not signals for you: they are for the information of your teacher.

- You should not begin to pack away or put on outdoor wear until your teacher tells you to do so.

- When told, stand and push in or put up your chairs; any litter should be picked up.

- Only when your teacher finally tells you to go may you leave the room.

Finally, but most importantly:

Teachers are in the position of parents/guardians while you are in school. This means in particular that:

- There is no excuse for rudeness, disrespect or insolence towards teachers.

- Any reasonable request from a teacher should be carried out at once and without argument.

Breaking either of these basic rules will be treated as a VERY serious matter.

Extracts from a booklet for teachers

REWARDS AND SANCTIONS

It is very important that the positive aspects of praise and reward should have great emphasis. Good discipline is, as we all know, based on mutual knowledge, respect the setting of known standards. It must have high priority.

Children appear to respond better to systems which recognise their difficulties and strengths. Anything which recognises that children have achieved what has been asked of them is desirable.

REWARDS

1. Credit marks are awarded to pupils who have produced an excellent piece of work or who have made a consistently good effort with several pieces of work. Staff are asked to enter and initial credits in the homework diaries. This ensures that both parents and form tutors see them when checking diaries regularly. The form representative enters credit marks in a book during form time which is then handed in weekly to the Head of Year. Three credit marks = one merit mark. Merit marks are announced during assemblies.

2. Merit certificates are awarded for outstanding achievements. They can be as a result of a consistently high standard of work (ie over a half a term or so), consistent effort, or a special event or situation where a recognisable and good attitude resulted in a wider benefit for the school. They are generally given out at the end of the term. Children who have taken a very full and active part in school life may well get one or two regularly each half a term.

3. Commendations can and should be entered in exercise books and homework diaries.

4. Recognition can be given to success of differing kinds in assemblies or form time.

5. Pupils' work can/should be displayed as much as possible. Pinboarding can be provided in rooms which are deficient.

6. Head/Deputy Heads/Heads of Department/Heads of Year are very willing, and indeed welcome the opportunity, to praise individuals for pieces of good work if these are brought to their notice.

7. Above all, praise and encouragement in lessons should be used as much as possible.

SANCTIONS

It must be emphasised that it is the primary responsibility of staff to deal with discipline themselves, by extra work or their own detentions. Colleagues are reminded that the Authority asks that the pupils should be given 24 hours notice of a detention and that it should last no longer than one hour. Indiscriminate detentions of a whole class cause more resentment and problems than they solve. Heads of Department should take responsibility for work and progress achieved by members of their department. After all this, various sanctions are possible. The following have been tried and offer hope of success:

1. late report cards of persistent offenders;

2. full report (ie signature for each lesson) for those absent from, or late for, lessons;

3. full report, as above, but for work and behaviour in lessons;

4. detentions (by subject teachers, heads of departments, form tutors or heads of year);

5. interruption of break and lunchtime privileges for bad behaviour;

6. 'punishment fitting the crime' – cleaning of graffiti, picking up litter, etc;

7. referrals to Form Tutor, Heads of Department, Head of Year, Deputy Head;

8. for most pupils, the greater sanction is to contact the parents and seek an interview with them;

9. exclusion ('cooling off') at the request of Deputy Head or Heads of Year. Only the Headteacher may actually exclude; and

10. suspension, leading to expulsion. This becomes a 'legal' issue and needs to be well documented.

A booklet for staff

INSIDE INFORMATION – THE WAY TO GOOD ORDER

THIS OUTLINE OF GOOD PRACTICE AND THE WAYS TO GOOD ORDER IS FOR YOU, PLEASE USE IT.

Acceptable standards	of behaviour, work and respect depend on the example of us all.
	• All have positive contributions to make.
Good order	has to be worked for: it does not simply happen.
	• **Set** high standards • **Apply** rules firmly and fairly.
Most important	of all:
	• **Expect** to give and to receive respect.
Everyone	at school is here for a purpose.
	• **Respect** every person • **Treat** everyone as an individual.
Relationships	are vital: relationships between everyone and at every level. **Take the initiative:**
	• greet and be greeted • speak and be spoken to • smile and relate • communicate.
'Problems'	are normal where children are learning and testing the boundaries of acceptable behaviour.
Our success	is tested not by the absence of problems but **by the way we deal with them.**

Don't react:	address the problem:

- avoid confrontation
- listen
- establish the facts
- judge only when certain
- use punishments sparingly.

Removal of privilege is the most effective strategy.

OUT AND ABOUT THE SCHOOL

All informal contact contributes to standards of behaviour. **Control** that **behaviour** by taking the initiative at every opportunity. **Expect to:**

- start the dialogue
- greet pupils
- deal with all misbehaviour – to ignore it is to condone it!
- set high standards of speech, manner and dress
- enjoy relating to pupils.

IN THE CLASSROOM

Create and sustain a positive, supportive and secure environment. **Well prepared,** stimulating lessons generate good behaviour and earn respect. **Expect to:**

- arrive before the class and begin on time
- be prepared for the lesson
- keep everyone occupied and interested
- extend and motivate all pupils
- mark all work promptly and constructively
- set homework regularly to schedule
- encourage creative dialogue – confidence in discussion is important
- keep an attractive, clean and tidy room
- maintain interesting wall displays
- use first names.

DO ALL YOU CAN TO AVOID:

- humiliating .... it breeds resentment
- shouting .... it diminishes you
- over-reacting .... the problems will grow
- blanket punishments .... the innocent will resent them
- over-punishment .... keep your powder dry, never punish what you can't prove
- sarcasm .... it damages you!

Please never leave pupils outside rooms. The 'problem' needs a solution not complicating. **Seek help** if you need it. **And do all you can to:**

- use humour .... it builds bridges
- keep calm .... it reduces tensions
- listen .... it earns respect
- be positive and build relationships
- know your pupils as individuals
- carry out any threats you have to make
- be consistent.

Always apply schools rules positively

MAINTAINING DISCIPLINE

Insist on acceptable standards of behaviour, work and respect. **Expect to:**

- apply school rules uniformly
- work to agreed procedures
- insist on conformity and school uniform
- be noticed and discussed, in school and at home
- follow up problems to their conclusion.

The majority conform and are co-operative. Deal immediately with the few who present problems.

- **Establish your authority firmly and calmly.**
- **Separate the problem from the person.**

Only if you cannot resolve a problem, refer it on to **one person.** Make sure it is pursued to a satisfactory conclusion.

SANCTIONS AND PUNISHMENTS

After-school detentions may be used, subject to approval from Head of Year/Head of Department, BUT make sure that transport home is available. If they generate resentment and provoke parents **detentions are counter-productive. Subject teachers** – consider:

- reprimand
- change of seat
- repeat of work
- withdrawal of privilege of working in class
- additional work
- clearing litter, cleaning – especially if related to misdeed
- referral to Tutor/Year Tutor
- use of Homework Diary notes to parents.

TUTORS – **consider also:**

- referral to Year Tutor
- contacting parents – via Year Tutor
- a group change with Head of School approval
- isolating pupil from peer group
- exclusion only in very last resort and after full consultation.

All staff always notify Year Tutors of matters to be recorded. Keep the record card up to date. **Records are vital.** Facts on the file save enquiry time – YOUR time – and make solutions more likely.

EMERGENCIES

In an emergency escort the offender to the most accessible senior member of staff. If the class cannot be left, send a reliable pupil with a message to a senior member of staff.

RESPECTING THE ENVIRONMENT

Our reputation for cleanliness, attractive rooms and well kept grounds is essential for our success. **We must recruit from outside our catchment area, so must offer a superior and appealing 'package' or be undersubscribed.** Maintain high quality in our surroundings, in general spaces and in the classrooms. The visual impact always should be attractive and stimulating. Litter, damage and graffiti have no place here. Accept only the highest standards of cleanliness.

Encourage pride in the school:

- insist on a clean room
- teach in tidiness, encourage tidiness
- leave desks in place and the board clean after lessons
- clear graffiti immediately
- remove/repair all damage, but, if you cannot, tell the caretaker
- deal firmly with offenders
- enforce the ban on chewing gum
- keep displays fresh and attractive
- keep your desk, shelves and cupboards tidy
- insist on litter-free buildings and site
- deal with offenders: to ignore is to condone!
- report damage immediately.

With the compliments of the management team.

South East Essex College
of Arts and Technology, Southend

Printed in the United Kingdom for The Stationery Office
J29611 C5 11/97 (14001)